Holistic Reading Strategies
Teaching Children Who Find Reading Difficult

Timothy Rasinski
Kent State University

Nancy Padak
Kent State University

Merrill,
an imprint of Prentice Hall
Englewood Cliffs, New Jersey   Columbus, Ohio

Library of Congress Cataloging-in-Publication Data
Rasinski, Timothy V.
    Holistic reading strategies : teaching children who find reading difficult / Timothy Rasinski, Nancy Padak.
        p.   cm.
    Includes bibliographical references and index.
    ISBN 0-02-398471-6 (alk. paper)
    1. Reading—Remedial teaching. 2. Developmental reading.   I. Padak, Nancy. II. Title.
LB1050.5.R33   1996
372.4'3—dc20   95-24839
                                                               CIP

Editor: Bradley J. Potthoff
Production Editor: Alexandrina Benedicto Wolf
Photo Editor: Anne Vega
Design Coordinator: Jill E. Bonar
Text Designer: Ed Horcharik
Cover photo: © J. Myers/H. Armstrong Roberts
Production Manager: Deidra M. Schwartz
Electronic Text Management: Marilyn Wilson Phelps, Matthew Williams, Karen L. Bretz, Tracey Ward

This book was set in Bitstream by Prentice Hall and was printed and bound by R.R. Donnelley & Sons Company. The cover was printed by Phoenix Color Corp.

© 1996 by Prentice-Hall, Inc.
A Simon & Schuster Company
Englewood Cliffs, New Jersey 07632

Photo credits: pp. 2, 9, 14,18, 27, 30, 62, 68, 76, 102, 110, 122, 137, 140, 147, 174, 188, and 194 by Anne Vega/Merrill/Prentice Hall; pp. 5, 48, 71, 88, 93, 150, 158, 161, and 202 by Scott Cunningham/ Merrill/Prentice Hall; pp. 35, 44, 55, and 86 by Barbara Schwartz/Merrill/Prentice Hall; p. 164 by Tom Watson/Merrill/Prentice Hall; and pp. 170 and 178 by Todd Yarrington/Merrill/Prentice Hall

Printed in the United States of America

10 9 8 7 6 5 4 3 2 1

ISBN: 0-02-398471-6

Prentice-Hall International (UK) Limited, *London*
Prentice-Hall of Australia Pty. Limited, *Sydney*
Prentice-Hall of Canada, Inc., *Toronto*
Prentice-Hall Hispanoamericana, S. A., *Mexico*
Prentice-Hall of India Private Limited, *New Delhi*
Prentice-Hall of Japan, Inc., *Tokyo*
Simon & Schuster Asia Pte. Ltd., *Singapore*
Editora Prentice-Hall do Brasil, Ltda., *Rio de Janeiro*

To our mentors, Jerry Zutell and Jane L. Davidson

Preface

This book is the result of several years of teaching and thinking; talking with children, teachers, and parents; and discussing between ourselves and with others—sometimes heatedly. We have struggled with many questions: What is the best way to provide instruction for children who are having difficulty learning to read? How should instruction for these students be different from instruction for children who are progressing along more normal lines? What are the proper roles of teachers and parents in the instructional efforts? And what is the best way to communicate our ideas about corrective instruction to teachers—those in training and those already working with children?

This volume is our best response to those questions and many others. It offers new instructional strategies for helping children in what we believe is an informal, easy-to-read, yet scholarly approach. The ideas presented here have been tried and tested in studies of effective instruction and, more important, in our own classrooms and tutoring rooms and those of teachers we have known and worked with over the years.

To be honest, we know there are many books that offer ideas for helping children who experience difficulty in learning to read. Most are based on a highly analytic, diagnostic-prescriptive approach that results in a recipe book of activities designed to remediate specific skills and subskills that have been diagnosed as areas of deficiency for the child. These books include lists of skill activities aimed at remediating everything from medial vowel sounds to homonyms to sequential comprehension difficulties. Approaches are described in detail and are meant to be implemented in the manner prescribed. But such books pay little attention to the instructional context or how various activities might form a coherent, logical, and effective whole.

Our book breaks with this traditional model. The instructional strategies and activities are arranged around general areas of focus, such as word recognition, fluency, vocabulary, and comprehension. Because we built the framework of this book around broad-based areas of concern, you now have a framework around which to organize your own understanding and approach to remedial and corrective reading instruction. All the instructional strategies and activities are meant to nurture and develop proficiency within that broad area; they are definitely not meant to remediate any skill or subskill.

The strategies are meant to be generalized to many situations so that informed teachers can mold and modify them for their own teaching and learning contexts. As you and your students work with these strategies, we think you will find that they offer supported opportunities to experience reading success. We like to think of our descriptions of the instructional strategies as the raw material. Teachers need to take this raw material and use it to meet the needs of their students without lessening the effectiveness of the activities. Indeed, because our presentation assumes that informed, sensitive, and caring teachers will mold the strategies to fit their own instructional contexts, we expect the effectiveness of the strategies to be enhanced.

Because we recognize that instruction is extremely dependent upon the context in which it occurs, we wanted you to hear the voices of teachers who have tried out these strategies in their own rooms. You will see how they perceive and provide corrective instruction, how they modify the strategies for their own use, what they like about the strategies, and why they choose them. We believe that, by reading about these teachers, your understanding of and insight into the activities will be deepened and enhanced.

This book includes another unique feature—our attention to how different strategies might fit together in whole instructional packages or routines. We offer opportunities for wide and guided reading that will help you form consistent and complete instructional routines that are predictable, successful, and effective.

We think you will like this book. Whether you use it as a textbook for a course or a handbook for working with children in a classroom or clinic, you will find that it contains ideas, suggestions, and discussions that will help you be the best teacher you can be.

We have one further note. In our long discussions about this book, we found ourselves using many terms to describe readers who find learning to read difficult: remedial readers, corrective readers, poor readers, less able readers, students who find reading difficult, and children who experience difficulty in learning to read. Because no term is completely satisfactory, we have used a variety throughout the book. Please recognize that the various terms we use are not meant to categorize types of readers who have difficulty reading. Rather, we have included many terms to describe the same concept—students who experience moderate to severe difficulty in learning to read in the classroom or clinic or at home.

Acknowledgment

A book such as this is more than the product of any two individuals. We had help. Among those we need to recognize are Linda James Scharp, Brad Potthoff, and Jeff Johnston at Prentice Hall, who shared our vision of a new type of book on corrective reading strategies and methods. Our mentors, Jerry Zutell at The Ohio State University and Jane Davidson at Northern Illinois University, have continued to influence our thinking and challenge us to consider problems in new ways. Our own students, including Wayne Linek of East Texas State University, Gay Fawcett at the Summit County, Ohio School Board, Betty Sturtevant at George Mason University, Olga Nelson at Eastern Michigan State University, Belinda Zimmerman with the Kent city school system, Karen Niles, and many others who have graduated or are on their way, continually provide us with fresh insights into working with children who find reading difficult. Finally, those teachers and children whose classrooms we have visited and whose stories we have told must be acknowledged and thanked. In many ways we can say that this is a book for teachers and children by teachers and children.

Timothy Rasinski
Nancy Padak

Brief Contents

Chapter 1   New Perspectives on Helping Students   2

Chapter 2   The Instructional Framework   14

Chapter 3   Developing Positive Attitudes about Reading   30

Chapter 4   Word Recognition   48

Chapter 5   Nurturing Fluent Reading   68

Chapter 6   Building Vocabulary   86

Chapter 7   Comprehension Development with Narrative Text   102

Chapter 8   Comprehension Development with Expository Text   122

Chapter 9   Writing Development   140

Chapter 10   Putting It All Together: Making Reading Programs That Work   158

Chapter 11   Involving Parents in Children's Reading   170

Chapter 12   Determining Instructional Needs: Observing Readers in Action   188

Appendices   208

References   256

Author Index   262

Subject Index   266

About the Authors   273

Contents

Chapter 1
New Perspectives on Helping Students   2

Defining Whole Language   3
Whole Language Classrooms   5
Corrective Reading and Whole Language   7
Principles of Whole Language and Corrective Instruction   9
A New Direction   11

Chapter 2
The Instructional Framework   14

Accommodation   15
    Students' Conceptual Needs and Beliefs   16
    Students' Instructional Needs and Beliefs   18
Developing Communities of Learners   20
How Much Time on What Kind of Task?   21
Establishing Instructional Routines   22
    Read Aloud   22
    Sustained Silent Reading   23
    Choice Time   24
    Mini-lessons   25
Creating a Literate Environment   25
    Room Arrangements   26
    Materials   26
What Do Teachers Do?   28

Chapter 3
Developing Positive Attitudes about Reading   30

Motivation to Read: A View from Children   32
What Affects Motivation?   33
Finding Out about Attitudes and Interests   34
Learning to Expect Success   36
    Exemplary Classrooms   37
    Conditions of Learning   38
    A Success-based Classroom   41
Learning to Value Reading   42
    How Do We Decide about the Value of Reading?   42
    Schoolwide Programs   43
    Classroom Programs   45
Putting It All Together   46

Chapter 4
Word Recognition   48

Old and New Ways of Word Recognition Instruction   51
    Phonics   53
    Language Experience Approach   54
    Key Words and Word Banks   55
    Word Sorts   56
    Word Walls   57
    Word Families   58
    Making Words   58
    Contextual Analysis   59
    Dealing with Longer Words   61
    Reading and Games   62

Multimodality Approaches to Word Recognition   *65*
Fluency Building and Wide Reading   *66*
Putting It All Together   66

Chapter 5
Nurturing Fluent Reading   68

Model Fluent Reading   71
Repeated Readings   72
Paired Reading   74
Tape-recorded Passages   75
Choral Reading   76
Marking Phrase Boundaries   77
Choice of Texts   79
Fluency Development Lesson   80
Oral Recitation Lesson   82
Shared Book Experience   83
Support-reading Strategy   83

Chapter 6
Building Vocabulary   86

Traditional Vocabulary Instruction   87
Good Ways to Learn New Words   89
Three Principles of Effective Vocabulary Instruction   90
List Group Label   91
Other Categorization Activities   93
Concept Map   94
Analogies   96
Word Histories   97
Games and Puzzles   98
    Wordo   *98*
    Concentration (or Match)   *99*
    Scattergories   *99*
    Balderdash   *99*
    Hinky Pinkies   *99*
Books about Words   100

Chapter 7
Comprehension Development with Narrative Text   102

Supporting Comprehension before Reading   105
   Jackdaws   105
   Related Readings   107
   Other Media and Activities   108
   Story Mapping   108
   Role Playing   108
Supporting Comprehension during Reading   109
   Directed Reading-Thinking Activity   110
   Think-Pair-Share   112
   Character Sketches   113
   Linguistic Roulette   113
   Imagery   114
Extending Comprehension after Reading   115
   Group Mapping Activity   115
   (Write and Share)²   116
   Agree or Disagree? Why?   116
   Bleich's Heuristic   117
   Sketch to Stretch   117
   Compare-and-Contrast Charts   118
   Reader's Theater   118
   Response Journals   120
Instruction to Promote Comprehension   121

Chapter 8
Comprehension Development with Expository Text   122

Prereading Activities   124
   Word Sorts   124
   Brainstorming   125
   Anticipation Guides   126
   K-W-L   128
   Building Background Knowledge   128
Activities to Support Students during Reading   129
   Directed Reading-Thinking Activity   130
   Dialectic or Double-entry Journal   132
   Save the Last Word for Me   132
Postreading Activities   133
   Distinctive-features Activity   133
   Herringbone   135
   Guided Reading Procedure   135
   Response Activities   136
Principles for Effective Comprehension Instruction   137

Chapter 9
Writing Development   140

Learning about Written Language   142
Why Should Readers Write?   143
Discovering What Children Know about Writing   144
Supporting Writers: General Principles   147
  Classroom Atmosphere: Lots of Writing   147
  Talk about Writing   148
  Support, Encouragement, and Acceptance   149
  Modeling and Corrections   150
Writing Activities   151
  Personal Journals   152
  Dialogue Journals   152
  Learning Logs or Content Area Journals   153
  Copy Change   154

Chapter 10
Putting It All Together: Making Reading Programs That Work   158

Guidelines for Program Development   160
  Focusing the Program   160
  Massed and Spaced Practice or Activity   162
  Consistency Over Time   163
  Proficient, Professional Instructors   163
Effective Instructional Programs   164
  Reading Recovery   164
  Cunningham, Hall, and Defee's Approach   165
  Success for All   166
  The Curious George Strategy   167
  Fluency Development Lesson   168
Just Do It   168

Chapter 11
Involving Parents in Children's Reading   170

Use Proven and Effective Strategies   172
Provide Training, Communication, and Support   172
Real Reading   173
Make Activities Easy and Consistent   173
Make Reading Fun   173
Provide Texts and Other Instructional Materials for Parents   174
Provide Ways to Document Home Activities   175

Be Consistent Over the Long Term   175
Successful Parental Involvement Programs   175
    Communication   175
    Incentive Programs   177
    Paired Reading   181
    Fast Start in Reading   182
    Backpack Programs   183

Chapter 12
Determining Instructional Needs: Observing Readers in Action   188

The Classroom As Setting, the Reader As Informant   190
The Value of Portfolio Assessment   191
The Importance of Observation   193
    Why Kidwatching?   193
    Professional Judgment in Making Diagnostic Decisions   194
    Observing Throughout the School Day   196
Techniques and Strategies   197
    Anecdotal Notes   198
    Checklists and Charts   199
    Conversations and Interviews   200
    Performance Samples   203

Appendix A
Award-winning Books   208

Appendix B
Poetry and Rhymes for Reading   222

Appendix C
Predictable Pattern Books   224

Appendix D
Series Books   228

Appendix E
Alphabet, Number, and Other Concept Books   230

Appendix F
Common Word Families   234

Appendix G
Maze and Cloze Activities   238

Appendix H
Meaningful Prefixes, Suffixes, and Word Parts   240

Appendix I
Magazines for Children   244

Appendix J
Bookmaking Ideas   248

Appendix K
Sample Letter to Parents   252

Appendix L
Professional Resources   254

References   256

Author Index   262

Subject Index   266

About the Authors   273

Chapter 1

New Perspectives on Helping Students

Whole language is one of the most powerful ideas that ever hit literacy education. In just about any elementary school in the United States or Canada you will find classroom teachers talking about and practicing whole language. Magazines and journals have maintained a constant flow of articles about whole language, and conferences on literacy learning are filled with speakers presenting new ideas and applications related to it. Even parents have begun to learn about whole language as teachers and students inform them about the advantages of learning to read and write in authentic literacy settings.

Nevertheless, although there is a great deal of talk and activity centered around whole language, the concept remains ambiguous. In some classrooms teachers read to their students daily and call the practice whole language. In other classrooms, however, students choose books to read and then respond to them in creative ways. Some teachers create integrated units of study in which students use their knowledge of reading, writing, and other forms of language to explore topics that touch upon and require knowledge of social studies, science, math, music, and other content areas. Still other teachers develop environments that make students want to read—creating inviting spaces for reading, stocking classrooms with interesting and provocative books and other reading materials, providing time for students to read, and introducing students to good books that they may not discover on their own. In each case we have described, teachers believe they are providing whole language instruction.

Defining Whole Language

What is whole language? We certainly don't have the definitive answer to that question—and we wonder if there is one. To a large extent, whole language is defined by the teachers who put it into practice. Manifestations can differ from teacher to teacher, school to school, and grade level to grade level. Nevertheless, saying that whole language depends upon the person who implements it does not help anyone understand the idea. So we'd like to share some of our thoughts about the subject.

We start with the belief, almost a cliché nowadays, that people learn to read by reading. Several recent studies have documented that students who are good readers in school read substantially more than less able readers during reading lessons and free reading time in school and at home. In one study, fifth-grade students who were the best readers in their classes read more in one day outside school than the poorest readers read in an entire year (Anderson, Fielding, & Wilson, 1988). How can we ever expect children to become good readers unless they read?

Our next assumption is connected to the first. We believe that children are most likely to engage in reading when they perceive it as meaningful, instrumental, and enjoyable in their lives. When students see that reading is useful for themselves, they are more likely to pull out books, newspapers, or other written materials and read with purpose and passion.

Proceeding from this assumption, then, we believe that the role of teachers, principals, schools, and parents is to make reading meaningful and enjoyable for students. Teachers need to help students master and make sense of the written symbols on the page. Equally important, they need to help students develop a passion for reading—to see that reading can be better than video games, watching sports on television, talking on the telephone, camping in the woods, playing soccer, collecting stamps or baseball cards, or any other activity in which students take pleasure and delight. Teachers do this best by sharing their own passion for reading with their students: for example, by talking about their own reading, reading to students, recommending books, and listening with interest to students talk about personal reading.

Clearly, whole language is not just another method. Rather, it is a set of beliefs, a philosophy that "aims to be an inclusive philosophy of education" (K. S. Goodman, 1992, p. 196). Frank Smith (1992) has described the philosophy this way:

> The original philosophy of whole language, even before it acquired the label, had nothing to do with methods, materials, or techniques. There was no attempt to tell teachers what they should *do* to teach children to read; rather, the aim was to tell teachers what their attitudes should be. The basis of the philosophy was *respect*—respect for language (which should be natural and "authentic," not contrived and fragmented) and respect for learners (who should be engaged in meaningful and productive activities, not in pointless drills and rote memorization). (p. 440)

In whole language classrooms, teachers create conditions and develop activities that make reading something that students will engage in wholeheartedly and enthusiastically. When students willingly engage in reading and teachers provide necessary instruction, assistance, modeling, support, and encouragement, students become more proficient in reading. Because instruction is aimed at students' needs and interests, students will see the importance of reading and remain active and engaged readers beyond the boundaries of the classroom. The goal of the whole language teacher, then, is not simply to develop students who can read but those who *want* to read and *choose* to read.

Whole Language Classrooms

How do teachers create conditions that make students want to read? As we mentioned earlier, teachers create whole language classrooms in various ways. But one thing nearly all whole language teachers share is an authentic excitement about reading. They are avid readers themselves and share their enthusiasm with students, telling them about what they are reading, why they choose certain books, and how reading affects them. A teacher also communicates this enthusiasm by reading to the class every day. In effect, the teacher is saying, "Reading is so important that I am willing to take the time to share with you some of the best stories and poems that I know. I want you to know about and enjoy these stories and poems, too." Students are much more likely to develop an enthusiasm for reading when they are in an environment where reading is treated as special and important.

Research is beginning to prove this point. In one study, students in a whole language second grade read more in school and at home than children from a more traditional, skills-oriented program (Mervar & Hiebert, 1989). Moreover, the whole language students read more at school than their skill-based counterparts by a factor of nearly three to one. In another study, intermediate-grade students from a school with a long-standing whole language tradition had considerably better attitudes toward academic and recreational reading than children from a similar school that embodied a more structured, skills-oriented approach (Rasinski & Linek, 1993).

Some of the biggest differences in whole language classrooms are found between grade levels. In the primary grades, instruction focuses on introducing students to the printed word and stories. Because many activities at this level are group-oriented, we would expect to find the teacher reading aloud and talking to the class about books every day. Groups of students would be engaged in reading oversized (big) books together. Usually the content of these books is patterned or very predictable (see Appendix C for

Whole language teachers are avid readers themselves.

titles). The pattern makes the books easy and fun to read and read again. Bill Martin's *Brown Bear, Brown Bear* is one of the best examples of a patterned book:

Brown bear, brown bear what do you see?

    I see a yellow bird looking at me.

Yellow bird, yellow bird what do you see?

    I see a purple cow looking at me.

After several group readings in which the teacher points to words as they are read, most children are able to read the story on their own and begin to identify specific phrases and words from the text.

Language experience activities are also a large part of reading instruction at this level. In language experience students share an experience, which can range from a field trip to the local supermarket to a visit with the school principal to a math or science activity. After a brief discussion of the experience, students dictate a text that summarizes what they learned or reflects their perceptions of the shared experience. As the children dictate, the teacher acts as a scribe, writing students' dictation on a large sheet of paper that hangs from the chalkboard. When the text is finished, students read and reread it, first with the teacher's help and later independently. Children are successful at reading this story because it is about an experience they have all shared, talked about, and composed. Once students are very familiar with the text, the teacher may begin pointing out individual words and letters. At this level we would also expect many opportunities for children to play together; read and look at books on their own and with peers; write their own stories and make entries in personal journals; and read individually to and with the teacher, classroom aides, parent volunteers, and students from other classrooms and grades. When students begin to develop an affinity for reading and some proficiency in fluent reading, the whole language teacher gives them even greater control over and choice about their reading.

Intermediate-grade students may engage in what many reading educators call reading workshop (Atwell, 1987). In reading workshop most reading instructional time involves actually reading real books, primarily ones that students have chosen themselves. Students' response to what they read is an important aspect of this approach. They may respond to what they have read in their personal journals or write to their teacher and peers. In addition, they may recast the story in a poem, script, skit, or visual art form. Students also have many opportunities to discuss their reading with peers and teacher in an informal, accepting environment. Of course, teachers at all levels introduce students to unfamiliar books and literary genres by reading regularly to the class.

Another feature, one not often mentioned, is characteristic of whole language instruction—a caring and personal relationship between teacher and students. This is not to say that whole language has a monopoly on caring in the classroom; caring teachers are present in all teaching approaches at all levels. In whole language classrooms, however, caring seems particularly visible to students.

As teachers talk with students and enter into relationships with them, negotiate classroom expectations together, and give students a degree of control over their learning while providing support and guidance, students learn that their teachers care about them and their progress as learners. When students feel trusted and cared for, when they truly feel that someone has their best interests in mind, they are more likely to learn with vigor, enthusiasm, and persistence and attain the high expectations that their teachers hold for them. This attitude of caring and cooperation is pervasive in whole language classrooms. It creates an atmosphere of warmth and acceptance that encourages students to become active rather than passive learners; take risks in their study and explorations; and expand their interests, inquiries, and expectations.

Corrective Reading and Whole Language

We now have a good picture of what whole language is like in regular classrooms. Less clear is how it works in situations in which teachers deal with students who experience considerable difficulty learning to read and require some adaptive instruction. Some people claim that whole language is fine for students who learn to read in a normal manner and at a normal rate but will not work with those who are not making it. According to this way of thinking, these children need a more structured environment in which reading is divided into small digestible units. Educators assume that it is easier for students to master smaller segments of reading and work alone or in groups with other children who also have reading problems than to deal with reading whole books and working with students of diverse ability. This approach is called a diagnostic-prescriptive model. Diagnose the specific skills in which the student exhibits the most difficulty, teach or remediate those skills, and (according to the theory that underlies this model) the student will achieve his or her lost proficiency in reading.

The idea may sound good on paper, but in reality it doesn't work. Richard Allington and his associates have studied remedial, special, and compensatory reading instruction for several years (Allington, 1987; Allington & McGill-Franzen, 1989; Allington, Stuetzel, Shake, & Lamarche, 1986). They report that current approaches to remedial reading do little good for students who manifest problems in reading. Instruction tends to rely heavily on skill, drill, and worksheet activities focused on isolated words, sounds, and letters. Students have few opportunities to engage in real contextual reading. What they do read is usually chosen for them according to perceived level and type of difficulty but hardly ever matches students' interests. Children work by themselves or with other readers experiencing difficulty in reading, and little of what they do in these special reading classes has any connection to what they are learning in their regular classrooms. Remedial instruction usually emphasizes word-perfect oral reading of uninteresting texts rather than acquiring any meaning from the text or developing attitudes and habits that will draw students to reading throughout their lives.

Allington argues that current approaches to remedial reading don't work to the level of effectiveness that justifies their continued use with children. Students get into special programs, and they never leave and never get better. They tend to remain behind classmates who achieve at more normal rates of progress. What usually changes in these students are their attitudes about learning, reading, and themselves. They begin to see themselves as failures and view reading as a meaningless and frustrating task—something to be avoided whenever possible. Allington and others say that it is time to reinvent remedial reading.

Those taking a broader perspective on educational reform share a similar view. The Commission on Chapter I was formed in 1990 to investigate the strengths and weaknesses of current programs and recommend alterations for the 1993 reauthorization of the federal legislation that provides Chapter I funds for school-based compensatory and corrective reading programs. The commission's report, released in December 1992, describes typical Chapter I instruction: "Children in Chapter I learn and relearn discrete low-level skills. They rarely know what it is like to attempt interesting content or to use knowledge creatively. Rather than experiencing the joy of wrestling with ideas, children are more likely to spend their time circling m's and p's on dittos" (Commission on Chapter I, 1993). The commission argues that it is time to reinvent Chapter I reading.

One way to reinvent remedial reading is to make instruction look, feel, and be more like whole language classrooms than skill-and-drill emporiums. Of course, critics will say, "Whole language is too soft; it doesn't provide enough structure; students will be overwhelmed by having to read real books and become actively and creatively involved in responding to what they read; students will be discouraged and frustrated by working with higher achieving classmates; students will not learn the basics of reading." We disagree. We feel that whole language is an innovative and exciting approach for helping students overcome their difficulty and dislike of reading.

At our university reading center, children are provided with instruction that we believe reflects the whole language philosophy. Children read books of their own choosing as well as exemplary trade books chosen by the teacher. They respond to their reading in creative ways—for example, by recasting their stories as scripts and performing them in readers' theater for their families. These children write every day in school and at home about topics of interest to them. They learn to like reading, understand that reading is enjoyable, and discover that it can help them in their own lives.

Parents see the difference that whole language instruction makes for their children, and they are universally pleased. They tell us how their children hated to read before enrolling at our center. Today those children not only look forward to the center sessions but also insist on reading to and with their parents at home. Parents tell us that students who had previously refused to pick up a book, even when Mom or Dad told them to, now choose to read on their own.

Good instruction is good instruction, whether it's for children reading four levels above grade placement or those who struggle with reading. If children learn to love reading and make good progress in learning to read in regular classrooms with a whole language orientation, then it makes sense that instruction with the same basic characteristics will work just as well for children who are having trouble learning to read. Certain adaptations may be necessary, but we feel that the principles that drive whole language in regular classroom settings are equally applicable in settings that address the needs of corrective readers.

Throughout this book we will describe various instructional strategies aimed at overcoming specific areas of difficulty in reading (such as attitude and motivation, word recognition, reading fluency, vocabulary, and comprehension). These are not precisely defined skills but broad areas that are essential to growth in reading. Difficulties in reading can often be attributed to problems in one or more of these areas.

Although we describe and recommend instructional practices, we need to make it clear at the outset that such instruction needs to occur within a larger framework of holistic and authentic literacy education. The strategies and practices we describe are generic and can easily be adapted and applied to nearly any instructional setting, with students of all levels of achievement, and with texts of any level of difficulty.

Principles of Whole Language and Corrective Instruction

What are the principles of whole language that directly apply to corrective reading situations and establish a general framework for corrective reading? Among the most salient are the following:

Use authentic and whole texts. If we want children to be able to read real books and other reading materials, they need to be given plenty of opportunities to read such material in their corrective reading instruction. By reading real stories, poems, and essays, students learn that reading is enjoyable and does have meaning in their lives. The workbooks and skill sheets of traditional remedial reading offer little enjoyment and sat-

Whole language instruction uses authentic materials.

isfaction for students, and they certainly have questionable applicability to students' real-life reading.

Focus on students' motivation and interest in reading.   Most students who are having difficulty learning to read also dislike reading. They have experienced pain and frustration in their reading instruction and associate reading with unpleasant experiences. Corrective instruction needs to help students develop more positive images of reading and themselves as readers. Teachers can accomplish this goal by helping students achieve success in reading, encouraging them to read material that is real and personally satisfying, and engaging in instructional activities that are authentic and enjoyable.

Maximize the amount of reading of connected text.   Students in traditional corrective reading programs often get few opportunities to read connected written discourse. Certainly, they read less than students in regular classrooms. Yet we know that the amount of reading one does is directly related to the growth in reading one achieves. We need to create situations that make students want to read real books on their own, both in and out of school.

Let students lead the way.   In traditional corrective reading classrooms, the teacher makes all the decisions about lessons for individual students, sometimes basing lessons on diagnostic test results or packaged instructional materials. Students have little voice in this process and often have difficulty making sense of the lessons or connecting the lessons to real reading situations. Consequently, motivation and interest are difficult to sustain.

We can best foster motivation and interest when students are involved in reading and learning that they care about. By encouraging students to select their own reading material and inviting them to react, ask questions, and seek answers, we can help students control the purpose, content, and direction for their literacy experiences. Learning is easiest and most efficient under these conditions.

Provide support when needed.   Students are in corrective reading placements because they have difficulty reading. They cannot read material with the same degree of fluency as more normally progressing students. Teachers need to be ready and able to provide support to make reading manageable and meaningful for students. This may mean reading to or with a student before asking her to read the text on her own, ensuring that she has sufficient background knowledge to understand the text, checking that the text chosen for reading is sufficiently easy for her to read, or asking her to practice reading a passage at home with her parents before reading it at school on her own. Readers should never have to struggle to the point of failure or frustration in any reading task or activity.

Sometimes support involves instruction in specific skills or strategies. But this instruction is not the focal point of the whole language curriculum as it has been in traditional corrective-reading programs. Nor is it provided for all readers. In whole language classrooms, teachers provide skill or strategy instruction as needed—only if they can see that lack of a particular strategy or bit of knowledge about reading is hampering a student's progress. That is, teachers do not make assumptions about student need; rather, they take their cues from student performance. Moreover, the instruction is embedded in real reading tasks so that it gives students opportunities to respond creatively to what they have read. This could mean creating a script or skit from the text read, writing their own version of a story based on personal experience, responding to the reading through art, or developing and sharing a critical review of the reading with classmates. By getting actively involved, students are forced to consider and react to the meanings implied in the passage. Not only are comprehension and satisfaction increased but creative response activities often become a means for classmates, parents, and others to celebrate students' achievements.

Focus on success. Traditional corrective reading programs are predicated on a deficit view of students. The assumption is that something is missing or wrong with a student, that instruction should fill in what's missing or correct what's wrong. This view focuses on weaknesses among readers—on what they can't do. Whole language philosophy, in contrast, focuses on what students *can* do. Teachers do not think about students as remedial or view their task as fixing what's wrong with learners. Rather, they view students from a developmental perspective: they believe that all students can learn and expect that they will. They realize that instruction should be based on what students know and are interested in and what they are able to do.

Everybody's a teacher, everybody's a learner. Whole language classrooms don't look much like conventional classrooms—no desks in rows, no isolated individual learners, no teacher behind a desk monitoring activity. Instead, students are learning from and with each other. Variety and choice are evident. And the teacher is a learner, too. Teachers learn about students by listening to and observing them in action; they value students and are genuinely interested in their thoughts and opinions. Together, whole language teachers and their students strive to create a learning community where everybody's a teacher and everyone learns.

Involve parents. Reading is not something that can be learned and practiced only at school. Ideally, reading is an activity that students will do at any time in any place. Making parents aware of what is going on in the school and encouraging them to help their children at home in ways that complement school instruction will reinforce and multiply the effectiveness of that instruction. Moreover, involving parents will make them greater stakeholders in their children's education and increase parental support for and satisfaction in the job that schools do. Effective reading instruction demands that teachers inform parents and get them involved in substantive ways in their children's development as readers.

A New Direction

Whole language has a legitimate place in instruction aimed at helping children who experience significant difficulty when learning to read. This book was written to introduce classroom and special teachers of students with reading difficulties to instructional strategies that fit within a whole language orientation. As do other books in this genre, we provide descriptions of instructional strategies and activities. As we suggested earlier, however, these strategies are not aimed at remediating any particular or precise skill such as learning consonant blends, mastering sight words, or determining the main idea of a paragraph. Rather, the strategies we present are organized under general areas of concern that can be diagnosed by simply listening to a child read and respond to questions about the reading, observing the child within the classroom during instruction and recreational reading times, talking with the child about how he or she perceives and feels about reading, and talking with the child's parents and teachers about how they perceive the child's progress and interest in reading. Our major topics include the broad areas of word recognition, interest and motivation for reading, reading fluency, vocabulary development, and comprehension.

We hope that teachers will find the outlines of successful and alternative strategies useful for helping children learn to read. But we do not intend these strategies be implemented in any prescriptive or lockstep manner. Rather, we recommend that teachers become familiar with the strategies and modify them for use within their own instructional settings. Not all strategies work the same way for all students or teachers. Informed teachers will take the essence of the strategies that they feel have the greatest potential for success; fit them to the needs and interests of their students; and combine them with other strategies to create complex and integrated lessons that synergistically support children's reading while engaging children in authentic, interesting, and enlightening literacy experiences.

We encourage teachers to use the strategies creatively to develop effective lesson formats but recommend that teachers implement those formats with a high degree of consistency. From one day to the next, the general lesson format should be consistent yet implemented with a variety of texts. This consistent application of effective instruction will minimize lost time, make lessons secure and predictable for students, and ultimately lead to significant gains in reading. Successful reading programs such as Reading Recovery or Paired Reading owe a large part of their success to the consistent application of instruction as well as the incorporation of strategies that engage students in real reading.

We encourage our readers to use this book as a handbook or reference guide. It is not a book to be read during a university course in corrective reading and then forgotten. Rather, it is meant to be read, reread, and consulted frequently as teachers search for instructional strategies that make reading real for students and overcome the difficulties and failures they have experienced in past attempts to become successful readers.

Chapter 2

The Instructional Framework

S arah, a seven-year-old, finds reading difficult. Yet when we chatted with her about reading, here's what she said: "Well, it's hard sometimes, but it's not boring. Reading is fun mostly. It's sort of like taking a vacation in your mind." Her difficulties with reading notwithstanding, Sarah's comments make it clear that she considers reading meaningful and satisfying. When we visited her classroom, we found out why. Every day, Sarah reads and writes in an instructional atmosphere that reflects the principles about literacy learning that we outlined in Chapter 1.

Betsy, a reading resource teacher, shared with us her views about reading and learning to read: "When I have a student who appears to be at risk, my questions to myself are simple: What does the child know? What can the child do? Given the answers to these questions, how can I adjust my teaching to support the child's learning? I no longer focus on what's wrong with the child. Instead, I examine my instructional program, the strategies and materials I use." Betsy adapts her instruction to respond to her students' interests and needs rather than expecting them to adjust to her agenda. The framework that guides her instruction provides students with daily opportunities to succeed as readers and writers in meaningful and satisfying ways.

In this chapter we explore some of the issues that Betsy and teachers like her encounter in their attempts to ensure that instruction and classroom interactions foster literacy learning. First, we address several general aspects of instruction that have an impact on what and how students learn. Then we describe several concrete aspects of the instructional environment, such as the creation of predictable routines. Together, these ideas and activities provide a conceptual and practical framework that allows principles about literacy learning to be realized instructionally.

Accommodation

Betsy's comments about her interactions with students focus on a concept that is critical to developing an effective framework for instruction: accommodation or environmental responsiveness to students' needs. Accommodation does not involve letting kids off the hook, lowering standards, or anything of the sort. It's simply a way to acknowledge that students *do* have their own interests and needs, an awareness that the teacher can use to create personal learning environments.

Suppose you're interested in developing an accommodating instructional environment. What can you think about? What can you do? The first step, and it's a big one, is to consider how *you* think about the teaching-learning process. Years ago, many people believed that teaching was simply a matter of transmitting knowledge from someone who had it to someone who didn't. As we argue in Chapter 1, however, we have learned that this concept of teaching and learning is inaccurate. Learning involves the construction of knowledge, not its transmission. Learning is something we do *with* students, not to or for them.

Those who think of teaching and learning in this constructivist way believe that students must make their own meaning as readers and writers. They don't try to tell students what a story means, for example, but they do create learning environments that support students as they figure out the story for themselves. This sort of accommodation (or environmental responsiveness) reflects students' conceptual and instructional needs and beliefs. Let's take a closer look at these two areas.

Students' Conceptual Needs and Beliefs

During the past two decades, literacy scholars have done a great deal of talking, thinking, and researching about the importance of students' conceptual schema (what they already know about a topic they are going to study or read about). We know that effective teaching-learning environments must accommodate and build upon the background knowledge that students bring with them to the classroom. Therefore, the question isn't *if* accommodations are necessary but *how* to accommodate and *what* implications such accommodations have for larger curricular issues. When teachers begin thinking about accommodations, they often become concerned about time. It takes time to teach from a constructivist perspective, time for students to think and talk about what they already know, and time for them to embed new learning in their already established network of ideas. As teachers, we have to decide if time spent this way is worth it.

Deb struggles with the issues of accommodation and time in her fourth-grade classroom (Watson & Konicek, 1990). Not too long ago, for example, she began a science unit about heat by asking her students to brainstorm a list of things that give off heat. In addition to the sun, stoves, and their bodies, the children mentioned sweaters, hats, and rugs. (After all, they had been hearing "put on your warm clothes" for years.) So Deb, sensing a need to address students' conceptual beliefs, said, "What could we do to find out which things give off heat?"

The children decided to wrap sweaters and scarves around thermometers. After 15 minutes, the thermometer readings hadn't changed. But rather than changing their beliefs, the children decided that the thermometers hadn't been wrapped up long enough. They resolved to keep the thermometers wrapped up overnight and predicted three-digit temperatures by morning.

By the next morning, nothing had changed. Deb asked students to write about the experiment in their science journals. They wrote entries such as "we just didn't leave them in there long enough" and "maybe some cold air got in them somehow." So the testing went on, with children hypothesizing, designing ways to find out (which included sealing the items in large plastic bags so that cold air couldn't seep in), and reflecting about the results of their experiments.

After three days, Deb realized that the children had given up their old beliefs but had yet to replace them with new ones. So she wrote two statements on the chalkboard: "Heat can come from almost anything, even sweaters and hats. We are fooled when we measure heat because cold air can get inside" and "Heat comes mostly from the sun and our bodies. Heat is trapped inside winter clothes that keep our body heat in and cold air out." The children decided which theory made sense to them and wrote reasons for their choices in their science journals. Some were still puzzled, so Deb said, "What could we do to find out?" The children went out to recess with thermometers in their hats to test this new hypothesis.

In their commentary about Deb's experience, Watson and Konicek (1990) note the following:

> [If she had begun the unit] in the usual way, she might never have known how nine long Massachusetts winters had skewed her students' thinking. . . . [Students] would have learned a little about the sources of heat, a little about friction, and how to read a ther-mometer. By the end of two weeks, they would have been able to pass a simple test . . . but their preconceptions, never having been put on the table, would have continued, coexisting in a morass of conflicting ideas about heat and its behavior. (p. 680)

By viewing teaching and learning as a cooperative construction of knowledge rather than its transmission, Deb enabled her students to learn about sources of heat. She was satisfied with her decision to accommodate children's conceptual needs, but she worried a bit about the time it took to do so. In her journal, she noted: "The kids are holding on to and putting together pieces of what they know of the world. But the *time* we are taking to explore what kids think is much longer than if I just told them the facts" (Watson & Konicek, 1990, p. 682).

Learning involves conceptual change. To teach for conceptual change, we need to establish instructional frameworks that stress relevance; involve lots of predicting, testing, and confirming; and offer consistent opportunities to talk things through with others. Authentic experiences, whether in the classroom (such as the ones Deb provided for her students) or outside it (such as field trips), offer students opportunities to develop new concepts and refine old ones. To some extent, the teacher's or students' related readings can achieve the same purpose. In any event, instruction focused on conceptual change should offer students plentiful opportunities to share what they know, think, and have learned. Of course, this takes time. But teachers like Deb have decided that the time spent is worth it because such accommodations allow students to make productive use of what they already know as they try to make sense of or understand how their world works.

Students' Instructional Needs and Beliefs

Surely, creating an instructional environment that accommodates students' academic needs makes sense. We invite students to read and write and observe them carefully as they do. We look for ways to support students' growth as literacy learners. We also look for ways to challenge students, to offer them opportunities to stretch and grow in an atmosphere that promotes success. These two notions, challenge and support, describe frameworks that effectively accommodate students' instructional needs.

Students' instructional beliefs, their assumptions about how one "does school," are equally important to the creation of supportive and successful instructional frameworks. Educational anthropologist James Heap calls these beliefs *cultural logic*. He says that people develop expectations, based on their experiences, about what to do and how to behave in certain cultures (such as classrooms) and use these beliefs to guide future actions. We think he's quite right. Consider, for example, the story of Johnny.

Johnny came to our summer reading program at the end of second grade because his parents and teachers were concerned about his reading. He wasn't making any progress, they said; he wasn't an independent reader. Johnny's tutor, Janine, verified his lack of independence. He knew what he knew, but he didn't have any strategies for solving problems in reading. For example, his only word-recognition strategy was to make wild guesses based on the first letter of unknown words.

So Johnny and Janine spent some time working on word recognition strategies that summer. She taught him how to use context by asking questions such as "what word would make sense there?" And she encouraged him to skip unknown words when he encountered them and then reread the sentence, looking for familiar words or word parts within unknown words. At the end of the summer program, Janine suggested that Johnny dictate a list of things to try when he encountered an unknown word. She hoped that the list would remind him of his options as a reader. Here's his dictation:

At the end of the summer program, Janine suggested that Johnny dictate a list of things to try when he encountered unknown words.

When I Get Stuck

1. You can skip them and then go back.
2. You can think about what's happened so far.
3. You can look at the pictures.
4. You can sound it out.

After Johnny completed the dictation and Janine read it back to him, they had the following conversation:

Johnny: [points to items 1–3] Did you know about these before?
Janine: Yes.
Johnny: Where did you learn about them?
Janine: At school.
Johnny: You know, [my teacher last year] only knew about how to sound it out.
Janine: Oh.
Johnny: Well, she should learn about them. They work better, and they're easier, too.

We don't know how Johnny drew the conclusion about his teacher, but we suspect that he came to it honestly by constructing knowledge based on his classroom experiences. We have known others like him, students who think that their goal as readers is to answer the teacher's questions correctly or that their goal as writers is to produce "pretty" copy with neat handwriting and no surface errors. Although both reading and writing may at times involve these issues, focusing on either as a solitary goal is a mistake. The point here is that students' experiences in school cause them to draw conclusions about "doing school," about what they should do as readers and writers. Depending on their nature, these conclusions can hinder learning, as they did for Johnny.

Classrooms based on the principles outlined in Chapter 1 and this chapter will reduce the possibility of students' drawing potentially harmful conclusions about what reading and writing are and what readers and writers do. Teachers and students must share assumptions about the purposes and goals of literacy activities and individual literacy lessons. For example, if a student believes his responsibility is to complete an assignment or answer the teacher's questions, the intended learning may or may not take place. "Teachers might see quite clearly that a certain exercise will improve a child's useful knowledge or skills, but unless the child can see some sense in the exercise, the instruction is a waste of time" (Smith, 1978, p. 97).

Instructional responsiveness to students' needs, or accommodation, involves conceiving of learning as the construction of knowledge. We must be sensitive to how students construct knowledge about content as well as knowledge about what to do as learners in whatever setting they may be placed. In many ways, this instructional responsiveness is at the heart of effective teaching. When we understand learning as the construction of knowledge, we also understand the importance of instruction that invites students to behave as real readers and writers. Moreover, we know the importance of tasks that spark genuine student interest in inquiry. Most of all, we know the importance of signaling that we care about what students know, think, say, and learn. We convey many of these understandings to our students subtly—by the questions we ask, the way attention is focused in the classroom, and our choice of instructional routines. In all ways, we signal to students that the classroom is a community of learners.

Developing Communities of Learners

As adults, we may perceive reading as a solitary activity. This is not so in classrooms: Reading is "a very social activity, deeply embedded in interactions with teacher and peers" (Cazden, 1981, p. 118). We know that literacy instruction should foster meaningful interactions with texts and among participants. But we also know that students determine what they should do and how they should participate in lessons by drawing conclusions about the tasks they are asked to perform. As Johnny's story illustrates, they may sometimes draw conclusions that we do not intend.

One conclusion we *do* want students to draw is that they're engaged in cooperative rather than competitive learning situations. In competitive situations, difficulties are cause for distress, particularly if everyone else seems to be coping well. This may lead students who find reading difficult to "believe that reading is a contest they will never win" and to "become more concerned about avoiding failure and embarrassment than with learning to read" (Winograd & Smith, 1987, pp. 308, 307). Moreover, scores, numbers of stories read, or other measures of reading often become more important in students' minds than the actual process of reading, their reactions to reading, or what they are learning as they read.

A competitive classroom atmosphere can actually cause students to make counterproductive decisions about participating in lessons. For example, students whose comprehension instruction consists of providing the right answers to the teacher's questions may decide that silence or "I don't know" responses are safer than risking failure. Having chosen this route, students' minds are free to wander, and little further learning can take place. Over time, all these decisions become part of students' beliefs about being a student.

Activities that foster cooperative involvement and joint problem solving are a much better alternative. In cooperative situations, students are likely to view problems as challenges for the group to consider instead of indications of their own inability. In addition, cooperation leads to better learning (Spurlin, Dansereau, Larson, & Brooks, 1984). Instruction based on active, cooperative participation among groups of students can support the development of a community of learners within classrooms.

What is a community of learners? Dictionaries tell us that communities are unified bodies of individuals with common interests who share ownership and jointly participate in community activities. Families are communities as are groups of friends. Classrooms can be communities, too, if the instructional framework invites learners to participate actively, share responsibility, explore issues of common interest, and interact cooperatively.

The ownership aspect of communities is also important. Community members can ordinarily make some decisions about if and how to become involved in community activities. Classroom communities should also feature choice. For example, students should often be able to choose what to read, how to respond to their reading, and whether they wish to work alone or with others. Of course, individual community members don't make *all* the decisions about involvement; so in classroom communities the teacher has choices, too. In fact, balance between teacher choice and student choice is one feature of a supportive instructional framework. In classrooms, learning is most assuredly a social activity. To foster the development of literacy learning communities, we must promote authentic, cooperative interactions among students. We must expect active involvement and invite student choice.

How Much Time on What Kind of Task?

Time is another important factor to consider in establishing a framework for instruction. Deb's young students showed her the value of taking time to teach for conceptual change. Time available for reading is equally important. For example, the Commission on Reading (Anderson, Hiebert, Scott, & Wilkinson, 1985) reported that students in basal-dominated classrooms spend up to 70 percent of their time for reading instruction completing up to 1,000 worksheets each year. That doesn't leave much time for reading, reflecting, discussing—all the things we know lead to reading growth. Indeed, findings from a series of studies reviewed by Rupley, Wise, and Logan (1986) indicate that time spent reading correlates highly with reading achievement. This certainly makes sense. To grow as readers, students need opportunities to read. So in planning instruction, teachers must think carefully about how much time will be available for reading.

The focus of attention during reading time, especially during reading instruction, is another issue related to time. One careful study of two 30-minute reading lessons revealed that students in a high-ability group spent three times as much time on task (that is, reading and discussing what they'd read) as students in a low-ability group (McDermott, 1978). Allington's research (1977, 1984) has found a similar dearth of contextual reading for less able readers. These substantial differences must have an impact on reading growth. Other studies have shown that teachers' discussions with better readers tend to focus on text meaning, but discussions with poorer readers tend to focus on decoding (Allington, 1978, 1980; McDermott, 1978). As a consequence, perhaps, better readers spend more time reading, thinking about their reading, and sharing their thoughts with others. In contrast, less able readers focus on the mechanics of reading while paying little attention to what the reading means or how they might respond to it.

Ability-group differences in teachers' responses to students' miscues have also been noted. For example, Allington (1978) found that teachers correct poor readers' miscues more often than they correct good readers' miscues. Further, the correction cues that teachers provide are more apt to be graphophonic (sound-symbol based) for poor readers and semantic or syntactic (meaning based) for good readers.

Thus, instructional environments can differ, even for students in the same classroom, with regard to how time is spent. Like others (for example, Good, 1987), we believe that

these differences are cause for concern. Too often, students who find reading difficult participate in lessons that emphasize decoding, rote drill, and meaningless practice. Given our
knowledge of the reading process and ways to support reading growth, we believe that this
sort of instruction does more harm than good. In fact, it can lead to what Keith Stanovich
(1986) calls the "Matthew Effect," a sort of rich-get-richer and poor-get-poorer situation
where the environment supports continued growth for good readers but actually thwarts
growth for those who find reading difficult. Instead, instructional frameworks for children
who experience difficulty in reading should feature an abundance of time to read and write
for meaningful, interesting, student-selected purposes.

Establishing Instructional Routines

Part of the solution to the problems we have identified lies in instructional planning—
specifically, the creation of predictable routines that together constitute daily opportunities for reading and learning to read. Routines are regular blocks of time during which
certain predictable types of activities occur. To some, the word *routine* connotes bore-
dom. Not so in whole language classrooms. The routines we describe in this section—
read aloud, sustained silent reading, and choice time—are anything but dull.

Read Aloud

Story time is a staple in most classrooms, as well it should be. Read aloud should be an
instructional routine in all classrooms, including those for students who experience difficulty in reading. The benefits are many. Listening to an interesting text read well is a
pleasure for all of us. In addition, through the literature read to them students encounter
new ideas, words, and concepts as well as interesting characters, situations, and places.
Another advantage of reading aloud, especially for those who find reading difficult, is
that it familiarizes students with the style and form of written language. It also provides
students with a model of what fluent reading should sound like. Often poor readers have
only other poor readers for models of oral reading. Finally, a special time for daily read
alouds powerfully demonstrates that reading is a worthwhile activity, important enough
to include in the busy instructional schedule.

Virtually any interesting material can be read aloud—fiction or nonfiction, picture
books or chapter books, poetry, articles, letters, and so on. And read alouds need not be
restricted to story time. Mary Beth frequently reads aloud to her students with learning
disabilities. "We have story time every day," she says. "But I also read to students during
science and social studies, sometimes just a paragraph or two and sometimes an entire
selection. Not just nonfiction either; I look for poetry and fiction related to the concepts
that we're working on. Sometimes the kids bring things in. Reading aloud in the content
areas is a great way to foster additional learning and to give students access to information that they couldn't read independently."

Students can learn a great deal about the nature and process of reading by listening to good books, poems, articles, or other types of text read aloud. They can also experience the rewards that reading can offer.

Sustained Silent Reading

Just as time is devoted every day to the teacher's reading aloud, so, too, should students have daily opportunities to read material of their own choice for their own purposes. To develop feelings of comfort and success as readers, students need consistent opportunities to behave as readers—to read. Toward this end, we recommend sustained silent reading (SSR) as another regular instructional routine. SSR is simply a period of time when everyone, especially the teacher, reads. (Other acronyms, such as DEAR [Drop Everything and Read] and SQUIRT [Super, Quiet, Uninterrupted, Independent Reading Time], describe the same activity.)

Harry introduces SSR to his first graders on the very first day of school. Initially, children read for only 5 minutes, but by the end of the year, SSR lasts for 20 to 30 minutes each day. He begins with such a brief time period because he wants the students to be successful in sustaining their reading: "Everyone can hang in for 5 minutes. After a week or so, I gradually increase the time." Two rules govern SSR in Harry's classroom: Children must be quiet, and no one may leave his or her seat. Children's desks are arranged in clusters, and Harry puts an extra stack of books on each cluster of desks so that children can easily select other books if they need or want them. Harry makes sure that he reads during SSR, and he asks visitors to the classroom to read as well. "My reading sends the message to the kids that reading is so important that I *want* to do it with you."

The SSR period always concludes with a brief sharing session so that children can read interesting parts of their books aloud or talk about what they have read. Harry also tells his students about what he's reading—what he likes, what difficulties he has encountered, and so forth. "I consider myself a model for the children," Harry says. "Just reading is an important part of this, and so is responding to what I am reading. But sharing tough spots is equally important, I think. The kids need to learn that everyone—even adults—has trouble with reading from time to time."

Of course, there are lots of other times during each school day when Harry's students can choose to read and choose what to read. "But SSR is a time when we all have our noses in books and all at the same time," Harry says. "We enjoy it, the kids get good practice, and I think it goes a long way toward helping children develop the 'reading habit.' In fact, I really know they're hooked when they start groaning about having to stop reading at the end of SSR periods. That's music to my ears!"

Some teachers wonder if SSR will be frustrating for students who find reading difficult. After all, they are asked to sustain an activity that has proved troublesome for them in the past. In our experience, however, we have found just the opposite: Even the most reluctant readers eventually find success with SSR. They begin trying to read because they know that reading is what they're supposed to be doing. As they experience success, their interest in reading and confidence in themselves as readers grows. In other words, success breeds success. Teachers can support this cycle of success by beginning SSR with short time periods, ensuring a plentiful supply of interesting reading materials at a variety of difficulty levels, and clearly communicating the expectation that SSR is a time when everyone reads.

Choice Time

A third block of daily time should be devoted to choice, a time when students can make their own decisions about what they wish to do as readers or writers. During choice time, students can do whatever they want as long as their activity is related somehow to reading or writing. Unlike SSR, when everyone reads, choice time involves many different literacy activities occurring simultaneously.

Choice time is fun to observe in classrooms because students are so productively busy with such a variety of tasks. Some read or write alone, and others read or write together. Some perform or share their work, and others prepare to do so. "If you don't look carefully, choice time can appear chaotic," Brenda, a fifth-grade teacher, observed. "And I suppose, in a way, it is. But all you have to do is talk to the kids to see that they are meaningfully engaged and interested. Boy! Talk about time on task!"

Some teachers and students establish informal rules for choice time. For example, they might decide to reserve certain portions of the classroom for children who need silence or establish a procedure for seeking the teacher's assistance. (Brenda's students simply list their names on the chalkboard, and she works down the list in order.) Other teachers prefer less initial regulation, opting to see if problems arise and inviting students to develop solutions if they do.

Because students are involved in a variety of activities during choice time, the teacher's role varies, too. Bobbi Fisher, a kindergarten teacher, describes her role during choice time (1991):

> I have six primary functions during choice time: (1) to set up the environment, (2) to facilitate the routine, (3) to teach, (4) to act as audience, (5) to kid watch, and (6) to enjoy the children. . . . [M]ost of the children are practicing independently or with peers, and I work with individuals and small groups of students . . . , although sometimes my role is to be an audience while children are performing or sharing their work. During part of each day I watch children and conduct formal or informal assessments, and occasionally I [simply enjoy myself] as a member of the classroom community. (p. 70)

Choice and response are critical features of all three routines we have discussed. During read aloud and SSR, students exercise choice over reading materials; during choice time, they also select their own activities. Response, which is encouraged in all three routines, helps students consolidate and elaborate on what they have read in personally meaningful ways. Thus, response activities help to ensure comprehension for struggling readers. Moreover, students learn to behave as readers by exercising choice and responding to what they have read.

Mini-lessons

The three routines we have discussed could together constitute "reading time." Or teachers could develop others, such as time for whole-group instruction or for using the strategies and techniques that we describe throughout this book. Mini-lessons about specific topics are occasionally useful as well. A mini-lesson is a short, focused instructional session that can introduce a new strategy or help students solve a problem they have encountered recently in their reading.

Topics for mini-lessons come from what learners need. The lessons themselves typically begin with the whole, focus on some part, and end with a discussion of the usefulness of the new strategy or information. One of the great things about mini-lessons is that they can fit naturally within other instructional routines. Suppose, for example, that the teacher makes a significant mistake during read aloud. This would be a good time to teach a mini-lesson about when and how to employ the strategy of rereading.

Betty makes frequent use of mini-lessons in her Chapter I instruction. Not long ago, for example, her upper-grade students were conducting library inquiry projects. "I noticed lots of kids just flipping through the pages," Betty said. "At first I thought they were just wasting time, but then I realized that they didn't know how to use tables of contents or indexes." So Betty taught a mini-lesson about these text aids. She began with the whole—in this case a brief discussion of the frustrations that students felt about their inability to use the reference books. She then told students about tables of contents and indexes and demonstrated their usefulness by using overhead transparencies taken from a book. Next, pairs of students practiced using tables of contents and indexes in books from the school library. Betty concluded the lesson by asking students how knowledge of tables of contents and indexes might help them. "The whole lesson took no more than 10 minutes," Betty said, "but the students really learned, probably because the topic was immediately useful to them."

Planning instruction in terms of routines helps teachers focus on what's important and ensures that classroom time will be well spent. Routines are also helpful for students because a predictable instructional environment fosters independence. Students can get about the business of reading and writing rather than always waiting for the teacher's directions.

Creating a Literate Environment

Creating a literate environment involves everything that we have addressed thus far in this chapter. Two other aspects of the physical environment can also affect opportunity to learn: room arrangements and availability of materials. Support, interest, variety, and choice are important concepts to remember when making decisions about either aspect because environments that reflect these concepts both encourage and facilitate literacy learning.

Room Arrangements

"User friendly" is a good way to think about effective room arrangements. Rooms should be organized so that students can read and write independently and efficiently. This means easy student access to reading and writing materials and well-defined areas for certain types of activities, such as a classroom library area or a corner where resources and editing supplies are available. Display areas, such as bulletin boards, should be used to celebrate children's work and promote books and reading. Even promotional materials should be student-designed and made.

Everything about the room arrangement should foster the notion of student ownership of the classroom and their reading. Some of the most exciting and lively rooms we have visited, places where children are engaged in real learning, have students' work displayed on tables, walls, and ceilings in the classroom; in the hallway; outside the principal's office; and, in some cases, outside the school itself. What a message this sends to children, parents, and the community about what goes on in school!

Although the specifics of room arrangement may depend on students' ages and curricular issues, the overall organization should promote group inquiry, encourage independence and responsibility, and cultivate student interest. Many classrooms feature reading centers and writing centers as special places. Reading centers have comfortable places to sit, nooks and crannies for curling up with a good book, bookshelves and book displays, and so on. It's amazing what a rug, a few pillows, and a rocking chair can do.

Writing centers have all the materials students need for writing organized for ready access. Classroom computers and writers' reference books are also typically located in writing centers. Other areas of the classroom, such as areas for read aloud or sharing, may be used for both reading and writing as well as instruction in other curricular areas.

Classroom setups are important because they, too, can support or hinder students' learning. Like so many other decisions we make as teachers, room arrangements reveal what we believe about how children learn and the best way to support their learning. Bolted-down desks in straight rows reveal one set of beliefs; classrooms arranged as a variety of interest centers where students' interests and work are taken seriously and celebrated reveal another.

Materials

A literate classroom environment offers a wide range of authentic materials for reading and writing. Materials should be conveniently available so that student readers and writers have easy access to what they need.

Materials should be conveniently available so that students have easy access to what they need.

Reading materials for beginners of any age should support and encourage them in their quest for meaning. Predictable materials are especially effective because they enable "the beginning reader to process the printed page in the same way as the mature reader, employing the predicting, sampling, confirming, and disconfirming strategies from the first" (Bridge, 1979, p. 507). Materials are predictable when it is easy to determine what will come next, both what the author is going to say and how it will be said. Students' own dictations are predictable because they use familiar language and the content is already known. Pattern literature is predictable for a variety of reasons, including repetition, use of familiar concepts, match between illustrations and text, and use of rhythm or rhyme. (A starter list of pattern literature is provided in Appendix C.) Both types of materials provide a familiar, dependable context for beginning readers.

Likewise, materials for students who are developing as readers should also be supportive and encouraging. Because reading interests and tastes differ, students need access to a variety of topics, genres, and formats. And because we read for many purposes, reference books, lists, written directions, menus, catalogs, and the like are legitimate materials for the classroom. (See Chapter 3 for more information about classroom materials, including the setup and use of classroom libraries.)

Jerry Harste says that effective literacy learning environments are "littered with print." This is a useful visual image for thinking about both room arrangements and availability of materials. Although organization is apparent, classrooms are arranged and stocked with materials so that students naturally read and write in the process of getting things done.

What Do Teachers Do?

The teacher has an essential role to play in developing and maintaining an effective instructional framework. This role is shaped by beliefs and attitudes as well as instructional skill. Teachers must expect all their students to learn, see the value of everything that students bring into the classroom, think that it's more important to focus on what students can do rather than on what they can't, and believe that learning is easiest when students have choices and their instructional opportunities are based on interest and relevance.

Moreover, teachers are models of literate behavior. Through what they do as well as what they say, teachers show students what it means to be a reader, how readers handle problems, what value reading can have in a person's life, and so forth. This role—teacher as model—is critical to the development and maintenance of an effective instructional environment.

Teachers' attitudes toward mistakes are also important. They find what's right about students' work. They encourage students to take risks, try out new ideas, learn new things, and expand their learning horizons. Taking these risks will lead to student errors, but teachers know that mistakes are an inevitable part of the learning process, part of the human condition. They communicate this attitude to their students through what they say and do.

Jackie taught developmental readers in college. Her reflections about that experience summarize key aspects of the instructional environment and the teacher's role:

> I think of my developmental reading students who were "conditionally admitted" because they weren't successful enough in their bottom-up, form-before-content schooling. Many blossomed in the nonthreatening environment I tried to offer. *All* were readers and writers; but more important, *all* were thinkers, and they repeatedly demonstrated this when invited to do so.
>
> I saw Brian again today. He was driving a campus bus and called to me as I walked across the parking lot. He's confident, majoring in English, and plans to be a secondary teacher. He's a junior, I think, but as a first semester freshman when he read my comments about his fine writing, he said, "No one ever said that to me before." How could his teachers of 12-plus years not see him as a writer? I think it's because they saw him as "at risk" rather than inviting him to take risks.

Jackie's comments concern a college-age student, while Betsy's, mentioned in the introduction to this chapter, depict first graders. Despite the significant differences in their students' ages, the two teachers share fundamental assumptions about literacy teaching and learning. More important, they believe that their students can learn, and they have developed instructional frameworks based on their assumptions and reflective of their beliefs.

Chapter 3

Developing Positive Attitudes about Reading

C hildren are born with the desire to learn. They are curious—interested in objects, people, and events in the world around them. Parents and others encourage this curiosity and, in general, support children's learning. Consequently, almost all children enter school wanting to learn, which includes learning to read, and expecting to do so successfully. And most *are* successful.

Something happens, however, when children repeatedly experience difficulty learning to read (or any other kind of learning). They may become frustrated or tired of failing. They may lose their enthusiasm for reading. Often their desire or motivation to read is stifled. All this is dangerous, of course, because these negative attitudes can hamper learning and the desire to learn.

"I learned about the importance of attitudes the hard way," said Barb, who recently left her third-grade classroom to teach a self-contained group of intermediate-grade students with learning disabilities.

> I knew the curriculum, and I had studied ways to accommodate students' learning needs. I thought I was all set. The first few days of school were all right, but something was nagging at me. A week or two into the year, it struck me like a bolt of lightning: I was surrounded by kids who *absolutely hated* reading! As I think back on it now, I guess I should have expected that. But it really took me by surprise. I wasn't prepared for the intensity of their feelings. After all, they're just kids.

Instructional planning for students who find reading difficult must include systematic attention to promoting and maintaining positive attitudes toward reading. In this chapter, we present some general principles for developing a literacy learning environment where readers will be successful and want to read. First, however, we provide an overview of several issues related to attitudes and motivation, from both the perspective of children who are motivated readers and the perspective of psychologists who study human motivation. Then we suggest some ways to find out about students' attitudes and interests in reading.

Motivation to Read: A View from Children

In this section, we report the results of two large-scale research studies designed to help teachers understand what motivates children to read. One study focused on why children select particular books to read, and the other examined motivation for reading more generally. Both studies, which were conducted by researchers associated with the National Reading Research Center, have implications for teachers who wish to help students develop and maintain positive attitudes toward reading.

Palmer, Codling, and Gambrell (1994) used questionnaires and interviews to explore the reading preferences, habits, and behaviors of 330 third- and fifth-grade students. They documented four powerful influences on children's motivation to read:

• *Prior experiences with books.* Children at both grade levels mentioned this category most often. Children reported reading books that their teachers or parents had previously read aloud to them or books based on television programs or movies they had seen. They also frequently mentioned rereading favorite books and reading series books. Palmer et al. (1994) believe the appeal of series books may be based on the fact that "the characters, setting, and general story structure remain consistent, but the plot provides new and challenging information" (p. 177).

• *Social interactions with books.* Children placed high priority on reading books that they had heard about from friends, parents, or teachers.

• *Book access.* Easy availability of books, both in the classroom and at home, was important to children. Most children reported selecting books to read from their classroom libraries, which underscores the importance of the quantity and quality of books available in the classroom.

• *Book choice.* Children were most motivated when they read books they had selected themselves. Often these were books that someone else had recommended, which suggests that choice and social interaction may be related in an important way.

These categories of responses point the way to classroom adaptations that can help struggling readers develop and maintain positive attitudes toward reading. Children need easy access to books and the freedom to choose their own reading material. Moreover, both teacher read alouds and consistent opportunities to talk about books with others appear to be critical in developing children's motivations to read. We agree with the researchers that "teachers are in a position to have a positive influence on children's motivation to read through careful planning with respect to the classroom literacy environment" (Palmer et al., 1994, p. 178).

Sweet and Guthrie (in press) have also explored children's reasons, goals, and motivations for reading. As a result of their research, they believe that children's motivations for literacy are "multidimensional and diverse" and that teachers must learn to recognize the characteristics of these motivations to foster long-term literacy growth.

Children in Sweet and Guthrie's research reported both intrinsic and extrinsic motivations. Intrinsic motivations, which originate in personal interests and private experiences, include *involvement*, or the phenomenon of "getting lost in a book"; *curiosity*, reading to satisfy personal questions or hypotheses; *social interaction*, which is similar to the Palmer et al. (1994) finding; and *challenge*, such as the challenge involved in solving a mystery. Sweet and Guthrie comment that intrinsic motivations have both short- and long-term value. In classrooms, children need strong intrinsic motivations to learn complex strategies, such as summarizing, and to benefit completely from integrated, student-centered instruction. The long-term benefit of intrinsic motivation is that children develop lifelong, voluntary reading habits.

Children in the Sweet and Guthrie study also reported reading for extrinsically motivated reasons—that is, for reasons that originate outside themselves, such as with their teachers or parents. Examples of these motivations include *compliance* ("because the teacher said to"), *recognition* ("to get as many points as I can"), *competition*, and *work avoidance* ("I am writing this story so I won't have to read my book"). Sweet and Guthrie believe that extrinsic motivations are powerful because they cause immediate attention and effort but are limited because motivation ceases when the particular task is concluded. Unlike intrinsic motivations, extrinsic motivations do not regenerate themselves.

Obviously, we want students to develop and maintain intrinsic motivations for reading. Just as obvious, unfortunately, is the fact that children who find reading difficult are not typically intrinsically motivated readers. So what are we to do? Understanding motivation from a psychological perspective can provide helpful information for solving this problem.

What Affects Motivation?

Psychologists who study people's motivations to achieve believe that two variables are crucial. The first is whether we expect to be successful. We are all more willing to engage in activities if we expect that we will do well. The value we place on successfully accomplishing the activity is the second critical variable. If we care about doing well, we are more likely to try to do well. Both expectations and value affect persistence with any task, including the task of learning to read (Wigfield & Asher, 1984). Our challenge is to create an instructional environment in which students are continually successful so that they learn to expect success and in which students come to value reading because it meets their needs and satisfies their interests.

Attribution theory attempts to explain how people think about why they succeed or fail at a task. Most of us think we succeed or fail for one of three reasons: *ability* ("I am/am not able to do this"), *effort* ("I tried/did not try to do this"), or *luck* ("My success/failure had nothing to do with me"). Research comparing ideas about attribution between students with high and low motivation has found differences that have instructional implications. Highly motivated students tend to believe that success is due to ability while failure is due to lack of effort. Poorly motivated students, on the other hand, tend to attribute success to luck but failure to lack of ability (Weiner, 1979).

Attitudes affect motivation, and motivation affects our thinking about why we succeed or fail. Moreover, those who repeatedly fail may begin to believe that they are incapable of success. This syndrome is often called *learned helplessness* because the feeling of helplessness is learned through repeated negative experiences. People with an attitude of learned helplessness frequently quit trying; they don't see what good it does to try because they are convinced that they will fail.

Fortunately, learned helplessness and other negative attitudes can be unlearned; that is, students who believe that they cannot learn to read successfully can begin to believe in themselves as readers. An environment where students come to expect success and where they value reading can help them overcome feelings of learned helplessness. To develop such an environment, we must first learn about our students' attitudes and interests in reading.

Finding Out about Attitudes and Interests

Children with reading difficulties often associate reading with failure, and this often leads to negative attitudes toward reading. Some may view reading as a chore, while others view it as a waste of time. Many may choose not to read so that they will not have to experience frustration or failure. But this grim portrait can be altered; that's what this book is all about. Finding out about children's attitudes and interests is an important first step in this process.

The best ways to find out about attitudes and interests are to observe children's behaviors in the classroom and ask students to share their ideas in conversation or writing. Questionnaires or surveys can also be used; several are available in professional journals (for example, Estes, 1971; Heathington & Alexander, 1978; McKenna & Kear, 1990). Although surveys are particularly helpful when dealing with groups of children, we should not rely solely on their results to learn about children's attitudes and interests. The purposes behind the questions are often transparent to children, who may respond with "right" answers rather than those that reflect their true feelings. Observations permit us to check survey responses against actual behavior, and interviews allow us to extend or clarify children's responses (Rhodes & Shanklin, 1993).

Careful observation may be the most effective way to learn about attitudes and interests. As we suggest in Chapter 12, observations should be conducted objectively, over time, and in a variety of situations. Observation is easier when the teacher focuses on key questions. With regard to attitudes and interests, it's important to focus on both independent and organized reading in the classroom.

Here are several questions that relate to independent reading:

How does the child react to independent reading?
Does she choose to read?
Does he appear to enjoy reading?
Does she appear to concentrate?
Does he use books as resources?
What types of reading material does she select?

Any or all of these questions might provide focus for classroom observation.

Observation can also be aimed at discovering attitudes toward reading instruction, which may be different from attitudes toward independent reading. This sort of observation can be framed by questions such as the following (Padak, 1987):

Does the child participate willingly?
Does he stay actively involved?
Does she seem able to concentrate?
Does he interact freely with teacher and peers?
How does she react when asked to read orally?
How does he react when asked to read silently?

See Chapter 12 for further information about observation, including suggestions for recording information.

Informal discussion can be another way to learn about children's attitudes and interests. For discussion to yield useful information, however, children must feel comfortable sharing their thoughts honestly. If not, discussions can be subject to the same "right answer" syndrome that often plagues written surveys or scales. Discussion can also confirm hypotheses generated through observation. Moreover, we can learn about interests by talking with children about hobbies, leisure-time interests, favorite books or authors, and so forth.

We can learn about interests by talking with children about hobbies, interests, and favorite books and authors.

Teacher-made surveys or checklists are yet another way to find out about students' attitudes and interests. To gather information about students' attitudes toward independent reading, for example, we might ask these questions:

Do you like to read at home? Why or why not?
Do you like to read at school? Why or why not?
Do you like to go to the library? Why or why not?

Survey questions can also yield information about students' attitudes toward reading instruction:

What's your favorite thing to do during reading instruction? Why?
If you could change one thing about our reading class, what would you change? Why?

Checklists or surveys are efficient ways to gather some initial information about children's reading interests. A simple approach is to prepare a list of broad topics, such as animals, real people, mysteries, sports, make-believe, humor, and so forth. Then ask children to check topics of interest or rank the topics by preference. We can also examine lists of books that children have read to draw some conclusions about their reading interests. Figure 3.1 provides additional questions that teachers frequently use to explore children's interests in reading, the types of things they enjoy reading, and their interest in reading and writing as activities.

Barb, whom we introduced at the beginning of this chapter, uses all these tools to find out about her students' attitudes and interests. "I usually give kids a couple of written surveys at the beginning of the year," she says. "It's a good way to start getting to know them and their interests, and I pick up a few clues about their attitudes, too, which are usually pretty negative." Next, Barb observes as children begin adjusting to her classroom. "I look for the good times—instances where children are actively involved as readers and seem happy to be here. I use these to plan instruction. That is, after I have figured out what children enjoy, I try to plan more and more sessions like that." Barb saves conversations about attitudes and interests until she and the children have gotten to know each other. "It takes a while for the kids to trust me, and I know that they won't share the real in-depth stuff until then, especially if it's negative."

Helping her students develop positive attitudes (or maintain them, if they're already positive) is important to Barb. She also wants to know about their reading interests because she uses this information to plan instruction, suggest books, and help children form interest groups for inquiry. She believes that written surveys can provide her with some of what she wants to know about her students. But observing and talking with them provide an even more complete and accurate view. Each year Barb uses what she knows about attitudes, motivation, and interests and what she learns about her students to develop a classroom environment where her students can learn to expect success and value reading.

Learning to Expect Success

Most of Barb's students, like others who find reading difficult, expect *not* to be successful as readers. As we noted earlier, they have developed these expectations based on previous expe-

Reading Interests

1. What sorts of books do you like to hear others read?
2. What's your favorite school subject?
3. If someone were going to buy a book for you, what would you want it to be about?
4. What kinds of stories do you like to write?
5. What kinds of magazines do you like to read?
6. What are your all-time favorite books?
7. Who are your favorite authors?
8. What section do you head for first in the library or a bookstore?

Interest in Reading

1. If you had a free day from school, what would you do?
2. Do your parents (or someone else at home) read to you? How often? Do you like this?
3. Do you read to your parents or someone else at home? How often? Do you like this?
4. Do you like to go to the library? How often do you go there? Do you usually find some books to take home?
5. Do you like reading by yourself? Do you like reading with others?
6. Where do you like to read at home? Is there a time of day when you like to read? How long do you usually read when you read at home? How often do you read at home?
7. What's the best way to become a better reader?

Figure 3.1
Reading interests and interest in reading.

riences in school as readers. Unfortunately, such expectations usually take time to change; this is especially true for older students who have experienced feelings of failure for more years than their younger counterparts. But there is good news: Students can and do change their expectations for success. Classroom environments where this sort of change occurs share some common characteristics that we will discuss in this section.

Exemplary Classrooms

Mike Rose (1994) spent five years searching for exemplary classrooms (preschool through high school) throughout the United States. He spent time with teachers and students in those classrooms trying to identify what the classrooms all had in common. He found four ways in which these diverse classrooms were similar.

- Students felt safe, both physically and psychologically.

- Teachers demonstrated respect for students, and students demonstrated respect for the teacher and each other. This attitude of respect fostered feelings of psychological safety.

- Authority and leadership were distributed in the classrooms. Students and the teacher shared responsibility for leading classroom activities. When appropriate, students had opportunities to be "experts." In other words, classrooms were characterized by community and cooperation (see Chapter 2).

- Students believed that classroom learning was vital. That is, they saw the importance of what they did as learners and believed that instruction was in their best interest.

We can use these four characteristics to develop a literacy learning environment that will enable students to learn to expect success as readers. For example, consider the issue of psychological safety. Most of us feel safe psychologically if we believe that others are interested in our ideas—that we won't be ridiculed or put down based on what we say. If others are interested, we are more likely to share our ideas. This sharing is likely to be successful because of others' interest.

That's a cycle that can help students learn to expect success: Others' interest leads students to try, which leads to success. Over time, the accumulation of these successful experiences can alter expectations about the likelihood of future success. In other words, providing a psychologically safe learning environment can reverse the thinking that initially led students to expect not to succeed.

Vital classrooms begin with vital teachers. Students will feel good about what they do when the teacher is excited and enthusiastic about both their abilities and the topics studied. Such an enthusiastic teacher can transmit a love of learning to students as well as help them learn to believe that they can be successful. In contrast, it's hard for a teacher to get someone else excited about an idea or activity when his language and actions demonstrate no real interest.

We've heard that the great anthropologist Margaret Mead was asked why children in some cultures find certain things easy to learn while those in other cultures find the same things difficult. Mead responded that children find it easy to learn those things that are valued by important adults in their lives and cultures. Teachers (and parents) need to communicate to children that reading is important and useful and that they expect children to learn to read successfully. Similarly, attention to the other features in Rose's exemplary classrooms, when applied to literacy learning environments, can help students learn to expect success as readers.

Conditions of Learning

Like Mike Rose, Brian Cambourne has attempted to understand "exemplary learning" and provide instructional suggestions based on his insights. Cambourne has studied the environmental factors and conditions that support children as they learn to speak their native languages. The findings of this research, which has been conducted over 20 years, offer another way to think about creating classroom environments where students learn to expect success as readers. Cambourne (1995) has identified eight conditions that are always present when language is learned. He believes that these conditions co-occur and are synergistic—that is, each affects and is affected by the others. The following paragraphs briefly describe each condition.

• ***Immersion*** refers to being immersed in or engulfed by what is to be learned. For example, young children are typically surrounded by conversation and other forms of oral language. In terms of effective environments for literacy learning, immersion refers to the quality, quantity, and availability of reading (and writing) materials. As we noted in Chapter 2, the classroom should be filled with interesting and attractive reading materials. Students should have ample opportunity to browse through materials and read them.

Although reading materials are usually dispersed throughout the classroom, the classroom library should house the majority. Every classroom should have a library that is stocked with a variety of books, at least 10 per child. To the extent possible, children should be involved in book selection for the classroom library; they should also be responsible for organizing and maintaining the library. (See appendixes A–E for books that could be included in a classroom library.) Children in the Palmer et al. (1994) study overwhelmingly reported selecting "most enjoyable" books from their classroom libraries. This finding points to both the quality of the classroom library and children's access to books as significant factors in motivating children to read. Dina Feitelson also experimented with factors related to book access and children's "ownership" of classroom libraries. Both factors led to increased engagement with books and reading, which led her to conclude that literacy growth can best be supported in an environment "in which an individual can discover that reading is interesting and fun and in which it is considered a virtue to be a 'reader' " (Shimron, 1994, p. 95).

• ***Demonstrations*** provide the examples and raw data that enable learning. Demonstrations occur naturally as others in the environment use what children are learning. For example, listening to others talk helps young children decide about the functions and forms of language. Cambourne notes that demonstrations associated with oral language learning always take place in a meaningful context and serve relevant purposes.

Likewise, demonstrations associated with using and managing classroom libraries as well as those that arise from peer discussions about books and reading help students find success as readers, which ultimately leads to their *expecting* to be successful readers. Classroom demonstrations of literate behavior are vitally important as well. This is one of the many reasons why classroom reading activities should be as authentic as possible: Students need repeated opportunities to engage authentically and successfully as readers to develop expectations for success.

The models of literate behavior that we provide as teachers, whether reading aloud, talking about a favorite book, or participating in an authentic story discussion, are also demonstrations. Teacher-as-model is a common theme throughout this book, but here we wish to underscore the affective nature of modeling. Students cite their teachers' behaviors as motivators for their own behavior (Gambrell, 1994). They can learn to appreciate reading from teachers who genuinely love to read. Teachers who demonstrate their own real, personal affection for reading are much more likely to have students who share that enthusiasm.

- *Engagement* refers to active participation in reading. This is influenced, of course, by attention, perceived need or purpose for reading, and willingness to make attempts. Children learn to talk because they actively try to talk. And they try because they believe they are capable of succeeding, see the value of learning to talk, and feel no anxiety about trying to do it.

So it is with learning to read. In fact, Cambourne believes that engagement is the single most important condition of learning. The feelings and attitudes associated with engagement—seeing value, being free from anxiety, and so forth—are remarkably similar to those Mike Rose found in his exemplary classrooms. The activities, strategies, and instructional routines included in this book are all designed to promote active participation or engagement—real reading.

- *Expectations* about the learner's ability and eventual success are communicated by others, both overtly and subtly. About learning to talk, Cambourne says, "Try asking the parents of very young children whether they expect their offspring to learn to talk. Pay attention to the kind of response you get."

We know that teachers' expectations have an enormous influence on children's learning. This has been a persistent finding from decades of research (for example, Good, 1987). At the root of this relationship are two facts: (1) teachers are "significant others" in their students' lives, and (2) expectations are often translated into behaviors, which in turn influence learning. Thinking through the impact of teacher praise or criticism may help us understand how this cycle works.

Consistent verbal encouragement, such as "You can do this, Jeremy. I know you can!" or "Good thinking, Marie!", can lead students to believe that they *can* achieve and *are* good thinkers. Such beliefs may lead to positive learning gains. Unfortunately, the reverse is also true. Excessive criticism, for example, leads to anxiety. And anxious people have divided attention; part of it concentrates on doing the task while the other part worries about how well they are doing. Thus, it's not hard to see how some children's attention problems in school could be due to anxiety. In fact, Cooper (1977) found that children's behaviors changed when their teachers stopped criticizing them. Children began to interact more positively with the teacher and their peers; they were also more actively involved in their academic tasks. Differential praise and criticism—that is, expectations—influence children's motivation to achieve.

- *Responsibility* refers to decision making and choice. Children learning to talk make decisions about what they will attempt to say and to whom. They also choose to pay attention to some noises and ignore others. Other people provide opportunities to learn, of course, but children decide the nature of the language interaction in which they will participate.

This condition is also applicable to the literacy learning classroom. Self-selection of reading materials, for example, which we address in this chapter and elsewhere in the book, fosters student responsibility for learning. Likewise, providing choice during instructional sessions (see Chapter 2) and encouraging choice in responses to reading (see Chapters 7 and 8) enable students to develop feelings of control and responsibility for their own reading.

- *Approximations.* Children don't wait to talk until they can enunciate fully formed sentences. Instead, they approximate or say whatever they can, and their attempts are received enthusiastically. No one worries about approximations because we know that immature forms of talk will eventually be replaced by more conventional forms. No parent frets that a child will continue saying "Da-da" into adulthood. Like learning to talk, learning to read and write are gradual, developmental processes in which first attempts are approximations of skilled, mature behavior. Beginning readers and writers need to be supported and encouraged in their efforts, just as beginning talkers do. Thus, positive attitudes toward and acceptance of approximations (or mistakes) are essential components of the psychological environment in the classroom.

• ***Employment*** refers to opportunities to use and practice oral language. Most of these opportunities occur in interaction with others, especially parents or caregivers, but children also practice talking to themselves. It should be obvious that oral language opportunities are authentic—real and functional for the language learner. Similarly, opportunities to read and write should be as authentic as possible in addition to being plentiful and consistent. Children should have opportunities throughout each day to engage with the written word.

• ***Response*** is the final condition of learning. Children get feedback and additional information as a consequence of their attempts to talk. They use this feedback to support further learning. As in the reading classroom, some of this feedback comes from adults in the form of praise or scaffolding to foster further learning. Students also need opportunities to respond in personal ways to their own reading. Response journals, poetry, discussion groups, artistic responses, notes to the teacher, skits, and music are just some ways for students to respond to their reading. Opportunities to respond to peers are equally important, as are times for quiet reflection so that learners can respond for themselves.

Tom, a sixth-grade classroom teacher, found that allowing students to give creative oral book reports on Friday afternoons really swelled enthusiasm for reading in his class. Some students who read books together did "Siskel and Ebert"-style reviews, others shared artwork and skits they had created, and still others brought in artifacts from home that represented special items and events from their stories. "I had expected the standard book report in oral form. I couldn't believe what they were coming up with, and they were selling the other kids on the books they had read. This was the start of a classroom book club for us," Tom said.

By tapping into students' responsibility and choice, employment, and personal response, Tom had unwittingly unleashed some previously restrained potential for making reading come alive for his students. Responsibility, employment, and response led to greater enthusiasm and motivation for reading, which led to even more reading.

A Success-based Classroom

Can students who find reading difficult learn to expect success? We believe the answer is a resounding yes! Moreover, we believe that such expectations are critical to long-term reading growth and the development of lifelong reading habits. And we believe that teachers can create success-based reading classrooms by using Rose's and Cambourne's descriptions as a framework for making instructional decisions.

That's what Barb did, and here's what she says about it:

When I realized how pervasively negative my students' attitudes were, I knew I had to do something. I did some reading, I talked to a few colleagues whose opinions I respect, and I did a lot of thinking and soul searching. I finally decided that it all boiled down to several key factors. I wanted students to see reading as vital and to be active, frequent readers. For this to happen, I knew I needed to provide lots of good books, to set aside blocks of time for reading, and to encourage kids to try to read what interested them. I also knew that my own attitudes would be critical. I really *did* respect my students as learners and expect them to be successful, but I needed to find ways to communicate these feelings to my students.

Quite a bit of this fell into the "easier said than done" category for me. But I believe the goals are important, so I made a plan. My system is based on those day-planner diaries that are all the rage these days. I have separate sections of a small notebook for the goals I want to achieve. In each section, I have made some notes about the kinds of things I think I should do to help achieve the goals. And then every so often I look at the goals and the plans and ask myself, "Have I been doing what I planned to do? What else could I be doing?"

This is the way I work at implementing the goals consistently throughout the school year. Other people will probably have other ways of doing this, but for me it's important to keep the goals in mind and to make and evaluate concrete plans. And I think my plans are working. I have seen a difference in students' attitudes. I believe that they are beginning to believe that they *can* do it.

Learning to Value Reading

Learning to expect success is only one part of the equation for helping at-risk readers develop and maintain positive attitudes toward reading. Learning to find value in reading is the other. It's easy to see how these two factors are related. For example, many of the things Barb did to help her students begin to believe in themselves as readers have the added benefit of showing children that reading is a worthwhile activity, one that's enjoyable and fun and can help them learn and satisfy their curiosities.

How Do We Decide about the Value of Reading?

We value what we find desirable, useful, or important. Our students' attitudes about the value of reading are no doubt influenced by their families and reading practices in the home. Children who routinely watch their parents and others at home read for enjoyment, learning, and getting things done come to see the value of reading for all these purposes. In this way, parents and others at home are powerful models for not only literate behavior but also the development of positive attitudes toward reading.

Children's peers may also influence their attitudes about the value of reading. If peers view reading as a desirable and important activity, this collective attitude encourages all members of the peer group to value reading. This is one reason for the powerful influence of social interaction around literacy activity.

Of course, teachers and classroom activities also influence the value that children perceive in reading. Gambrell (1994) says that children value reading in classrooms that feature "choice and voice": choice in what to read, whether to read, and how to respond to reading; and voice in terms of the teacher's and peers' respect for children's ideas.

Guthrie, Schafer, Wang, and Afflerbach (1995) provide another view of the development of positive attitudes about the value of reading. They studied the influence of classroom experiences on children's interest in reading by analyzing results from the National Assessment of Educational Progress (NAEP), a standardized instrument administered to thousands of 9-, 13-, and 17-year-olds across the U.S. They found several aspects of instruction that were associated with increased amounts of reading (which itself was associated with increased reading achievement) and high interest in reading:

- *Social interaction.*   Students who said they read many books also reported spending lots of time talking with others about books, reading in general, and writing, both in and outside the classroom.

- *Cognitive strategies.*   Guthrie et al. (1995) believe that teachers created interest in reading in part by helping students find and understand books that met their needs. That is, teachers provided the instruction in reading strategies that students needed in order to read to fulfill their own purposes. Moreover, students who were interested and voracious readers often reported that their teachers asked them to share their opinions about their reading, think about how books were alike and different, and support their ideas with reference to books they had read.

- *Personal significance.*   Interested and voracious readers reported that reading was personally significant for them. They also credited their teachers with supporting these feelings. They said their teachers gave them freedom of interpretation, choice in reading material, and time to discuss reading with peers.

Guthrie et al. (1995) conclude that these factors converge to help students see the value of reading, which in turn sustains long-term motivation for reading. Thus, they can provide a firm foundation for an instructional program that helps students view reading as valuable. Special programs to promote positive attitudes can also help students view reading as valuable. In this section we describe several programs that appear to work particularly well. Some are schoolwide efforts, and others involve single classrooms.

Schoolwide Programs

Reading Millionaires (Baumann, 1995; O'Masta & Wolf, 1991) is a schoolwide program with a single goal: Collectively, students and staff attempt to read independently for 1 million minutes over a specified period of time. Like other schoolwide programs, Reading Millionaires takes a bit of organizing. For example, a plan needs to be developed for reporting the number of minutes read. In addition, someone, perhaps a group of students, needs to tally all those minutes.

Reading Millionaires can be simple or elaborate. A simple version might involve only advertising the start of the project, periodically announcing total minutes read, and celebrating the achievement of the goal. In some schools, the principal agrees to do something—usually silly—if children reach their goal. At one school, for example, the principal agreed to spend a whole day sitting on the roof; at another, the principal tried to milk a cow while the entire student body watched.

Baumann (1995) describes some additions to Reading Millionaires that made the program successful in her school. For example, she occasionally held raffles for paperback books, with return of the record of minutes read as the "ticket" for the raffle. She also created a "Reading Hall of Fame" bulletin board that spotlighted classes that had been especially voracious readers. And the parent organization in her school funded the purchase of small mementos for participating students, which were presented at a schoolwide celebration after the goal of 1 million minutes had been met.

Some schools hold annual *read-ins,* which are somewhat like slumber parties that focus on reading. Larger schools may hold read-ins by grade levels; smaller ones often combine primary grades for a read-in and intermediate grades for another. At some schools only students and staff participate; parents are invited to attend at others.

All read-ins involve children and books. Here's how one might look. Early on Friday evening, children (and parents) return to school with books, sleeping bags, and pillows. All assemble in the school gym or multipurpose room where they are joined by teachers,

Some schools hold read-ins, which are like slumber parties that focus on reading.

the principal, and other volunteers. Activities for the evening focus on books and reading. Children and adults read silently. Oral reading to partners or larger groups by both children and adults is also featured. Stories are told; readers' theater or puppet renditions of stories may be performed. There are also times for physical activities and snacks. On Saturday morning, everyone involved leaves the read-in after having spent a night sharing the fun of reading and enjoying the companionship of others.

Schoolwide reading projects can involve the *community,* too (Rasinski, 1992). Some schools form alliances with senior citizen homes or centers, and children travel there occasionally to read aloud for their senior buddies or listen to stories the buddies read. Pen-pal relationships may also develop. If they are able, the seniors may sometimes visit the school.

Community connections can also be made in more subtle ways. For example, children might create posters advertising the joys of reading and then ask local stores to display them. Some schools hold "Reading Days" at local malls. This usually involves some sort of visual display about reading, a few rocking chairs, and groups of children rocking and reading. Teachers and children can build floats for local parades that focus on books and reading. Some schools even have book parades that involve children parading through the school neighborhood dressed as book characters or holding posters about their favorite books.

Classroom Programs

Most teachers are familiar with Book It!, a national reading incentive program sponsored by Pizza Hut. The rules for participating classrooms are relatively simple. The teacher specifies the number of books to be read each month, and children who achieve the goal receive coupons for small pizzas. Teachers in some communities have sought similar support from local businesses (for example, fast-food restaurants or movie theaters) so that their students can be rewarded for independent reading. The key here is to connect the extrinsic motivator with promotion of the intrinsic value of reading. Teachers need to promote reading for the love of reading, not just for pizzas and prizes.

Classroom Choices is modeled after the annual Children's Choices project, which is jointly sponsored by the International Reading Association and the Children's Book Council. Children's Choices involves groups of children from all over the U.S. reading and rating new books. Their favorites are published each October in *The Reading Teacher*. Some states follow similar procedures to select favorite books among school children residing in the state. These projects are usually sponsored by the state reading or language arts groups. Teachers who are interested in participating should contact these groups for further information.

Classroom Choices is the same as the national and state projects but runs on a much smaller scale: the classroom. It works like this. For a school year (or a shorter specified period of time), children vote on their favorite books. In some classrooms, books are subdivided by genre, such as favorite make-believe book, favorite true story, and so on. Different ways of tallying votes are also possible. For example, children can simply vote yes or no about whether or not they liked a book. Each book's tally is the number of children who liked it. This can result in some interesting "run-off" discussions at the end of the voting, for many titles may receive unanimous support. Another option is to allow weighted votes, such as a 3–2–1 scale, where 3 is "Terrific! You have to read this book!" and 1 is "I wouldn't bother if I were you." Tallying these weighted votes and determining averages for titles can be an interesting and functional math lesson for older students.

Cheryl has a Classroom Choices project in her second-grade classroom each year. "I started because I noticed that the children were sharing good books with each other naturally," she says. "And so I thought, 'Why not go farther with this?' " Her project begins in early fall each year and ends at the spring recess. "We always write a class letter to the winning author. We tell him or her about the project and explain what we liked so much about the winning book. If we write early enough in the spring, the author usually responds in some way before school is out. Boy, do the kids love that!" Cheryl has found that her Classroom Choices project encourages children to read and share good books with each other. "It *is* a competition, in a way," she says. "But the books are competing and not the kids. I like that aspect of it. I also like the opportunities that arise to talk about what makes good books good, if you know what I mean."

All these special programs invite children to engage in authentic reading activities, encourage cooperation rather than competition, and feature celebration of children's abilities as readers. Although each program involves some external motivation, the programs are built on the assumption that internal motivation for reading will naturally develop when a spark for reading is ignited by the externally motivating activity. In other words, special programs can be valuable but alone cannot sustain long-term motivation for reading. Beyond these sorts of programs, teachers need to encourage social interaction around reading, provide necessary strategy instruction, and help students view reading as a personally significant and rewarding activity.

Putting It All Together

We want students to develop and maintain positive attitudes about reading and themselves as readers for at least two critical reasons. First, these attitudes allow students to develop the motivation they need to sustain interest in reading and persist in their efforts to become better readers. Second, it's not enough to know how to read; it's equally important (some would say more important) to value reading. That is, our goal should be to help students become both competent and avid readers.

Accessibility and availability have major influences on children's choices to read. A classroom environment that nurtures an interest in reading has the following characteristics:

- The teacher is enthusiastic about books and consistently supportive of children as readers.
- Children have easy access to many well selected books.
- Children have regular time to browse, choose books, and read them.
- Books are the subject of much comment and discussion.

- Appreciation for reading is developed through cumulative personal experience and response.

Students who find reading difficult often have negative attitudes about reading and themselves as readers. These negative attitudes can shut down further learning. So it's important for teachers to consider where the attitudes have come from, how they may hamper learning, and what to do about them. In this chapter we have provided a few specific ideas and many more abstract principles that can help teachers think about the relationships among attitudes, motivation, and reading.

Chapter 4

Word Recognition

Reading involves the construction of meaning from a written text. Unless the reader has some understanding of the text, we can hardly say that he is reading. To construct meaning, however, it is essential that the reader quickly, accurately, and effortlessly recognize the words in the text. By *recognize* we mean the ability to translate written symbols grouped into words into their oral representation, even if that translation is done within the reader's head, as in silent reading.

The less efficient a reader is at recognizing written words, the more mental energy she has to devote to the task. Thus, less mental energy can be devoted to making sense of the text as a whole. We want readers to become so efficient at word recognition that they can decode words with as little effort as possible so that all their attention can be focused on making sense of the author's message. Words familiar to students from previous encounters should be recognized instantly or automatically—that is, without the use of conscious attention. Unfamiliar words (often longer or content-specific words) should be recognized quickly and accurately by using effective word recognition strategies.

In our work with students who experience trouble with reading, we have noticed that an overwhelmingly large number demonstrate difficulty in word recognition and fluency. They labor over too many words, need to repeat many words several times before pronouncing them correctly, hesitate for a long time before attempting unfamiliar words, and seem to treat reading as a task of "getting the words right" rather than comprehending the text. When reading is so labored, slow, and frustrating, we have to admire students who persevere and are able to make any sense out of what they read. Nevertheless, despite their incredible efforts, they find reading much more difficult and frustrating than it should be. Just think how successful these children would be if they didn't have to struggle with figuring out the words and could devote all their mental resources to making sense of the passage.

Word recognition is a contentious area of reading theory and research. Some well-respected scholars argue that readers do not need overt instruction in learning to recognize words. These scholars believe that good word recognition develops as a result of reading for meaning. This may be true for many readers much of the time. But even the most proficient reader occasionally encounters an unknown word. Therefore, having strategies for figuring out words is essential.

Of course, less proficient readers—the children this book aims to support—are likely to experience even more frequent and debilitating problems with words. Children who manifest difficulties in word recognition read less text during their free reading than more proficient readers. As a result, they make smaller gains in word recognition. Without effective intervention they will continue to fall behind and associate reading with frustration and failure.

We agree that word recognition develops as a result of daily and sustained reading experiences, but we are also convinced that good word recognition is essential to proficient reading and needs to be developed through direct instructional interventions as well as wide reading. Word recognition should be developed to the point where it is so efficient that it doesn't seem to play a large part in the reading process. Listen to the good readers you know. They recognize words so effortlessly yet precisely that you hardly pay attention to their word recognition. What you do notice is their ability to process the text in a way that makes meaning easily accessible to reader and listener.

Some theorists who argue against attention to word recognition are really criticizing the way it has traditionally been taught. Here we agree wholeheartedly. Much word recognition instruction is divorced from meaningful texts. Often it is designed to be completed without the help of a teacher or other people, includes incessant and meaningless drill on words or parts of words in isolation, assumes that learning is most effective when learners passively respond to stimuli provided by the teacher or textbook, and requires the student to learn rules that describe certain letter-sound generalizations. Such approaches are not the most efficient, effective, or meaningful ways to develop proficiency in word recognition.

We have found that word recognition develops best when it is an integral part of meaningful and authentic reading experiences. Children learn to deal with words when they are actively involved in interesting and constructive experiences. The following principles help us create instructional experiences that keep students' attention focused on reading while allowing them to explore the nature and structure of the written words that form the text.

• Word recognition instruction should be an inherent part of real reading experiences. It should proceed from a whole text to examination of parts of the text and then back again to the whole. That is, word recognition instruction should begin with reading a text; move gradually to considering particular words and parts of words from that text; and end with a return to the text in the form of rereading, responding, or reading something related to the text as a whole. Moreover, after instruction in a skill or strategy, students should have the opportunity to consider its usefulness or applicability to their reading.

• Word recognition instruction should allow students some freedom to explore, make, and play with words. A sense of playfulness with words encourages the risk-taking behavior that leads to insight. By thinking about and acting upon words they create for themselves, children develop a thorough understanding of how words work.

• Instruction should include daily and extended times for group and independent reading of authentic texts that offer opportunities for students to put their word recognition competencies to use. Students need many chances to apply their knowledge of word decoding to the essential purpose of reading: making sense of printed discourse. Only in this way will students be able to master word recognition strategies and, through exposure to a multitude of words in their reading, make their subsequent recognition of words more efficient and effortless.

• Word learning requires students to see words repeatedly. But rather than see words daily on lists or flash cards, students need to see words in a variety of texts. Multiple exposures are the result of seeing the words in multiple passages that contain the target words. Sandy McCormick (1994, 1995) has called this principle of word recognition instruction Multiple Contexts/Multiple Exposures. Her own work with children experiencing difficulty in reading demonstrates the power of this principle.

• Choice of materials for use in word recognition instruction is an important consideration. Materials that repeat certain words, word parts, or phrases provide a natural context for repeated exposures. Verse poetry, chants, lyrical songs, and predictable pattern books provide near-perfect textual environments for word recognition (see Appendixes B and C). These authentic texts naturally focus the reader's attention on words and how they work. Series books (see Appendix D) are also excellent choices for reading and word recognition. Many of the same words and concepts find their way from one book in a series to another. Moreover, the familiarity of characters, plot, and authors' style make series books highly predictable (and successful) reads for all readers.

Texts of students' own composition can be powerful tools in word recognition instruction. Because students' own words and ideas are expressed in the compositions, familiarity with the words and story line are guaranteed. Creative teachers also generate texts—stories or poems—that highlight and employ words that students are studying. Adding a personal touch by including students' names or familiar settings and events can make such texts even more inviting and predictable. The excitement of knowing the author of a text is added incentive to read it well.

A key to text choice is ensuring that a selection does not contain so many unfamiliar words that it overwhelms the reader. Optimal texts are usually short and contain words with which students already have some familiarity. Too many new words might create frustration and too great a focus on word-perfect reading rather than making meaning.

• The teacher's role in word recognition instruction is to help students understand and use basic word recognition strategies and then immediately apply them to real reading. Teachers should never treat word recognition development as an end in itself but constantly and vigorously turn students' attention to applying the strategies in real reading. Teachers should be very cautious about testing students' skill in applying various strategies when their actual reading indicates that they are able to recognize the words they encounter. Word recognition should never be treated as a set of skills that should be mastered and tested outside actual reading. In fact, skill in word recognition is not worth much unless it can be applied to the task of reading.

Old and New Ways of Word Recognition Instruction

Traditional word recognition instruction can be characterized by lists of words in isolation, flash cards, and repetitive drill in practicing these words in isolation. We feel that this approach to word recognition has serious problems, and the number of children who have difficulty learning to recognize words suggests that they, too, have serious problems with the old way.

You will notice that many of the activities in this chapter can be extended into flash cards and word list reading activities. While we accept the goal of getting students to read words instantly, accurately, and effortlessly without referring to graphophonic, structural, or context cues, we are cautious about recommending the use of flash cards or word list activities. Such practices tend to communicate the message that reading is simply a matter of getting the words right rather than making sense of the passages. Moreover, they suggest that word-by-word reading is the appropriate way of processing text. Even more important, there is little that is inherently interesting or worthwhile in reading a set of isolated words.

The best alternative to word list or flash card reading is real contextual reading. In real reading students practice words and phrases, work to comprehend the author's message, and learn and enjoy the fruits of their efforts in ways that real readers do. One of the most enduring findings in all reading research is that good readers read a lot and poor readers read little. We must learn to maximize the amount of contextual reading that our students do because it is the best kind of practice for improving their reading.

Jane works with students who have significant difficulty learning words, yet she chooses not to engage in flash card activities with them. Here's why:

> I don't use flash cards for a number of reasons. I know it sends a message to the kids about what's important about reading. It's also a very inefficient activity. As one student is looking at a flash card, the other students I'm working with are usually thinking about something else. I prefer to encourage my students to read. Through wide reading they will encounter the words on the flash cards. And they also deal with contextual clues, phrasing, and making sense of the passage. Real reading makes a lot more sense than the humdrum flash cards.

The approach that we advocate for word recognition instruction features a great deal of student choice about and ownership over words. Students will more easily and enduringly learn words that are meaningful to them and their friends. Word recognition should provide opportunities for students to think, talk about, act on, and use words and elements of words and consider how they work. To become good at recognizing words, students need to know how words work and how elements from known words can inform readers about unknown ones. This is accomplished by discussing words with others, thinking about words, playing with and acting on words, and using words in the context of real reading and writing, not by mindless drill and memorization.

What follows is a description of various word recognition strategies that work. We have used them in our classrooms and clinics and know that they are effective. As with all instructional strategies, however, they should never be given to students in a mechanical or uniform way. Teachers need to design lesson formats that both meet students' needs and match their own styles of teaching.

Phonics

Apparently, reading teachers and clinicians either love or hate phonics. Some see phonics as indispensable to proficient reading. Others view it as something that bogs students down as they try to make sense out of text.

Phonics refers to the relationships between sound and spelling patterns within written language and the reader's use of this knowledge to decode unknown words. We believe, and research tends to confirm, that phonics knowledge is extremely useful to readers. Some readers develop and use phonics knowledge naturally. Others need to be guided by knowledgeable teachers to understand and use phonics generalizations. For us the question isn't whether phonics should be taught. Rather, we ask for whom and how?

We disagree strenuously with the uninteresting, mindless, mechanical way in which phonics is taught in most classrooms today. Indeed, we are convinced that many children end up in remedial reading classes and get permanently turned off from reading because of the incessant skill-and-drill activities and worksheets that have been foisted on them. In some classrooms first and second graders spend more time saying "buh, aah, tuh; baaaat; bat" than they do reading real, interesting books. As a result, we see many unmotivated children in remedial reading classes who think that reading is more about sounding out the letters than trying to make sense of the passage.

Steven Stahl (1992) has identified several principles that may help guide teachers in their development of phonics instruction for their classrooms or clinics. Among the principles are the following:

1. Phonics learning should proceed from what children already know about reading. It should gradually move from an understanding of stories toward an analysis of letter-sound relationships within the stories that students have read. Phonics, as part of a total word recognition program, should proceed from whole to part. Moreover, phonics and word recognition instruction is only one part of the total reading program, whether in a classroom or a remedial reading situation. Students, first and foremost, need to read and talk about what they are reading.

2. Phonics instruction should be clear, direct, and brief and focused on real words and text. Workbooks and worksheet activities in which children circle pictures, color, cut and paste, and so on do not help them learn the essentials of phonics.

3. Phonics instruction should focus on reading words, not learning phonics rules. It should lead directly to students' using their new-found knowledge to read words and stories. When children encounter unknown words, teachers should model or explain how phonics knowledge can be used to unlock letter patterns and decode the words.

4. Phonics instruction should focus on onsets and rimes within syllables, with the ultimate goal of students' noticing letter patterns within words. Onsets are the part of a syllable before the vowel, and rimes are the part of the word from the vowel to the end of the syllable. Rather than focusing on individual letters within words and syllables, students who deal with onsets and rimes can attend to larger segments of words and syllables that are more easily recognized and more consistent in their pronunciation.

5.   Invented spelling helps develop students' knowledge and application of phonics. Teachers need to encourage children to experiment with the writing/spelling system through their own spellings of words. Even though these spellings may not be conventional at first, they allow children to apply their knowledge of sounds, letters, and letter patterns in their own writing. Preliminary work in this area suggests that children who are encouraged to invent their spellings are better at decoding than those who learn to spell and read in more traditional programs.

Many of the instructional activities described in this section deal with elements of phonics. Children need to learn how to use phonics, but only within an environment of real and purposeful reading.

A final principle we would add to Stahl's list is to teach only those generalizations that students don't know but need to know. If a child demonstrates mastery over a phonics element, there is no need to teach it. That student's time would be better spent practicing the knowledge in real reading. Of course, this means that teachers have to be good observers of students' reading behavior—teasing out what they know from what they don't by watching students read, talking with them, and observing them in interactions with others.

Language Experience Approach

The Language Experience Approach (LEA) to reading is often associated with beginning reading instruction, but we have found it to be a excellent format for providing word recognition instruction at a variety of levels. In LEA, students use texts that they have composed; therefore, they have the important benefit of dealing with stories and words with which they are already familiar. Students own the text and words.

In the basic form of LEA, students dictate, either individually or in a group, a brief text of their own to the teacher. The teacher acts as a scribe by writing down the students' text on a sheet of large chart paper or, if the dictation is done by one child, on a sheet of notebook-sized paper. Students can read the story easily and successfully because the story is their own. After several readings of the story over a number of days, students become familiar with many of the words and are able to identify them more effectively in other reading settings. In fact, Russell Stauffer, an LEA pioneer, suggests that students be given their own copies of dictations and directed to underline the words they can recognize each time they read the texts.

Once children have become adept at reading the whole text, we often begin what we call the process of decontextualization. This simply means that we begin to focus attention on parts of the text as we strip away parts of the context. Initially, students' success in reading the story may be due to their use of context (such as pictures or familiar phrases) as well as familiarity with the whole passage. Decontextualization requires students to take a closer look at individual sentences, phrases, words, word parts, or even letters and letter combinations.

One way in which teachers decontextualize is by using sentence strips and word cards from the passage. Paula is a Title I teacher who has had great success using LEA with a number of her students. She tries to do at least two texts each week. For example, on Monday she might discuss an interesting experience from the previous week with her

Language experience activities can lead to effective word recognition instruction.

students. After the discussion the group dictates a story related to the experience, which Paula writes on chart paper. At the end of the session the students and Paula read the dictation several times—chorally, individually, orally, and silently—and with Paula reading while the children follow along.

On Tuesday, after a few rereadings of the story (as well as stories from previous lessons), Paula engages in decontextualization activities with her students. She creates a second copy of the text on chart paper and begins to cut this copy into sentences strips in front of the students. Together the group practices reading the sentences and puts them in their original order to remake the story. They also experiment with reordering the sentences to alter the meaning of the story. After some work with sentence strips, Paula cuts the strips into phrase strips and word cards that are also practiced, sorted into various categories of the students' choosing, put together to form new sentences, and played with in other ways. Students and teacher experiment with changing the beginning, middle, and end of several words to make new words. Paula also types out the story on regular-sized paper; she makes copies for all students to read on their own in school and at home to their parents.

On Wednesday, Paula may continue reading the story and messing around with its words and sentences, depending upon how well the students have learned the story and its parts. She also will begin a new LEA story with her class about the interesting speaker who came to school on Tuesday. She will make it a point to return to Monday's story periodically over the next several weeks.

Key Words and Word Banks

Key words and word banks are forms of decontextualization that give students some personal control and investment in the words they are to learn. This personal ownership of words provides a powerful incentive for students' learning. A key word is simply one that the student chooses from a reading. She chooses the word because she finds it interesting–the way it sounds, the word's length, or what it represents. Children will often choose words that are well beyond those typically found in materials for a particular age or grade level. But because the words are their own, students learn them easily and recognize them quickly in future reading. We have seen kindergartners and beginning first graders choose and learn words such as *microphone, carriage,* and *malevolent.*

When key words are written on index cards, they become part of a student's word bank. A word bank is a collection of words taken from students' reading and chosen by the student and his teacher. We have found that one or two story words chosen by the student and one chosen by the teacher are sufficient to maintain an active word bank. Students may choose any words they like, but teachers might choose those that can be generalized into other words by substituting letters or adding word parts. (For example, *dog* can be expanded into *doggy* or can be part of a word family that includes *log* and *jog.*) Children should have control over the size of their word bank as well as the words that go into it.

One idea is for students to keep two word banks: one in which they keep words they're learning, and another in which they keep words they can recognize on sight. Students choose the bank appropriate for each word and decide when a word moves from one bank to another. Words in both word banks can be practiced, sorted, used to make sentences, or used to play word games with other people. Moreover, teachers can use the contents of students' word banks to teach phonic principles. For example, students can sort their *a* words into groups according to the sounds that *a* makes in the words.

This immersion and practice with words develops students' proficiency in word recognition. For each LEA story, Paula has each student select some key words. Students write their key words on cards and share them with the group, telling why they chose their particular words and making up sentences that include the words. Paula also chooses a word that students write on cards and add to their word banks. From the most recent LEA story, Paula chose *table,* which she will use to illustrate the words that can be made from the *able* word part and discuss the "consonant plus *le*" generalization.

Once or twice a week Paula's students warm up for reading by reading their word bank words with a partner. Partners also use their word bank words to make sentences. At least once a week students sort their word bank words into categories that Paula provides or that students think of. Students also use their word banks for games such as word match (duplicate sets of word cards are laid face down and players have to find matching pairs) and word war (the word played with the most letters and read correctly wins the war). In addition, Paula uses the word banks to practice alphabetizing and other word-related concepts such as word families and phonics generalizations.

Word Sorts

Word sorts are activities that invite small groups of students to categorize words according to some dimension identified by the teacher or a student. Word sorts allow students to use their knowledge and learn from and with each other. Teachers can choose to focus on particular word elements, depending on student need; or the activity can be totally student-centered. Moreover, word sorts work particularly well when students in small groups sort the words from their individual word banks.

Paula uses word sorts with her students several times each week as part of their word bank activities. After a mini-lesson on syllabication, Paula has her students work in groups of three to sort their word bank cards into words containing one, two, three, and more than three syllables. On other occasions she has students sort words by initial consonants, vowels sounds, long and short vowels, prefixes and suffixes, and other word characteristics with which she wants her students to become familiar. "I think it's important for students to put into practice the strategies we are exploring. Word sorts give students the opportunity to test their knowledge with words they are already familiar with, and the sorts allow me to observe how well students have grasped and can use the strategies. I think it's also important to note that when groups of students use word sorts they actually teach and reinforce each other as they go."

Students can also sort their words into their own creative categories, an approach that Paula sometimes uses with her class. After a few minutes of sorting, groups of students try to guess (infer) the categories created by other groups. Sometimes Paula simply asks each group to explain its way of categorizing. "But they really prefer the guessing," she says. "It's like a game to them, but I'm constantly amazed at the high level of thinking."

Word Walls

One of our goals in word recognition instruction is to create a physical environment in the classroom that encourages word exploration and play. One step toward creating such an environment is through word walls. Pat Cunningham describes word walls as one aspect of a four-part instructional strategy in reading (Cunningham & Cunningham, 1992). We like to think of them as part community word bank, part graffiti wall, a place where students feel free to write their own words and commentaries.

A word wall begins when the teacher places a large piece of butcher or chart paper on a classroom wall. Every day the class adds a word or two to the wall. The word may be related to a current event in the world or local community. Teacher and students explore other words related to the chosen words for the day and then write the related words on the wall, often connecting them with lines like an idea web. Teacher and students also look for letter patterns in the chosen words and brainstorm other words that contain the pattern. Students practice and refer to the words on the wall often. In some classrooms students may use the word wall to jot down some of their own words or ideas. These are then read by all students and result in lively oral and written discussion.

Sherrie is a fifth-grade teacher. The first thing a visitor notices in her room is the word wall that takes up an entire bulletin board. One day the word *portage* was selected for the wall because a student came upon it in his reading. (Portage is the name of the county in which the school is located.) After talking about the meaning of the word, Sherrie and her students added and discussed other related words (either by meaning or structure). Among them were *canoe, river, port, porter, portable, sort, porous,* and *sage.* Sherrie reports that each word wall fills up in less than two weeks. She leaves it up for a few days after it is filled because she finds that students often refer to the words in their own writing or discussion and are continually adding words that connect to the ones on the board. Even though the wall may not look very neat after several days of student contributions, Sherrie notes that it is important to the class as a whole because the words are meaningful for students and the wall itself is a joint venture to which all students feel the need to contribute.

Word Families

Many words that children encounter in their reading are made up of common word parts or rimes. Recognizing the *an* word part can help students decode words such as *can, pan, ant, pant, fantasy,* and so on. Indeed, almost 500 primary words can be derived from the following 37 word parts (Stahl, 1972):

-ack	-ain	-ake	-ale	-all	-ame	-an
-ank	-ap	-ash	-at	-ate	-aw	-ay
-eat	-ell	-est	-ice	-ick	-ide	-ight
-ill	-in	-ine	-ing	-ink	-ip	-ir
-ock	-oke	-op	-or	-ore	-uck	-ug
-ump	-unk					

See Appendix F for other common word families and letter patterns. Such knowledge can help students figure out unknown words.

Mel makes good use of word family instruction with his primary and intermediate-grade students who have difficulty recognizing words. Every three to five days he introduces a new word family to his students. The first thing they do is brainstorm as many words as they can that contain that word part. Using a large sheet of chart paper, Mel writes down his students' choices as they are called out. The paper is hung in the classroom, and students add new words to the chart as they are discovered.

Mel encourages his students to use the words from the word family in their writing, class work, and individual poems. He also reads his own poems and poems written by former students that contain the word family under study. Later, Mel demonstrates how knowledge of the word part can help students decode unknown and lengthy words. For example, after working on the *at* word part Mel helped his students see how knowledge of *at* could help them figure out *Atlantic* and *cattle.*

Making Words

Making Words is another activity that Pat Cunningham considers to be part of a comprehensive reading program (Cunningham & Cunningham, 1992). The activity has several key features. Students make up their own increasingly complex words by concretely manipulating a limited set of letters. Those who find word recognition difficult are often overwhelmed by the seemingly endless number of letters and letter-sound patterns they need to deal with. But limiting the number of letters to between five and eight helps students focus on the essential characteristics of a few letters at a time. As with most activities, we recommend that students work in pairs or small groups so that they can learn more thoroughly by talking with and teaching each other.

Making Words begins when the teacher selects a word of between five and eight letters from students' previous reading. After passing out enough one-inch squares of paper for each letter to each group, the teacher calls out the letters of the word and students write down one letter on each slip. Now the fun begins.

Mel makes words with several of his primary Title I classes. He begins by asking student pairs to arrange the letters to make two-letter words. Then students call out their constructions, and Mel writes a few of the words on the board. Mel also tells students words and observes as they work to make them with their letters. Next, students work through three-, four-, five-, and six-letter words. Mel writes many of these on the board as well. At last he challenges his students to use all the letters to come up with the original word and other words that can be made from the entire set of letters.

Using a few of the words written on the board as examples, Mel explores some of them with the group, noticing word families and moving from one word to another through letter changes. "What would I have to do to change *part* to *art* to *par?* To change *art* to *arch?* To change *par* to *parka?*" Mel often cuts up a transparency into squares and does the activity with his students on an overhead projector so that students can see the manipulations. Sometimes he does the same with large index cards and a pocket chart. Making Words is quick and fast paced. Students learn, in a very concrete way, that words and the letters that form them can be manipulated in a variety of ways. Mel has found that his students like the fast pace of the activity and the fact that they are actively involved throughout the 10- to 15-minute session.

Contextual Analysis

In addition to analyzing letters and letter combinations to decode or recognize words, proficient readers use context to help them figure out unfamiliar words. In other words, readers use the meaning of the passage and sentence as well as their own knowledge about the world to predict unknown words. For example, consider the following sentence:

The mail carrier was bitten by a ____.

Readers can figure out the unknown word by combining the information in the sentence with what they know about the stereotypical predicament of postal carriers on their rounds. Combining this information leads to the prediction or inference that the missing word is most likely *dog*. Thus, a reasonable prediction can be made without using any letter or phonic information from the word itself.

We can help readers use context by asking them to think about what an unknown word might be based upon the meaning of the passage rather than always advising them to "sound it out." Similarly, teachers can occasionally explain to their students how they figure out unknown words in their own reading. Some experts call this explanation of one's problem-solving process "think alouds." Making such subtleties clear and apparent to students is what teaching is all about.

Another activity that helps develop readers' use of context is the cloze procedure. Cloze may seem like an odd name, but it is based upon the psychological understanding that humans attempt to provide closure or completeness to incomplete illustrations or objects. In the cloze procedure the reader attempts to impose closure on incomplete linguistic data by using the contextual information available in the passage. The teacher deletes words from a passage by marking over certain words with a marker or retyping the passage with blanks for the deleted words. Here is an example of a cloze activity taken from *Stega Nona's Magic Lesson* by Tomie dePaola:

> Bambolona, the baker's daughter, was angry. Every day, summer, fall, ____, and ____, she had to get up before the sun to bake the ____. Then, piling the ____ on her head, she went to deliver them.

When creating a cloze passage it is a good idea to leave the first sentence intact so that the reader can establish a mental framework for the text.

The reader's job is to use the context before and after the deleted words to identify the deletions. After completing a passage with 20 to 30 deletions, students share their guesses with one another and discuss the clues they used to make their predictions. The teacher may also provide the words actually used by the author. Cloze activities work well in groups as students verbalize their own strategies for predicting words with their partners.

There are several variations possible with the cloze. Students unfamiliar with the procedure or who are dealing with a difficult text may be overwhelmed by a passage containing many deleted words. The task can be made easier by placing possible answers next to each blank or listing all the deleted words at the end of the passage. The activity is then called a maze or multiple-choice cloze.

> One day Bambolona said, "Papa, there is too much ____ (work, noise, money) to do. I need some ____ (fun, work, help)."
> "Get up earlier," her father said.
>
> "But I get up now before the ____!" said ____. "And I'm the last one in town to ____ to bed."
> "That's the way things are," ____ father said as he went out the ____ on his way to the ____.
> (Bambolona, square, her, go, door, sun)

Good readers simultaneously employ both context and letter information to decode words. Cloze activities can be designed so that students integrate both sources of information about words. Here's an example from Gary Paulsen's *Hatchet:*

Somehow the plane was still flying. Seconds had passed, nearly a m____, and the plane f____ on as if nothing had happened and he had to do something, had to do something but did n____ know what. . . .

He st____ one h____ toward the p____, saw that his fingers were trembling, and touched the pilot on the chest. . . .

The pl____ lurched again, hit more t____, and Brian felt the nose dr____. It did not d____, but the n____ went down slightly and the down-angle i____ the speed, and he knew that at this angle, this slight angle d____, he would ultimately f____ into the tr____.

In this passage readers employ both context and the beginning letter or letter combination, which are the most salient graphic cues for readers trying to recognize the missing words.

Key elements in using the cloze procedure successfully include choosing texts that are challenging but not overwhelming, giving students time and assistance in predicting the missing words, and encouraging students to share the strategies and clues they used in identifying the unknown words. Other examples of cloze passages are found in Appendix G.

Karen, a Title I teacher who works with primary-grade children, finds that many of her students get so hung up on sounding out words that they fail to attend to the meaning of the passage. They often come up with responses that are nonwords or words that fail to fit the meaning of the passage. Karen designs cloze passages for these children. She chooses stories that students have read a few days previously and found interesting. "This ensures that the students have a familiarity with the content and that they have a motivation for reading." As students become more adept at using context she may choose unfamiliar passages that come from a sequel or are written by a familiar author.

She may also add challenge by increasing the number of blanks within a given passage but always ensuring that enough context is available for making good predictions. As a rule of thumb, Karen provides at least four words of actual text for every word she deletes when developing her most challenging cloze passages.

To Karen, the student talk is what really counts in cloze activities. "I think that the most important part of the cloze activity is when we talk after the groups have had a chance to fill in the blanks. Students talk about the various strategies they used to figure out the blanks. This is where you see the lights go on in students' heads as they say to themselves, 'Oh yeah! I didn't think about doing it that way.' "

Dealing with Longer Words

Long words can daunt young and struggling readers, and initially these unfamiliar words are often difficult to handle as whole units. Even when proficient readers come to longer words, they tend to break the word into manageable chunks and then apply some of their basic word recognition strategies to the chunks until they become familiar with the word. There are several strategies that readers can use to break longer words down into more manageable units.

Compound words.   Compound words are combinations of two whole words. Compound words can first be broken into their constituent words. For example, *everybody* can initially be broken into *every* and *body* and either identified as a whole word or analyzed into smaller units.

Affixes.   Prefixes and suffixes often add to the length of words. After searching for compounds, readers should look for common prefixes and suffixes and separate them from longer unknown words. For example, *telephone* can be broken into the common prefix *tele* and the base word *phone* and decoded from these two major parts. Similarly, *government* can easily be broken into the base word *govern* and the common suffix *ment*.

Letter patterns.   Earlier in this chapter we discussed the idea of helping students become familiar with common letter patterns, which we also called rimes and word families. A good strategy for helping students deal with long words is to encourage them and give them practice in finding these patterns in longer words. Research in word recognition suggests that this pattern search, combined with contextual confirmation, is the way that proficient readers read. Therefore, teaching students to employ this strategy can be highly effective. In the word *literature,* for example, there are several patterns that students can use to decode the word. *It, er,* and *ture* should be familiar word parts to students who have had opportunities to play with words and word families.

Reading and Games

The best way for students to put their word recognition strategies to use is through plenty of contextual reading. Through actual reading, readers become adept at using helpful word recognition strategies. Moreover, through repeated exposure to many

Games can provide enjoyable practice in word recognition.

words, they add to their sight vocabularies—words that can be recognized instantly at sight without having to rely on any recognition strategy. Thus, reading actually reduces the number of words to which readers have to apply decoding strategies.

Occasional games can add a different dimension to reading instruction while giving students enjoyable practice at recognizing words. Most are simple, and many are variations of popular television game shows. Here are a few of our favorites.

Scrabble.   In this classic board game, players are challenged to construct words from a limited set of letters that fit within an array of letters already on the board.

Hangman and Wheel of Fortune.   Players are required to guess unknown words and phrases by calling out possible letters within the words and having the letters entered into the word frame. Players have a limited number of opportunities to call out letters that might fit into the unknown word or phrase.

Wordo.   This game is a variation of Bingo. In Wordo, blank bingo cards are randomly filled with words that students have been practicing (see Figure 4.1). Using no particular order, the teacher or game leader calls out the words, their definitions, or sentences containing the words in which the target word is left blank. Players find and cover up their word squares as the words are called or identified. (Dried lima beans are excellent inexpensive markers for covering words.) The first player with a complete line of words running across, down, or diagonally is the winner.

Match.   Match is a variation of Concentration, a memory game that is popular with young children. Match is played with 15 or 20 matching pairs of word cards. The cards are randomly laid in a grid on a flat surface. Players uncover two cards at a time, saying each word as it is turned over. If the two word cards contain the same word, the player keeps the cards and is allowed to uncover two more cards. Play continues until all cards have been matched and removed from the playing grid. Then players count their cards, and the player with the most cards is declared the winner.

Word War.   In Word War, a variation of the popular card game War, each player has a deck of cards. (One child can use her word bank deck and deal it out evenly to all players.) Each player plays one card at a time by uncovering the card at the top of his deck, saying the word, and laying it on the table. The player who plays the word with the most letters and says the word correctly wins the round and takes the cards played by the other players. If there is a tie between two or more players, each player involved in the tie uncovers a second card and says it. In this tie-breaking round, the player with the most letters wins all the cards played in the entire round. Another tie results in another tie-breaking round.

Gary, who teaches remedial math and reading to intermediate-grade students, finds that word games, while not a central part of his instructional program, do create an added sense of playfulness and spontaneity. He reserves one day every two weeks for word games and uses quick games whenever he has a few minutes at the end of a class session with students. "Students respond well to the games; and the games make our word study more like playing around with words, which is how I want them to think of it."

Although there are many commercially prepared games for reading, we think that teacher and student-made games or games adapted by teachers and students are best. Teachers and students have ownership over these games, and it's easier to use students' own words under study in the game.

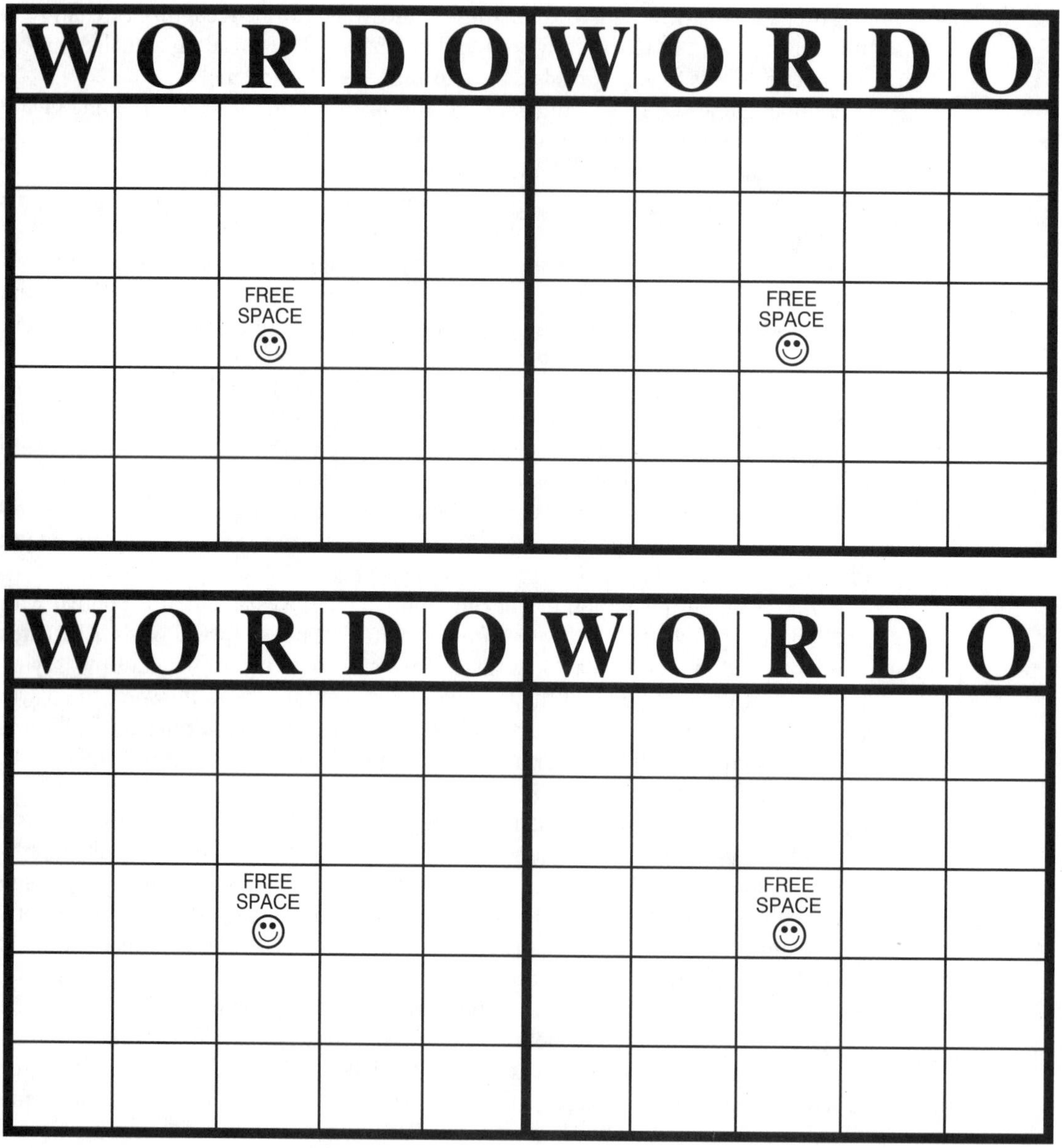

Figure 4.1
Blank Wordo cards.

Multimodality Approaches to Word Recognition

For some children word recognition is a struggle even when instruction is provided in various effective strategies. They seem unable to perceive common familiar words and have tremendous difficulty seeing patterns in longer unfamiliar words. One approach for helping these children involves the use of several sensory modalities. This is often referred to as the visual-auditory-kinesthetic-tactile approach (VAKT). *Kinesthetic* refers to the position and movement of body parts, hand, and mouth in recognizing words. *Tactile* refers to touch. An early version of this approach was described by Grace Fernald (1943) who developed a multimodality approach that she used successfully with children having extreme difficulty in learning to recognize words.

In VAKT approaches students initially learn words of their own choosing by seeing, saying, tracing, and touching printed versions of the word until they can trace or write the words without looking at them. Thus, students perceive the word visually and auditorily as they say it and see it. Kinesthetic perception is accomplished through the body movement involved in saying and tracing the word, and tactile perception happens when the student touches the written word as she says or traces it. The learned words are developed into a word bank and then used in language experience stories created by the student and teacher.

As students become more adept at perceiving words and word patterns (often children with severe reading difficulties take two or more months of instruction before beginning to recognize words without having to trace them), the teacher begins to reduce some of the modality support. Students might be asked to trace the words in the air while looking at a printed copy or move to the point of recognizing and writing words just from seeing and saying them. Students also move from reading their own stories to reading commercially published storybooks, beginning with easy texts and moving progressively to more challenging ones. Eventually, students should learn to recognize new words by recognizing familiar patterns in them, as most proficient readers do.

The VAKT approach is labor intensive. It usually needs to be implemented over a considerable length of time and is most effective when individual instruction is provided. Thus, it should be viewed as a method of last resort for children experiencing severe difficulty in word recognition. Nevertheless, teachers can use variations and portions of multimodal approaches within their regular classroom or clinical instruction.

Kim is a Title I teacher who does just that. One group of second graders has had considerable difficulty recognizing and remembering the words they encountered in their reading. When these children add words to their word banks by writing the words on blank cards, Kim has them trace each word several times while slowly saying the word. Then she asks them to turn over the word card and write the word on a piece of scratch paper. Similarly, she encourages students to use their fingers to trace words added to the group's word wall when they go up to the wall to practice the words or make an entry. "I really find that for these students the added practice of touching and tracing the words makes them easier to remember. And I found that I only had to do this for about eight weeks. Students quickly began to pick up key patterns in words. When they hit unfamiliar words, they began to trace them on their own. They saw the value of the tracing and touching without my even having to tell them."

Fluency Building and Wide Reading

Learning how to decode words accurately is only part of how proficient readers deal with text. They also read with fluency. That is, they read effortlessly and expressively in phrases and other large chunks of text, not word by word.

In Chapter 5 we discuss instructional strategies that teachers can use to help students become more fluent in their reading. Activities such as repeated or practiced readings, supported reading (as in paired or choral reading), listening to fluent reading, and developing an awareness of fluent reading are just some of the ways in which teachers can provide instruction and support in fluency. Fortunately, the strategies for building fluency also help students with word recognition. Studies have found that students who engage in fluency-building activities such as repeated readings or paired reading also make substantial improvement in their ability to recognize words accurately and quickly. Thus, we hope that as you read the instructional strategies in Chapter 5, you will keep in mind that these strategies can be used successfully to help children who experience difficulty in decoding written text.

Once again, we repeat an idea that we can't emphasize enough: Wide and authentic reading must be at the heart of all successful reading and word recognition instruction. All readers, whether proficient or struggling, need to read real reading material of their own choosing. Through wide, in-depth reading, children get the opportunity to practice their word recognition strategies. Moreover, by encountering new words and becoming exposed to words and word parts that appear frequently, students begin to recognize many words automatically.

Reading programs that successfully help children learn to read, overcome difficulties in learning to read, and develop a genuine love of reading seem to have one thing in common: Students read plenty of connected discourse. They read daily in their regular classrooms; for a large portion of their corrective or remedial reading time; and at home, encouraged and supported by parents. The more children read, the better they become in all aspects of reading—word recognition, fluency, attitude, vocabulary, and comprehension. As Gary has told us, "You can't expect children to *learn* to read if they don't get the *chance* to read. . . . You have to read!"

Putting It All Together

Knowledge of instructional strategies is only one part of developmental, corrective, or remedial reading instruction. The other part is designing coherent instructional packages that use selected strategies in informed ways. Sensible instructional packages begin and end with students who are reading real texts. Word recognition should be a small but consistent part of instruction if students are experiencing difficulty in this area. We do not recommend that teachers try to use every one of the instructional activities presented here. Rather, choose a small number of strategies that seem to make sense for the needs of your students. The chosen activities should be applied consistently from one day to the next. Thus, instruction becomes predictable for students, and time can be used efficiently for actual instruction rather than explaining a new activity or managing behavior.

That's how Mary designs instruction for her students with word recognition difficulties. She works with groups of five students for 30 minutes a day, five days a week. She begins the instructional period by reading a short story or poem to the students. Next, the group chorally reads and rereads the same text but presented in an enlarged format (perhaps on chart paper). Previously introduced stories are also read. Then students choose a word or two from the text to add to their word banks. For 5 or 10 minutes students work in pairs on various word bank activities including word sorts and games. Three days a week Mary works with students on word family exploration, and on the other two days the group works through a cloze passage taken from passages the students have recently read in Mary's class or their regular class. In several weeks she plans to substitute Making Words for the word family instruction. Each instructional period ends with sustained silent reading. Students also make entries into their learning log journals.

Mary wishes that she could have more time to work with this group of youngsters, but her instructional periods are all business. Because students are familiar with the routine, they are highly engaged in reading throughout the lesson and benefit well from the instruction. Progress is being made and sustained where once it was painfully slow.

Word recognition is only one part of learning to read proficiently. But it is an important part, and many children who experience difficulty and frustration in reading do so because of a lack of ability to recognize words accurately and quickly. Word recognition should have two major aims: to help children learn to decode unknown words, and to help them recognize familiar words quickly or automatically. The best way to accomplish both goals is to provide a little direct instruction in word recognition and a lot of guided authentic reading experiences. Thus, what has been learned through instruction can be applied immediately and repeatedly in real reading situations.

Chapter 5

Nurturing Fluent Reading

Accuracy in word recognition is not enough to ensure proficient reading. On the surface, students often exhibit good word recognition skills, reading with few noticeable errors. A slightly deeper analysis, however, may show that they read with excessive slowness and choppiness; their oral reading seems dull and expressionless, almost belabored, as if they are getting no satisfaction or enjoyment from the reading. Most likely, these readers have significant trouble in achieving fluency.

Reading fluency is not an easily defined concept. It may mean different things to different people. Yet most people can tell when they are listening to a fluent reader or speaker. Words such as "quick," "with expression," "good phrasing," or "read in a meaningful way" indicate fluent reading. We agree that all these terms, and others, are valid indicators of reading fluency.

One of the best ways to think about fluency is to consider that it deals with larger, multiple-word units of texts. Disfluent readers read so slowly that they appear to deal individually with each word they encounter. Fluent readers, on the other hand, read quickly enough and with appropriate phrasing and expression so that they are clearly working with larger units of text. Phrases, clauses, and sentences are more important units of text and meaning for fluent readers.

Why is the ability to read quickly and in appropriate textual units so important to proficient reading? After all, many teachers and reading educators dismiss reading speed as an appropriate goal of instruction. We like to use the analogy of fluent and disfluent speakers when discussing the importance of reading fluency. Fluent speakers actually help listeners understand their message. They speak fast enough so that the listener can quickly process the message. They speak in meaningful phrases and embed expression and pauses into their speech to help the listener make sense of the speech as easily as possible. Disfluent speakers, on the other hand, speak in such a slow, labored, and word-by-word fashion that it is difficult for the listener to make out the intended message.

In the same way, a fluent reader efficiently processes the text's surface-level information to make it as easy as possible to comprehend. Word-by-word, expressionless, labored, and slow reading diminishes the reader's ability to understand the text. Those listening to disfluent oral reading often have similar comprehension problems.

Is fluency a problem among elementary children who have difficulty reading? We think that problems in fluency are a major contributor to reading difficulties. Recently we studied elementary-grade children from a large urban school district who were referred for special tutoring in reading in the Title I program. As part of their initial diagnostic assessment, children read and answered questions about two passages that were near their grade placement. From this reading we were able to measure students' word recognition, reading fluency, and comprehension. Fluency was measured by rate of reading. We found that students' performance tended to be below grade level in all three areas. Word recognition and comprehension, however, were not drastically below grade level. Only reading fluency was significantly below grade-level expectations for these students. These students' reading performance was dramatically and consistently marked by excessively slow and labored oral reading. It was fairly obvious to anyone listening to these children read that they were struggling to make it through the passages and that comprehension was likely to suffer as a result of their lack of fluency.

We believe that reading fluency is a significant obstacle to proficient reading for elementary students and many older readers experiencing difficulty in learning to read. Students with whom we work in our university reading center confirm this observation. A large majority of children referred to the center for corrective reading tutoring manifest significant problems in achieving fluency.

There are several ways to assess readers' level of fluency. Perhaps the quickest and most effective assessment is simply to listen to children read orally. Teachers know what good fluent reading should sound like. Students who lack fluency are easily detected if a teacher listens to the quickness, phrasing, and expression of their reading. For teachers who desire a more quantifiable method for assessing fluency, reading rate offers a relatively simple and direct approach. An easy way to calculate rate is to ask a reader to read a text orally in his normal manner. The chosen text should be at or slightly below grade level in difficulty. Time the reader, and at the end of 60 seconds tell him to stop. Then count the number of words that were read. This is the reader's rate in words per minute (wpm). Do this procedure a few times. If you have a copy of what the child is reading, you can simply mark each 60-second boundary in your copy of the text without interrupting the child's reading. Either way, you need several 60-second samples so you can calculate an average rate. Compare the student's oral reading rate against the following second-semester grade-level estimates:

Grade 1: 80 wpm
Grade 2: 90 wpm
Grade 3: 110 wpm
Grade 4: 140 wpm
Grade 5: 160 wpm
Grade 6: 180 wpm

If the reader's rate is consistently and substantially below the appropriate grade-level rate, you can assume that he is experiencing difficulty in achieving fluency.

Reading to students is a wonderful way to model fluent and expressive reading.

Model Fluent Reading

Fortunately, several holistic approaches for improving reading fluency are available. These approaches tend not only to improve fluency, but also can have a positive effect on proficiency in word recognition and students' feeling of success as readers.

Children who have difficulty in reading often don't know what fluent reading should sound like. They have not developed a good self-awareness of fluent reading. They are often segregated into groups of children with similar difficulties. When they hear someone read, it's usually someone like themselves—disfluent and frustrated. Most of us would agree that learning something is difficult if we don't understand what it should look or sound like. That is why modeling fluent reading, commonly called reading aloud to and with children, is especially important for less able readers.

These children need to know what fluent reading sounds like. They need to develop models in their minds of what fluent reading is. Reading to children helps accomplish this goal, which can be further reinforced by talking with children about fluency after read-aloud sessions. Before the read aloud begins, a teacher might ask students to listen for variations in voice, phrasing, rate, expression, or volume. After reading, a teacher might ask students, "How did I communicate love or hate or fear or excitement with my voice during the reading?" Getting students to listen for various aspects of fluent reading and then talk about them is a first step toward getting students to read fluently on their own.

Another appropriate practice is for the teacher to read a text aloud to students before asking them to read it on their own. This preview reading helps students develop a sense of how that particular reading should be done; it will also conveniently and unobtrusively introduce students to words they may not have encountered before in print.

Terri knows about modeling fluent reading for her third-grade class. She recognized early in the school year that several of her lower-achieving students were not fluent in their reading. She has developed a program that involves her students in paired and repeated reading, which we describe later in the chapter. But an equally important part of her fluency instruction involves reading to her class every day:

> About once or twice a week I try to talk with the class about fluency after my reading. At first I had to ask them specific questions about my reading. After a few weeks I only had to ask, "What did you think about my reading?" They began talking about my voicing, phrasing, rate, emphasis on words, and how I used these elements to help convey meaning. Now when I ask my students to read orally, I remind them to think about fluency. Not only do they think about it, they read with greater ease and expression. Even the lower kids have gotten into this. I think I've noticed them more because they've made the greatest gains of all.

Terri will frequently read a passage to students and then ask them to read the passage to themselves or aloud to a partner. She believes that preview reading is a good alternative to asking students to read the text silently or introducing them to the text through a discussion or other activity not directly related to the text reading itself. "This way students get a good introduction to the passage itself because they hear and understand it before they actually read it themselves."

Repeated Readings

The method of repeated readings is a simple instructional procedure in which students are asked to practice reading one passage several times until they achieve a predetermined degree of fluency, usually defined in terms of rate or word recognition accuracy. Like musicians or athletes, readers must practice certain passages to achieve fluency. Although the activity itself may be simple, the effects of repeated reading are quite powerful. In an early study of this method, Jay Samuels (1979) asked students diagnosed as learning disabled in reading to practice reading short texts until they could read a passage fluently (85 wpm). Samuels found that his students exhibited progress on not only the passages they were practicing, but also other passages that they read without practice. In other words, the benefits of repeated readings were internalized and transferred to new passages. Other studies (Dowhower, 1987; Herman, 1985) have validated Samuels's original finding that repeated reading can help improve students' fluency, word recognition, and comprehension.

Teachers often ask, "How can we persuade students to read a passage more than once?" In some classrooms teachers have difficulty getting students to read a text even one time. The whole language answer to this dilemma is to create situations in which students have a real reason to read a passage more than once.

In writing classrooms the desired outcome for most writing is some form of publication. In a similar fashion, the natural outcome for practiced reading should be some form of performance. Teachers need to think about ways and reasons for students to read for another person or a group. Poems are meant to be shared orally with others. So are play scripts. Teachers can use poetry, scripts, or dramatic reading as a vehicle for repeated reading. Another idea is to encourage students to practice reading short stories so that they can share them with reading buddies in another class or grade. Some students are motivated by the opportunity to work with a friend. Pat Koskinen and Irene Blum (1984, 1986) found that repeated reading could be used successfully in group situations called paired repeated reading. In this version of repeated readings students read a passage to a partner several times. The partner's role is to provide positive feedback and assistance. After several readings, the roles are reversed. Koskinen and Blum found that students enjoyed the alternative format and demonstrated strong gains in fluency, word recognition, and reading for meaning in as little as 15 minutes a day, three times a week, for five weeks.

For some students, fluency difficulties may be so severe that performance is not a reasonable option. Examining the difficulty level of their books and other reading material is a first step in working with these students. After all, everyone can become disfluent when the reading material is very difficult. After students develop the fluency habit by practicing with easy, predictable texts, they can return to more challenging material.

Some children in our reading and writing center's tutoring program enjoy reading their texts into tape recorders. They then listen to their oral reading and, with the tutor, decide how to make the next reading more fluent. This process may be repeated several times until the child is satisfied with the sound of her reading. At that point a more public performance may be planned. Through tape recording and analysis of repeated readings, children develop fluency and an awareness of their own progress in becoming fluent readers. Another suggestion is to track students' performance as they practice reading texts. Then, using a simple graph of reading performance, teachers can show students the progress they are making in increasing their reading rate or decreasing the number of word recognition miscues over several readings of the same text.

Sheila noticed that several students in her class exhibited difficulties in reading fluency. When asked to read orally, they read at an excessively slow rate with little attention to meaningful phrasing and expression. It became increasingly evident to Sheila that these students had developed a negative attitude about reading and themselves. They balked at any opportunity to read aloud and began to cause disruptions during any type of in-class reading. Sheila decided that these students needed opportunities to engage in repeated readings with relatively easy texts so that they could experience success in reading. She made arrangements with Tim, a first-grade teacher in her building, to pair each of her sixth-grade students with a first grader. The reading buddies would meet once a week, and during each visit the buddies would read a book to one another. The sixth graders were encouraged to choose books that were appropriate for first graders. These were the very type of books that were ideal for her disfluent sixth-grade readers. Sixth graders practiced their books diligently throughout the week. By Friday they had their books down pat, and when they shared their books with their buddies, they glowed about their reading success and the awe they inspired in the first graders.

The program has continued for several months now, and Sheila is delighted with the progress her students have made. "These students have begun to believe in themselves again as readers. They see that they can read fluently and that their reading can have an impact on other children. When I provide instruction for these students they can relate it to their work as tutors and buddies."

Her students have yet to tire of the program after 14 weeks. Indeed, they have thrived on their weekly sessions. Nonetheless, Sheila has begun to think of other ways for her students to have authentic purposes for reading to others. These include reading at home to parents and developing partnerships with residents of a nearby retirement center. "It really doesn't take a lot for something like this to work," Sheila says, "just someone willing to honestly listen to these children read and give them encouragement. After experiencing so much failure in reading, these kids need to practice to get good and they need people to tell them that they are good."

Paired Reading

In the 1960s the professional literature began describing a new approach to corrective reading (Heckelman, 1969). The procedure is called the Neurological Impress Method (NIM) and is really much simpler than its monster of a name implies. Basically, NIM involves pairing a good and a poor reader. The readers sit side by side and read one text aloud and together.

Early descriptions of NIM had the good readers directing their voices into the left ears of the poor readers to imprint the sound-symbol match into the less able readers' heads. Early research about the approach was impressive. Tutors and tutees were asked to read together for relatively short periods of time, usually no more than 15 minutes per session. Using this type of format, Heckelman (1969) found that poor readers were able to make substantial progress in relatively short periods of time. One student, for example, made gains of 5.9 grade levels after doing NIM for a total of $7\frac{1}{4}$ hours over 6 weeks. The average gain was 1.9 grade levels for 24 students over the same time period.

For whatever reason, NIM never really caught on in the United States. You'd hear about it now and again in a professional article or meeting, but you never heard about many teachers actually using the method with their less able readers. But this was not the case in England. Researchers there developed an activity that was very similar to NIM, which they called paired reading. Perhaps the more easily understood name has helped its popularity.

Paired reading was originally intended for use with parents and their children as a way to supplement children's reading at school. The approach calls for parent and child to read one text aloud and together. Normally, the parent reads in a moderately loud voice at a pace that tends to pull the child along. No reading into the child's ear is required. In easier parts of the reading or when the child wants to read on his own, the child signals the parent who then stops reading aloud or reads in a whisper at a rate that shadows or slightly trails the voice of the child. As soon as the child begins to experience difficulty, the parent returns to her original role as leader.

Keith Topping (1987), who has led the paired reading movement in England, reports that students can make remarkable progress in a short period of time. Asking parents to work with their children for only five minutes per night, he reported that children who had been experiencing difficulty in learning to read could expect to make three to five times their normal progress in word recognition and comprehension. Because children and parents read connected texts together fluently, it is easy to expect that fluency would be positively impacted as well. Topping (1989) has also indicated that paired reading can work with good results in situations where peers or other adults take on the role of tutor.

Katherine has been a Title I reading teacher for the past 15 years in an inner-city school. She takes seriously the Title I mandate to involve parents in her programs to improve her students' reading. But until a few years ago, she had lots of problems with the parent involvement programs she designed. "We had all kinds of problems. Either the parents didn't show up for the training program, they didn't follow through and I didn't have the time to follow up with every child, or the program was more fun and games and really didn't involve sustained reading on the part of the child."

After hearing about paired reading at an in-service workshop, she decided to try it out with her students and their parents. She arranged for one-hour training sessions at various times throughout the day and advertised it furiously. Most parents came and were enthusiastic about paired reading. "This was something they could do with their children pretty much on their own," Katherine recalled.

On Fridays students bring in the record sheets that document the amount of paired reading that parents and children have engaged in during the previous week. Then children select a new book to read for the upcoming week and get a new record sheet. Parents have stayed with the program. As Katherine notes, "they see that it works, and I do too. Children who do paired reading with a parent make significantly more progress during the year than those who don't. Paired reading is one of the best strategies for helping our less able readers that I have ever seen or tried."

Tape-recorded Passages

For some students, paired reading just may not work. They may not have a parent, sister or brother, or other relative who can read with them in the paired-reading format. One alternative is to provide students with an audiotape of the text to be read so that they can listen to the text on tape while reading the written version. Marie Carbo (1978) has studied the use of tape-recorded passages with less able readers and calls the approach "talking books." In Carbo's research, learning disabled readers were given a trade book along with an oral version of the text on tape. Students read the texts while simultaneously listening to the tape. After using this approach for only a few weeks, Carbo reported that her students made gains in reading that were significantly beyond what would normally be expected for students at their grade level. Using this approach, students learned to read fluently what they were previously unable to read at all. Other research has reported similar positive results with elementary readers.

Although a wide variety of commercially prepared texts with tapes are available for purchase, we believe that tape-recorded passages prepared by the teacher or someone else in the school may be more effective than the commercial versions. The commercial

Listening to stories on tape while reading them helps develop fluency.

tapes often have sound effects that may draw students' attention away from the passage. They may not provide a word-for-word rendition of the passage, be read at an inappropriate rate for students, or have unconventional or inadequate signals for page turns or other aspects of the written passages that students should notice. These potential difficulties can easily be overcome if the teacher or an aide, student, or parent helper prepares the tapes. In addition, students may find the voice of the teacher or some other familiar person comforting and encouraging.

Ted uses tape-recorded books in his elementary Title I reading program. Students who manifest difficulties in reading fluency choose a book and tape from the extensive library of taped books that he has collected and made over the years. Students are asked to learn a book over several days on their own and to come to class on a designated day and read the book (or a portion of it) to him. Ted believes this activity gives students some control over and responsibility for their own learning; at the same time, they learn to read and enjoy a good book. "Most of my students really like learning to read these books on their own. It's really an accomplishment they can feel proud of." Once students have become familiar with Ted's format for the tape-recorded versions of the books and developed some degree of fluency, he invites them to make their own taped books to add to his library and be checked out by other students. Students like listening to books taped by their classmates.

Choral Reading

Choral reading is similar to paired reading in that less able readers receive on-line support while reading. But in choral reading, the support is given to a group of readers. Choral reading has become something of a lost art in elementary schools. In past generations, students learned and chorally recited poems, songs, famous speeches, interesting passages from stories, and other selections. With this approach, even the least able reader is able to join in as much as he dares without risk of failure or ridicule. After several readings he is able to read the passage on his own with considerable fluency. Today, however, with so much emphasis on silent reading, children have few opportunities to engage in this community form of reading.

Choral reading can capture the interest of readers through antiphonal reading and other variations. In antiphonal reading the class is divided into groups (girls and boys, January to June birthdays and July to December birthdays, and so on). Then different parts of the text are assigned to each group. The entire group may read some parts, and individuals may read others. Thus, the choral reading becomes a complex and orchestrated arrangement. Students enjoy deciding on parts for antiphonal reading. To do so, of course, they must read the text several times, which is good fluency practice, and think about how different groups of voices can convey meaning. In addition, assigning parts and directing practice with the texts helps students develop ownership over their reading and fosters a sense of a reading community. In choral reading activities, less able readers benefit from the support they receive from the group, the camaraderie and joy of participating in a group activity with peers who have a variety of abilities, and the valuable practice of reading one text in a variety of ways.

In Elizabeth's second-grade classroom, choral reading is a way of life. At the beginning of each morning she uses choral reading to warm up the class to reading and language. She usually finds a short suitable poem for the class to read together. She either writes out the poem on chart paper or puts it on an overhead transparency so that all the children can see it. Her routine is to read the poem to the class first, talk about it with the children, then invite them to read it chorally several times and respond to it through discussion. She says:

> I really like doing this at the beginning of each day because it helps create a sense of togetherness and community in the class. After reading it a couple of times I might ask four or five individual students of varying ability in reading to read it to the class. Choral reading really lets those less able readers shine with their peers! Later in the day when I'm working with those readers who are struggling in reading we will usually go back and practice the poem together some more and do some word analysis activities with it. Really, you can create a whole lesson that's fun and interesting from this initial group choral reading.

Not every day means a new poem. Sometimes Elizabeth will reintroduce students to an old favorite, and about halfway through the school year, she begins to share with students her role of initially reading the poem to the class each morning. The day before she gives a selected student a copy of the poem for the next day and asks the child to practice reading it at home and lead the class in reading it the next day. For some less fluent readers, she will supply a tape-recorded version of the poem to aid their practice.

Marking Phrase Boundaries

An important part of reading fluency is the ability to read in syntactically and semantically appropriate phrases. Meaning is embedded in multiple-word chunks of text or phrases, not in individual words themselves. Thus, one of the tasks of the fluent reader is to read in these phrases or chunks. Peter Schreiber (1980, 1991) has theorized that many readers characterized as disfluent suffer from a poor ability to phrase text appropriately while reading. This may be due to a lack of sensitivity to semantic and syntactic cues that mark phrase boundaries in the text, or disfluent readers may have routinized their word-by-word reading and not have automatic recognition of most words. Regardless of the cause, the end result is continued difficulty in fully understanding the text.

Consider the following sentence:

The young man the playground equipment.

At first reading the sentence may sound like nonsense. That is because you probably chunked or phrased the text as most readers would: after the noun *man*. However, in this contrived sentence, if you chunked the text this way, your comprehension suffered—there is no verb phrase. What you need to do is rephrase the text (hint: *young* can be a noun and *man* a verb). With the rephrased text the sentence is easily understood. For readers who have difficulty in determining appropriate text boundaries, many sentences can give them similar comprehension problems.

One method to help students overcome this difficulty is repeated reading. Schreiber has noted that repeated reading activities give the reader practice in discovering the text cues that mark phrase boundaries. Another approach is to mark or highlight phrase boundaries in the text itself, using a pencil slash or vertical line to specify the boundary (see Figure 5.1). A review of the research shows that marking phrase boundaries has considerable potential for improving reading performance and comprehension, especially with less able readers (Rasinski, 1990).

Ted has found that marking phrase boundaries for students is very helpful for his less fluent Title I students:

> If we are studying a short passage or poem that I want students to read orally, I will lightly mark phrase boundaries in the passage with a pencil and run enough copies of the text for each student. I use single slash marks for within sentence phrase boundaries and double slashes for the ends of sentences. After talking about the role of the marks, we might read the passage chorally and attend to the phrase and sentence breaks.

Later, as students become fluent and phrase-sensitive to the text, Ted will give them another copy of the same text without the slash marks. He feels that this is a good way to get students to transfer their newly learned sensitivity to phrase boundaries to passages in a conventional format.

As a variation and follow-up to using phrase-marked texts, Ted will give students copies of another passage that will be read orally. He asks them to read the passage to themselves and mark their own phrase boundaries. This is followed by a discussion of the marks and the need to read in chunks or phrases. Ted notes that his students appear to make real progress in their ability and desire to read in appropriate phrases when reading both orally and silently.

> Grant was not a military genius/who took brilliant gambles/and made flashing strikes.// His position/ as one of America's premier field commanders/was the result/of more solid qualities:/a wide vision of the war/and what had to be done to win,/balanced judgment,/dogged courage,/common sense,/and good luck/at the right time.//[1]
>
> Today/Kevin and I turned out/for track. //Mr. Kurtz,/the coach,/gave us a pep talk/about the importance/of taking part/and doing the best we can.// He said/it's not the winning,/it's the competing that's important.// He stressed/looking for improvement/within ourselves.//[2]

Figure 5.1
[1]From Robertson, J. I. (1992). *Civil War! America becomes one nation* (p. 79). New York: Knopf.
[2]From Cleary, B. (1991). *Strider* (p. 126). New York: Morrow.

Choice of Texts

The texts chosen for reading can aggravate or ameliorate fluency problems. More often than not aggravation is the result. Students with fluency difficulties are often given texts that are too difficult for their current level of progress in reading. Such texts ensure disfluent reading and perpetuate students' evaluations of themselves as poor readers. In dealing with fluency problems, teachers should always attempt to choose texts that are relatively easy in terms of word recognition and syntactic complexity. If the text is challenging, they should provide sufficient support before and during reading to ensure success. Reading easy texts helps students develop power and self-confidence in their reading.

Predictable or patterned text is particularly well suited to helping students develop fluent reading. These texts are written in a distinct and easily detected pattern that makes them not only easy to read but also require readers to attend to the pattern through phrasing and expression. Bill Martin's *Brown Bear, Brown Bear* is perhaps the best-known example of a predictable or patterned book. The text follows a clear pattern that most beginning readers will discover and employ after as little as one reading.

Brown bear, brown bear, what do you see?

I see a red bird looking at me.

Red bird, red bird, what do you see?

I see a yellow duck looking at me.

The pattern is easily discernible, and the passage is both readable and fun.

Later, students can use the same pattern to create their own stories, as Martin himself has done with his book, *Polar Bear, Polar Bear, What Do You Hear?* Most school or public librarians can supply teachers with patterned books written for a variety of reading levels and interests. A bibliography of predictable pattern books is located in Appendix C.

Patterned texts can also be found in poetry and song lyrics for children. Verses have the particular advantage of being short (thus lending themselves to repeated readings) and appealing to a variety of grade levels. Children's verse is also written in rhyme, which makes the poems even more appealing and predictable. (Poetry collections that we have found useful are listed in Appendix B.) For example, Shel Silverstein's *Where the Sidewalk Ends* and *A Light in the Attic* contain poems that are sure to delight children of all ages. Many poets write verse for children, and several published poetry collections can be read for both sheer enjoyment and to build fluency. Teachers and children can also compose their own original verse or verse modeled after favorite poems, which can be put together into class collections and used for reading.

Jean's students are in transitional second grade because they did not successfully complete the first-grade curriculum during the previous year. They have particular trouble emerging into conventional forms of reading. Jean has found that predictable books and poems are great ways to capture the reading interest of students who previously spent most of their reading time doing worksheets and unsuccessfully manipulating letters and sounds. Each day she introduces one or two new predictable stories written in the form of big books or poems written on chart paper. She explains, "The large texts allow the reading to be a community and choral reading experience."

As the lesson begins, students read several patterned stories and poems from previous lessons—perhaps *Brown Bear, Brown Bear,* Joy Cowley's *Mrs. Wishy Washy,* or Sue Williams's *I Went Walking.* Jean points to the words and lines in many of the stories. After reading them several times as a group and asking individuals and pairs of students to read them, Jean helps students detect individual letters, word parts, and words. She makes word and letter cards and has students match and name the cards with words and letters in the stories. She has students work in groups to find words from the stories that begin or end with particular sounds, letters, or letter combinations.

After several minutes spent looking at various aspects of the familiar texts, Jean introduces her students to a new book. Her routine includes showing students the cover or telling them the title and asking what the story may be about. She asks students to brainstorm various possible plots and select the most plausible. After this discussion she reads the text to her students, pointing to individual words as she reads. Students then talk about the story. Were their predictions correct? What did they like about the story? Were there any particularly interesting words? After a brief discussion Jean rereads and points to the words again. Then she invites the class to join her in a third reading. After a few more choral readings she moves on to other activities. But she makes sure that the text is available for her students so that they can read and explore it on their own during free time. In upcoming days, the class continues to read the patterned story and explores in more detail the sentences, words, letters, and sounds in the text.

Fluency Development Lesson

So far we have been discussing individual aspects of successful fluency instruction, but lessons that employ more than one aspect will increase the effectiveness of instruction. One example of this principle is the Fluency Development Lesson (FDL) (Rasinski, Padak, Linek, & Sturtevant, 1994). We devised the FDL for teachers who work with primary-grade children experiencing difficulty in achieving even initial stages of fluent reading. The FDL combines several principles of effective fluency instruction in a way that maximizes students' engagement in authentic reading in a relatively short period of time and requires cooperation between two or more students. In the schools in which we tried it out, the FDL was a supplement to the regular reading curriculum. Implemented at the beginning of each day, it took 10 to 15 minutes to complete. Teachers made copies of brief passages (50–150 words) for each child. Often the passages were in verse form.

A typical Fluency Development Lesson looks like this:

1. The teacher passes out copies of the text to each student.
2. The teacher reads the text to the class while students follow along silently with their own copies. This step can be repeated several times.
3. The teacher discusses the content of the text as well as the quality of her reading of it with the class.
4. The entire class, along with the teacher, reads the text chorally several times. The teacher creates variety by having students read in antiphonal and echo styles.
5. The class divides into pairs. Each pair finds a quiet spot, and one student practices reading the text to her partner three times. The partner's job is to follow along in the text, provide help when needed, and give positive feedback to the reader. After the first three readings, the roles are switched. The partner becomes the reader and reads the text three times as well.
6. Students regroup, and the teacher asks for volunteers to perform the text. Individuals, pairs, and groups of up to four perform the reading for the class. The teacher makes arrangements for students to perform the text for the school principal, secretary, custodian, and other teachers and classes. The performing students are lavished with praise.
7. Students are instructed to take the passage home and read it to their parents and other relatives. Parents are asked to listen to their child read as many times as they would like and to praise their child's efforts.

During our work with the FDL, teachers implemented it three to four times a week from October to June. We found that nearly all children benefited from the lesson: Their overall reading achievement, word recognition, and fluency experienced greater improvement than did a comparable group of children who received a more traditional type of supplemental instruction using the same passages. The greatest gains were made by students who were the poorest readers at the beginning of the year. Teachers and students who used the FDL liked reading and talking about the enjoyable passages, the opportunity to read chorally and with friends, and the noticeable improvement the approach offered students.

Maria has used the FDL in her class for more than two years. As a result, she has seen several of her second graders make extraordinary progress in reading. "The main thing about this lesson is that it allows children to be successful in reading. Even though this is second grade, several of my students essentially begin the school year not reading. These kids need intensive help in word recognition and developing fluent reading habits. I honestly think that FDL is one answer to helping these youngsters."

At the beginning of the year she asks parents to purchase a particular collection of poems for children. Each day, whenever possible, Maria and her students explore one or more poems using the FDL format. She has made one significant modification that she feels (and we agree) helps reinforce students' word recognition learning. After each FDL she asks students to choose a favorite or interesting word from the poem, write it on an index card, and add it to their personal word banks. These banks are then used in word practice and word sort activities. (See Chapter 3 for a complete description of these activities.) Students like the opportunity to work with others when practicing their reading and enjoy performing their readings for others. Indeed, Jean (whom you met earlier in this chapter) has recently worked with a first-grade teacher to develop a program where second- and first-grade readers are paired for reading practice in much the same way as in the FDL.

Richard Allington (1983) and others (Anderson, 1981) have argued that fluency is a neglected goal of the reading curriculum. If it isn't a focus of instruction and teachers' don't feel that the development of fluency in reading is important, then we have little reason to wonder why so many children in corrective reading programs manifest difficulties in fluency. It may be a while before all reading professionals recognize the importance of fluency in reading. Until they do, the strategies described here may remain within the domain of teachers who work with children experiencing difficulty rather than in the regular reading curriculum where they also belong.

Oral Recitation Lesson

Hoffman's Oral Recitation Lesson (ORL) is another fluency-instruction model that integrates several key characteristics of effective fluency instruction (Hoffman, 1987; Hoffman & Crone, 1985). The ORL consists of two components. The first, the direct instruction component, begins with a comprehension subroutine. The teacher reads a story to the students and guides them in discussion and analysis of the content. This analysis results in a story map that identifies basic story elements such as characters, setting, major episodes and events, and resolution. Students use the story map as a guide in writing a story summary.

The second subroutine is a practice phase in which the teacher models reading segments of the story. Then students practice the segments individually and chorally. In addition to the modeled reading, the teacher talks about fluent reading and leads students in practicing elements of effective expression during oral reading.

The third subroutine is a performance phase in which students read self-selected segments of the story for others. Students reap positive comments from their classmates after the performance.

In the second component of the ORL, indirect instruction, students work for 10 minutes every day on passage segments from the direct-instruction component of the lesson. Each student practices reading in a barely audible voice, a method called soft reading. During this time the teacher checks the progress of individual students. The ORL is meant to cover several days, normally two to four instructional periods. The format has been found to lead to improvements in fluency and reading comprehension (Aslett, 1990; Reutzel & Hollingsworth, 1993).

Shared Book Experience

The Shared Book Experience (SBE), another integrated lesson format for developing fluency, was derived from whole language theory and is based on the assumption that learning to read is a social experience and that children need positive guidance and support in group reading experiences (Holdaway, 1979). The use of authentic and enlarged trade books (big books) is its most salient characteristic.

In the SBE the teacher faces the students with an enlarged text at her side. After discussing the cover, title, illustrations, and other characteristics of the book, she asks students to make predictions about the content of the story. This is followed by the teacher's dramatic reading of the story and a discussion of the text. The book is then reread several times, with the teacher offering support and encouraging children to join in the reading, especially during repetitive parts of the text. Throughout these rereadings the teacher draws students' attention to words, word patterns, letters, and other language elements in the text, often using a word window to isolate individual words and letters.

As students become proficient in this shared big-book reading, they can be given conventional-sized versions of the same text for individual practice at school and home. Although students may read several stories during a lesson, their work with a particular story may stretch over several lessons and days. Thus, students develop a repertoire of big books that they may request, revisit, and reread. Research has found that SBE results in more positive reading for young readers than traditional code-emphasis instruction (Ribowsky, 1985) and the Oral Recitation Lesson (Reutzel, Hollingsworth, & Eldredge, 1994).

Support-reading Strategy

The Support-reading Strategy (SRS) was developed by Morris and Nelson (1992) in response to the needs of a group of low-reading second-grade students. SRS contains several fluency instruction elements and is meant to be integrated into a traditional class using basal materials. It follows a three-day instructional cycle that lasts 20–25 minutes at a time.

- **Day 1.** The teacher reads a story to a small group of students in a fluent, expressive voice. Throughout the reading the teacher asks students to clarify text information and predict upcoming events. Teacher and students then echo-read the story, with the students reading from their own books. The teacher monitors individuals' reading and provides assistance, support, and encouragement as necessary.

- **Day 2.** Students are divided into pairs that include a good reader and a less proficient one. The pairs reread the story, alternating pages as they go. The children are then assigned a short segment (100 words) from the story. In pairs, the students read to their partners who provide help as needed. Finally, if there is enough time remaining, the pairs reread the entire story, alternating pages so that each child reads the text that was read by his partner in the initial partner reading.

Repeated Reading

- Students practice reading texts until they achieve fluency.
- Students perform texts for interested audiences—peers, younger students, family members, and so on.

Paired Reading

- Student selects book.
- Student and parent (or other good reader) read book aloud together.
- Parent's reading slightly leads or follows, depending on student's need and desire.
- Student logs paired-reading activities.

Choral Reading

- Teacher or students select text and determine or assign parts (if it is antiphonal reading).
- Teacher reads text aloud; students listen and read along silently. Discussion may follow.
- Teacher and students read text together.
- Choral or antiphonal choral reading is performed.

Tape-recorded Passages

- Teacher or other competent reader prepares audiotapes of texts.
- Student selects book and tape. She reads and simultaneously listens to book several times.
- Student performs book or a portion of it for an audience.

Fluency Development Lesson

- Teacher selects short text and prepares copies for students.
- Teacher reads text; students listen and critique reading. Discussion may follow.
- Teacher and students read text together.

Figure 5.2   continued
Procedures for fluency.

- **Day 3.** During a seat-work period, individual children read their assigned parts to the teacher; and the teacher checks the reading for word recognition accuracy.

Many students in this program had made virtually no progress in reading during the preceding 11 months and were still at the initial stages of reading development when they began SRS. After six months of SRS, their reading ability had increased substantially (Morris & Nelson, 1992).

The activities we have described in this chapter share a common purpose: to help students develop the ability to read fluently. This goal is important because fluent readers are better able to identify unknown words and comprehend text. For example, the repeated

- Student pairs take turns reading the text to each other. Listeners provide assistance and positive feedback.
- Students perform the text for interested audiences.
- Students add words from text to their word banks.
- Students read text at home for parents.

Oral Recitation Lesson

- Teacher reads story to class.
- Story discussion is followed by the development of a story map.
- Students write story summary.
- Teacher models reading of story and discusses fluency.
- Students practice segments of story.
- Students read or perform texts for others.
- Students "soft-read" (practice) segments of story on their own, for 10 minutes per day.

Shared Book Experience

- Teacher discusses and reads a big book to the class.
- Teacher and students reread book several times over several days.
- Teacher draws students' attention to segments of text (words, word parts, letters).
- Students read smaller versions of the book on their own at school and home.

Support-reading Strategy

- Teacher reads story; students predict upcoming events.
- Teacher and students echo-read story.
- Student pairs reread story, alternating pages once or twice.
- Students practice 100-word segments with partners.
- Students read assigned segments to the teacher, who checks reading accuracy.

Figure 5.2, continued

readings embedded in fluency activities allow readers to develop their sight vocabularies naturally and without special emphasis or instruction. Moreover, knowing that one's reading sounds good boosts self-esteem. Students enjoy these activities, and the success they engender helps them develop positive attitudes toward reading and about themselves as readers. Finally, these fluency activities frequently involve joint decision making and cooperative activity and performance, all of which develop a sense of community among students.

Each of the fluency activities highlighted in this chapter has been proven and endorsed by teacher practice and professional research. All the approaches work with many types of texts but may be most appropriate with short, predictable pieces such as poetry or patterned books. Figure 5.2 summarizes the steps involved in each of the activities we describe in this chapter.

Chapter 6

Building Vocabulary

One of the earliest findings in reading research was the association between vocabulary knowledge and reading proficiency (Davis, 1944). Good readers tend to know many words and understand many concepts, and people who know many words tend to be good readers. That finding makes sense to us. To understand what you encounter in print, you need some understanding of the words that make up the text. Moreover, as you read, you encounter new ideas, concepts, and words, and you see existing ideas, concepts, and words in new ways. As a result, your knowledge of words grows. Indeed, readers' knowledge of words is one of the most potent predictors of their reading comprehension (Anderson & Freebody, 1981).

That's the good news, but there's also some bad news. If reading frustrates you or gives you little enjoyment, you may choose to minimize the amount of reading you do. This decision leads to fewer encounters with new and interesting words; and as a result, your growth in reading is slowed, and the process of reading becomes even more difficult and frustrating. The cycle continues—but in the wrong direction.

Many students who encounter difficulties in reading have limited word knowledge. Particularly when they read instructional texts, they may be overloaded with the vocabulary and overwhelmed by the conceptual load of the text. Reading is slow, laborious, and frustrating; learning is impeded. In fact, when readers at any achievement level confront text that contains a large number of unfamiliar words, their comprehension of the text suffers. Thus, it is imperative that all teachers engage students in regular vocabulary exploration, particularly teachers in specialized subject areas who introduce uncommon and unfamiliar vocabulary words as well as those teachers who work with students who experience difficulty in reading.

We like to think of vocabulary exploration as word play or having fun with words. Nevertheless, those aren't the words that characterize traditional forms of vocabulary instruction. Before we present our instructional suggestions, let's take a look at how vocabulary is currently taught in many classrooms at grade levels around the world.

Traditional Vocabulary Instruction

Nearly every person who has attended school in the United States can remember being regularly assigned lists of words to learn. More often than not, the words had little or no connection to what students were studying in other curricular areas; they might even have been words that students had never encountered before. The weekly assignment usually went something like this: "Find and write a definition for each word" or "Use each word in a sentence." At the end of the week students were normally tested over the words, and within a short time following the test the words were probably forgotten and never thought of again!

Unfortunately this type of vocabulary instruction continues in some classrooms. Yet most teachers, not to mention students, would agree that such an approach rarely increases vocabulary. It just doesn't work. The approach only adds to many students' frustration with words and reading, magnifies their negative attitudes toward reading, and contributes to alienation and lack of growth in reading. Moreover, students may come to believe that words and concepts really aren't very important, at least not beyond the test on Friday.

There are at least three reasons why such approaches are exercises in futility. First, the words have little connection to students' existing knowledge or what they are studying in other subjects. Learning new ideas, concepts, and words involves connecting or integrating the new information into what learners already know. If students have little background knowledge about the new words and concepts or can't see the connections, then the process of integration will be hampered. Learning will not occur efficiently or effectively.

Second, finding definitions or using words in sentences doesn't ensure understanding. Official definitions can be just as confusing as the words they are supposed to clarify, and sentences that students compose often demonstrate a remarkable lack of understanding. Take, for example, the following sentences from student compositions, compiled by Richard Lederer in his book *Anguished English:*

Children learn new words through direct experiences.

Socrates died from an overdose of wedlock.
Solomon, one of David's sons, had 500 wives and 500 porcupines.
The inhabitants of ancient Egypt were called mummies.

In what way do the students who wrote these sentences have command over the major concepts in the sentences?

Finally, this age-old method of vocabulary instruction is no fun at all. It's drudgery, and that's how students treat it. The unfortunate consequence is that students may learn that any type of word exploration is boring.

Vocabulary instruction doesn't need to be boring. Indeed, it can be a delightful and insightful experience for many students. To be truly effective, word play must be based on words that students need to know or have some interest in. Therefore, we must help them see connections between unknown words and familiar words and concepts. We must also make sure that the activities intended to enrich vocabulary are explored in an interesting and playful manner. When students become interested in and knowledgeable about words, reading fluency and comprehension will take a major leap forward.

Good Ways to Learn New Words

Before we share specific instructional activities, we want to describe two of the very best ways for students (and all of us, for that matter) to learn new words and concepts. Learning words and concepts is not exclusively a school activity. Children learn thousands of words and word meanings before they ever set foot in a school. How? They learn most words and concepts through life experiences that they later discuss with their parents and other important persons in their lives. When a child goes to McDonald's, she will learn about hamburgers, cheeseburgers, French fries, and McNuggets. A visit to the dentist can help someone learn about dentists, X rays, cavities, and novocaine. Our life experiences, no matter what age we are, give us wonderful opportunities for learning new words and concepts, especially if we discuss our experiences with others. Even a summer vacation to Europe or the Black Hills of South Dakota will lead a child or an adult to new words to discover in a rich and concrete context. All experiences are important, and teachers should remember the great opportunities available to expand student vocabularies through direct experience—everything from school field trips to investigations within and around the school itself.

We also learn words through secondhand or vicarious experience. Movies, television shows, and reading are examples of ways in which we share experiences that we have not actually had ourselves. Reading, in particular, is a superb way to increase vocabulary. We mentioned previously that reading is associated with vocabulary growth. The reason should be clear. As we read, we encounter words that may be unfamiliar or only partly familiar. The context of the story (the story's meaning, synonymous words, and illustrations) helps us understand more about these words.

We feel that reading is far superior to other forms of vicarious experience for learning vocabulary. Movies and television often deal with situations viewers are familiar to and incorporate words that are not new. Such events are often directed toward a lowest common denominator—those viewers with the smallest conceptual and vocabulary backgrounds—so that everyone can understand the story. In reading, however, authors often take readers to new experiences, even within familiar situations. And authors choose vocabulary that is rich and interesting—words that create a particular mood, feel, or texture. In other words, reading gives readers many opportunities to learn new words.

Thus, teachers have another reason to encourage reading in and out of school: Reading expands readers' vocabularies, which makes further reading easier. Listening to stories read by the teacher or parent can have much the same effect. Indeed, because elementary-grade students have limited word recognition abilities, they are usually able to comprehend stories at a higher level of sophistication when they listen than when they read. So reading to students can have an even more powerful effect on students' vocabulary development than their own reading, and its facilitative effect is well established in the research (Cohen, 1968). Now you have one more reason to read every day to your students, no matter what grade or age they are. A simple way to expand this effect is to take a few minutes after a read aloud and talk with students about the interesting words they heard as well as their meanings and use.

Three Principles of Effective Vocabulary Instruction

Students can also learn and explore words through direct instruction or word play activities. Five minutes of word play every day can go a long way toward expanding vocabulary and improving comprehension. But as we have already seen, traditional vocabulary instruction can be deadly to students' interest and growth and is largely ineffective. Nevertheless, there are alternatives to word lists and memorization. Vocabulary researcher William Nagy (1988) offers three principles that are characteristic of effective vocabulary instruction:

1. *Vocabulary instruction should be integrative.*   That is, it should help students connect new words with their existing store of words and knowledge. Students need to learn, for example, that *bull pen* is a word connected to baseball in general and pitchers in particular. That sort of connection makes words memorable. A dry, abstract, or out-of-context definition may not stick with the student. Vocabulary instruction, like all instruction, should move from what students already know to what is new for them. Their existing knowledge serves as an anchor for their learning.

2. *Vocabulary instruction needs to include repetition.*   To learn words students need to see, hear, and use them many times in many contexts. It is the unusual learner who can see a word once and know it. For most of us, multiple exposures to a new word cements it and its meaning in our memories. Repetition should not involve simple or drill-like repetition of words on lists or flash cards. The repetition needs to be within meaningful contexts.

3. ***Words and concepts are best learned when they are presented in meaningful ways.*** Meaningful repetition can occur very simply when a teacher connects a read-aloud experience with student reading and a direct experience concerning the same topic. These meaningful contexts provide the repetition that helps to ensure thorough learning of the words. This notion of meaningful repetition makes thematic units of study so inviting. Through such units students are exposed to words and concepts several times and in several meaningful contexts over the course of the unit study. Meaningful use means not only seeing the words in meaningful contexts, but also thinking about and using them in meaningful ways. When students use new words in ways that are meaningful for them, their understanding is enhanced, and they develop more flexible control over the use of the words.

In the remainder of this chapter we present specific instructional strategies that share these characteristics. We recommend flexibility in your use of these strategies. They can be applied before students read to acquaint them with specific words they will encounter. They can also be used within a regular classroom framework of general word exploration or play. Whether students' vocabulary is broadened for a specific topic or the more general purpose of fascination with words, their overall reading will improve as well.

List Group Label

List Group Label (LGL) is a generic vocabulary and background-building activity that can fit within almost any curriculum area of reading and can be used at any age level. The activity draws upon students' own knowledge of a topic and then invites them to work to organize that information. Because the students supply most of the material for the activity, its difficulty is controlled by the students themselves.

Here's how LGL works:

1.   The teacher or students choose a topic for study. It may come from a subject area, an upcoming reading, a theme to be explored by the class, a holiday, and so on.

2.   Students, working in groups, brainstorm all the words they can think of related to the topic. As they are called, the words are listed on the chalkboard or a sheet of paper so that everyone can see. The teacher may also participate in this activity and call out a word or two that he wants entered into the mix. After brainstorming, students may be asked to explain words that are unfamiliar to the group.

3.   Once students exhaust their store of words, they organize their list by choosing two or more words that share a common characteristic, listing them together and supplying a title or label that describes the category. This new organization is also recorded, on the chalkboard if the whole group is working together or on sheets of paper if the students are working in small groups. Students categorize and label the categories until the list is exhausted.

4.   Next, students try to add words to the categories on their organized lists. When a meaningful organization is imposed on a list of concepts, students usually find that

related concepts can be more easily recalled from memory. Students might discuss the reason why. (The answer is that organization assists memory.)

5.   If students are working in groups, each group shares with the entire class its method of categorization and the words that group members chose to add. Lively discussion should take place as students analyze words and concepts for shared and defining features.

6.   Students can extend the activity, if so desired, by transforming their list of organized concepts into a semantic web (Figure 6.1) or prototypical informational outline. The final product as well as the related discussion introduces students to new concepts and can act as a guide and background for further reading and writing on the topic.

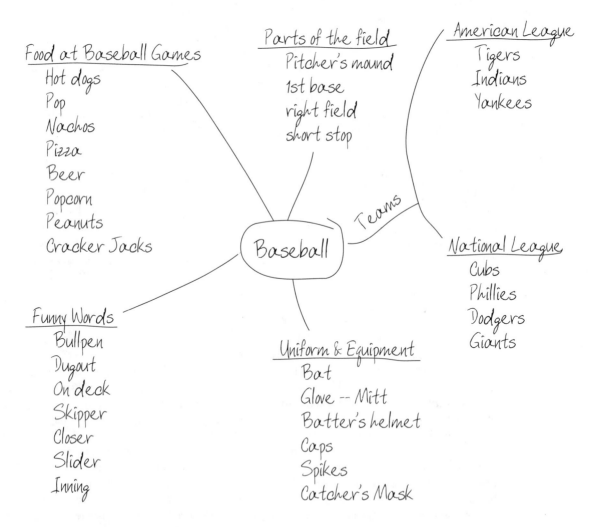

Figure 6.1
Semantic map for "baseball."

Categorizing words allows students to explore their meanings.

Karen, a Title I teacher, likes to use LGL when she introduces students to a new set of readings. She finds that students like to brainstorm their own words and mention and explain words that are unfamiliar to others. "The part I like best about this activity," she explains, "is that it gives students some control over the process. They're not reading and analyzing my set of words or a set of words provided by the textbook. My students love to do this, and all students, even the brightest, learn new words or new ways for thinking about words they already know. If you think about it, LGL requires kids to do some pretty sophisticated and creative analysis of words and concepts."

Other Categorization Activities

As students put similar concepts together, the process of categorization helps them make their world more manageable. It also gives students the chance to meet new words and think about familiar words in new ways. List Group Label is a great way to get students to categorize words and concepts, but it is not the only way. Word sorts, which we have mentioned in several chapters in this book, also challenge students to categorize words. If your students maintain a word bank in the form of a deck of word cards, you can ask them to sort their words into categories that you name. For example, when teaching word recognition skills, we ask students to sort their word bank words by number of syllables, beginning letter sounds, vowel sounds, affixes, and so on. This activity gives students practice with the words, focuses their attention on aspects of words that we want to reinforce, and gets them thinking about ways in which words might be analyzed and categorized. Later, we might ask students to sort their cards into more semantic categories such as things found at home and things found at school, indoor words and outdoor words, words related to fun activities and words related to work activities, and so on.

Word sorts can also be done with words provided by the teacher and related to a topic under study. For example, if the class is studying animal life, the teacher might present words such as *bear, dog, elephant, mouse, horse, tiger, giraffe, wolf, rabbit,* and *coyote.* Word sort categories could include North American and non-North American animals, predatory and nonpredatory animals, domestic and wild animals, and so on. Sometimes students can sort the same set of words in a variety of ways, which helps them think about the features of words. In the animal-life sorts, for example, students can think about bears as North American *and* predatory *and* wild.

In these kinds of word sorts the teacher provides the students with the categories. Therefore, they are called closed sorts. Open sorts, on the other hand, encourage divergent thinking among students. The teacher presents words, often derived from something students either will read or have read, and then asks students to work in pairs or small groups to arrange the words into meaningful groups. When they have finished, students share their reasoning with the rest of the class.

Another categorization activity is one we simply call Pair 'Em Up. It requires students to justify their thinking as they pair up words. The teacher (or a student) presents three words to the group. Students need to determine which two go together and provide a justification for the pairing. Recently, we observed a second-grade class that had a few extra minutes before heading off to lunch. After introducing the activity the teacher called out, "Trees, sky, and dirt."

One student said, "Trees and dirt go together because they both are on the ground."

"OK," said the teacher. "Anyone else have other ideas?"

Another child responded, "Sky and dirt because they're not alive."

A third child answered, "I think it's trees and the sky because trees grow into the sky."

Then a fourth said, "Hey, how about this? Trees and sky go together because they have long vowel sounds."

After a brief discussion on the merits of each response, the teacher had students continue the activity in pairs. The idea behind Pair 'Em Up is not so much to get the correct answer as to challenge students to think about the many ways in which words can be connected to one another. This flexible categorizing helps students create both depth and breadth in their vocabulary.

Concept Map

When a List Group Label activity is converted into a semantic map, students are able to detect visually the connection between words and higher-order or categorical concepts. For many students the visual display is helpful in developing the notion that words are connected to one another through meaning.

A refinement of this notion can be found in what is sometimes called a concept-of-definition map, which we like to refer to simply as a concept map (Schwartz & Raphael, 1985). A concept map is literally a visual representation or map of the definition of a concept or word. Besides defining particular words, concept maps help students understand how words and concepts are defined—that there are various ways to define a word. One can define words by contrasting words or concepts (using opposites) or identifying the hierarchical category to which they belong. Subordinate categories or examples can also help clarify the meaning. Finally, words or concepts can be defined by their essential characteristics or properties. Figure 6.2 is an example of a completed concept map.

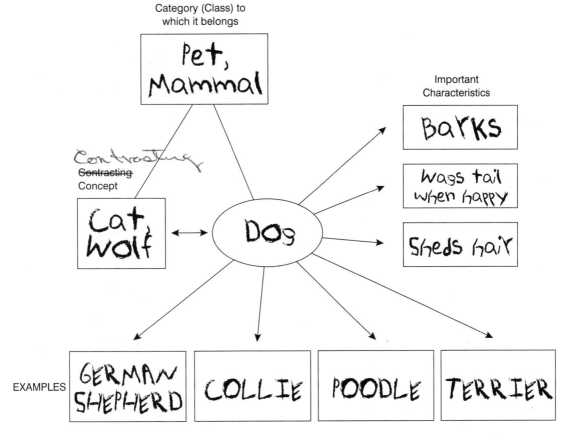

Figure 6.2
Concept map for "dog."

When using a concept map, the teacher usually begins by presenting only the word to be defined, which is written in the center. As a class or in several smaller groups, students define the word by filling in the various elements of the map. Small-group work can demonstrate very divergent thinking: some groups are conventional in their definitions while others are more creative. All maps are acceptable, however, as long as students can successfully defend their decisions.

Wayne, a fourth-grade classroom teacher, has used concept maps for several years with students.

> We do a word a day—I choose from current events or what we are studying in a thematic unit, or I'll ask a student to think of a word to share with the class. You need to choose words for which higher-order concepts as well as examples or subordinate concepts exist. We usually do it at the beginning of each day as a sort of warmup for the class. Most of the time the students work in small groups or pairs and then share their work with the class. What I really like about concept maps is that they help students understand how words are defined and that they don't need to rely totally on a dictionary to provide meaning for a word.
>
> Once the maps are done I'll put them on display in the hallway or we'll create our own classroom dictionary that consists of a set of maps put in alphabetical order and bound into a book or three-ring binder. It's interesting to see how students will look over the maps on display or actually leaf through the class concept-map dictionary. I know I'm touching some of the kids' interest in words through this and some of the other word activities we do.

✳ Analogies

Analogy problems are another word activity that Wayne plays with his class. Analogies are formal statements of the relationship between several words or concepts and are usually in the form *A is to B as C is to D* (sometimes written as *A : B :: C : D*). Here's an example of an analogy problem that Wayne has used:

Abraham Lincoln is to the Civil War as William McKinley is to what?

To solve the problem, we must determine the relationship between the first pair of words or concepts (in the previous example the relationship is "president" to "war during his term") and then apply that relationship to the next pair. When we determine that McKinley was president during the Spanish-American War, we find the answer.

As you can see, analogies can easily be applied to nearly any topic or subject area. Moreover, they promote sophisticated reasoning by requiring students to determine or infer the relationship between word pairs and extend the relationship to a second pair to solve the problem. Again, the focus of this activity is helping students make connections between words and concepts to create greater depth of understanding.

Wayne finds that his students enjoy doing analogies, but he adds:

> I always make sure I present them as a type of play or as riddles to solve. I think kids get a kick out of trying to figure these out and then explain their reasoning to the rest of the class. What's really neat is when I ask students to create a few analogies as a response to their reading, using words or ideas they encountered. Once they get the idea of what analogies are, the best analogies come from the students. We have a ball playing around with them. I find that through analogy play my students are more able to think flexibly about words and think about various ways that words might be related.

Because the analogies are developed from students' own interests and areas of study, difficulty level is self-controlled. (This is also true with List Group Label.) Analogies can be used successfully with primary-grade children as well as older students.

Examples of Analogy Problems

Steering wheel is to car as handlebar is to _____. (part to whole)

Night is to day as win is to _____. (opposites)

Storm is to rain as blizzard is to _____. (cause and effect)

Mt. Everest is to the Himalayas as the Matterhorn is to _____. (geography)

Boat is to ship as firearm is to _____. (synonym)

Word Histories

Words often have interesting histories. Exploring the origins of words with students helps them develop indelible memories as they link specific words with stories of the words' origin. In addition, they learn to appreciate the historical context of certain words and concepts. For example, a teacher might mention that *tank,* a heavily armored military vehicle, was originally used as a code word among the Allied powers to help conceal the vehicle's development and existence from the Axis powers during World War I. That interesting story not only describes the word and concept but also helps students understand an aspect of world history.

Learning the origin of place names, particularly those within their own community, is a great way for students to link history with vocabulary play and development. In a local elementary school, Jeanine, an intermediate-grade teacher of students with learning disabilities, interests children in words by relating the stories and rationales for place names in nearby communities. Jeanine works in Summit County, the county in which Akron, Ohio, is located. She invites students to speculate on the origin of the county's name. A few students know that *summit* refers to a high place and suggest that Summit County contains the highest point in the state. Jeanine compliments her students for a good guess and then shares the real story of Summit County: It was the highest point on the Ohio and Erie Canal, which ran from Lake Erie to the Ohio River. Her story leads to a discussion about the numerous canal locks located in the county, their purpose, how they worked, and their relation to the type of land on which that part of the canal was built.

Jeanine notes that the origin of the name *Akron* is also related to summits. She points out that the city's name is derived from the Greek word *akros,* which means "topmost." Then she challenges her students to find other words that include the *akro* or *acro* word part and determine how they might also contain a meaning for high place. Within minutes students find *acrobat, Acropolis,* and *acrophobia.* After everyone discusses the meanings of these words, Jeanine ends her mini-lesson with "akros = summit or high place" written on the chalkboard. Students have a clear idea of what these words mean and how they fit into the texture of their own communities. Familiar place names such as Pittsburgh, Pennsylvania, Florida, Baton Rouge, Vermont, Montana, Los Angeles, Palo Alto, and many others can evoke interesting and important stories about words and histories.

Many English words are derived from other languages such as Greek, Latin, French, and Spanish. Helping students gain insight into words and word parts from other languages will give them strategies for understanding many of the new words they encounter. Appendix H lists some common word parts derived from Greek and Latin that will help students unlock the meanings of many other words they encounter. A more complete list of Greek and Latin word roots can be found in *The New Reading Teacher's Book of Lists* (Fry, Fountoukidis, & Polk, 1985).

At first glance, exploring word histories with students seems like it can be a lot of fun. But when we share these ideas with teachers, the first question they ask is often, "But how do we find out about words and where they come from? We can't be expected to have all these words and their histories at our fingertips." The solution to this problem is as close as the local public library. Just ask the local librarian where you might be able to find a few of the many books written about word histories. Starting with these resources, you can begin to design your own captivating entrée into the world of word origins for your own students.

Games and Puzzles

Vocabulary learning should be fun, and one way to bring this spirit into vocabulary is through games and similar activities. It is easy to create variations of well-known games that students will find engaging and entertaining. Here are just a few that we have found are student pleasers.

Wordo

This is a form of bingo, using Wordo cards that are almost identical to bingo cards. (See Chapter 4 for an example of a Wordo card.) Choose 24 words to review and play with. Students randomly write one word in each square, leaving the center square as a free spot. The teacher then randomly selects one word at a time and presents the definition, an antonym, or a sentence with the target word missing. Players need to figure out the word and cover it with a marker. As in bingo, a player wins when a vertical, horizontal, or diagonal line is covered. Then a new game starts. Each game can last 5–10 minutes.

John has used Wordo with his Title I students as well as when he taught fifth grade.

> At the beginning of the year I run off a hundred or so of the Wordo sheets and cut them into individual cards. Then we're ready to play whenever we have the time, and the students and I want to play. They really like it. I think they'd play it every day if they could. I like to give out a cheap prize to the winner of each game. I have three empty coffee cans and place a prize in two of them. In the third is a slip of paper that says "Zonk." Thus, even when a student wins, there's an element of surprise and chance in their winning a prize.
>
> I've found that after a while, rather than my saying the clues or giving the antonyms, a student can do that job too. It gives them extra practice in playing with the meanings

of words. Of course, a student will want to play emcee for only one or two games. Then they'll want to get back and play the game!

Concentration (or Match)

In Concentration two decks of cards are laid out in a grid. One set of cards contains words to be learned and practiced; and the other set contains definitions, synonyms, or antonyms or some other way of matching the first set. As in the television version of the game, players (or teams of players) uncover pairs of cards trying to find a match. If a match is made, the player takes the cards and keeps playing. If no match is produced, then the cards are turned back over; and the next player takes his turn. Players who find the most matches win the game.

Scattergories

Scattergories can be played in either its commercial version or adapted for instructional use. In the adapted version a set of 5–10 letters is determined and listed vertically on each player's paper. Then a category is determined—for example, vegetables, countries, presidents' last names, or rivers. (This is best done by developing the categories before playing, listing each on a slip of paper, and then selecting one from the group for each game.) Working with a time limit of one or two minutes, individuals or groups of players think of words that begin with the given letters and fit the category. Players with the greatest number of unique words (words chosen by only one individual or team) win that round.

Balderdash

Here's another game that is available in both commercial and adapted forms. An adapted version goes like this. Each player chooses an uncommon word from the dictionary. When it is a player's turn, she presents the word and a definition—either the real definition or one made up by the player—to the other players. The other players individually guess whether the definition is the correct one or not. The presenting player gets a point each time she fools another player.

Hinky Pinkies

Hinky Pinkies are word riddles that students love to solve and to make on their own. The answer to a Hinky Pinky is two or more rhyming words. For example, a cold place of learning is a *cool school*; an obese feline is a *fat cat*. Students need to put their word knowledge to use to solve and make up Hinky Pinkies. A variation of Hinky Pinkies uses alliterative combinations of words instead of rhymes. Thus, a sleepy flower might be a *lazy lily,* and a 4,000-pound farm vehicle would be a *two-ton tractor*.

Hinky Pinkies are fun and easy and take little time to develop and play. Many teachers save them for when they have a few extra minutes in the school day. Other teachers we've seen have used them as alternative assignments in various content areas. After studying the states, students in one class were asked to describe states using Hinky Pinkies. California was described as *west, warm, and wild* while Florida was the answer to what is *fun in the sun*.

Regular, but not exclusive, use of games and puzzles adds another dimension to vocabulary learning. Students will appreciate the variety that these games can bring to the study of words and concepts. Often students will get into the spirit of things and exercise their creative talents by developing their own vocabulary games and puzzles.

Books about Words

There are several trade books for children that explore words and word meanings in a playful manner. In the *Amelia Bedelia* stories by Peggy Parish, for example, Amelia constantly misinterprets common expressions and idioms, which results in humorous situations. Similarly, several books by Fred Gwynne use illustrations to show misunderstandings of words and figures of speech (*A Little Pigeon Toad*, *The King Who Rained*, and *Chocolate Moose for Dinner*). *Daffy Definitions* by Joseph Rosenbloom presents nonconventional but clever definitions. Marvin Terban has developed an entire genre of word-play books that range from funny palindromes (*Too Hot to Hoot*) to funny eponyms (*Guppies in Tuxedos*). Joke and riddle books as well as crossword-puzzle books provide interesting word-play activities and opportunities to share with students.

The strategies and activities we have outlined in this chapter have the potential to increase students' interest in and knowledge of words, which in turn will have a positive effect on their reading. Informed teachers have been modifying and using these approaches to fit their own curricula, teaching situations, and styles of teaching to meet the needs and learning characteristics of their students. These teachers integrate and mass these approaches in planned and purposeful ways. They do not use them on a hit-or-miss basis— once or twice a week for a few minutes or when there is a lull in the instructional day. Instead, they incorporate these strategies into their own framework of teaching.

Most teachers, especially at the elementary level, teach a variety of subject areas. Even those who specialize in one subject area may teach a variety of topics and subtopics within the subject. These teachers recognize that within any one subject area there are new words and concepts that students will need to understand and use in order to learn successfully and efficiently. They use the selected strategies and activities in this chapter to present these new concepts and words to students. Thus, the vocabulary activities become an essential element of subject-area reading and learning.

Teachers also promote vocabulary learning by massing the activities we have presented in this chapter. In other words, using the activities, many teachers will put together a 10–15 minute vocabulary lesson three to five times per week in which students explore and play with words. The words may be tied to a particular subject or curricular area but don't have to be. Teachers and students find words from their interests and hobbies; current local and national news; or upcoming important events, anniversaries, and holidays. Then they play with them. Thus, students develop an interest in, improved knowledge of, and greater flexibility over learning and using words they encounter in their lives.

Rich, a third-grade teacher, does what he calls "Wordshop" three times per week. "I like to play with and learn new words," he says, "and I try to share my enjoyment with my students." He continues:

> For about 15 minutes, on Mondays, Wednesdays, and Fridays right before lunch, we play with words. We might do three or four activities during this time such as a couple of analogy problems, introduce the origins of two or three words, or learn about some Latin or Greek roots, and play a game like word Concentration or Wordo. It's really fast-paced, and the kids like it. Best of all I see many of them playing with words on their own!

Word knowledge or vocabulary may not be all there is to reading, but it is an important part. And it's a part that challenges many of our students who have difficulty reading. Many students think of word learning as drudgery; as a result, they avoid it or make inefficient use of their time and efforts for learning words.

Word learning need not be that way. Tapping into students' own interests and knowledge; employing interesting, effective, and challenging learning activities; allowing students to collaborate with others in shared learning experiences; and creating a playful environment in which words are played with, played on, manipulated, and used in a variety of ways can make the difference between vocabulary instruction that hinders reading and vocabulary instruction that nurtures reading.

Chapter 7

Comprehension
Development with
Narrative Text

Comprehension is what reading is all about. For example, the Commission on Reading (Anderson, Hiebert, Scott, & Wilkinson, 1985) defines reading as the "process of constructing meaning from written texts, . . . a holistic act" that depends on "the background of the reader, the purpose for reading, and the context in which reading occurs" (p. 7). Whether we're reading a novel, a technical manual, or a number from the telephone directory, comprehension is involved. Thus, a primary goal for literacy instruction, regardless of age, grade level, or achievement level, is to help students develop into purposeful, independent comprehenders.

This goal is essential for students experiencing difficulty in learning to read. Indeed, most of the at-risk readers we have encountered over the years are neither purposeful nor independent as readers. Instead they try, usually in vain, to guess at desired responses. Even sadder, they simply choose not to participate at all. Effective comprehension instruction can make all the difference for these children.

What's important in comprehension instruction? What kinds of discussions or activities can help students construct meaning from print? How can we foster students' thoughtful interaction with text? These are critical questions for teachers to consider as they plan instruction, and answers to them abound. The Commission on Reading (Anderson et al., 1985), for example, suggests that teachers engage students in discussions and provide instructional activities that do the following:

- Cause students to focus on relevant information, synthesize the information, and integrate it with what they already know
- Provoke thought and motivate higher-level thinking

These suggestions are certainly sensible, but we would also add several others:

- Comprehension instruction must involve students as readers in real reading situations. Instruction must keep the process whole and real rather than focus on artificial bits and pieces that draw attention away from the real purposes for reading. In other words, completing exercises about specific skills won't enhance comprehension as effectively as reading something that is interesting and then talking about it with others.

• Instruction should help students focus on meaning for themselves as thoughtful readers. In other words, children should work to develop their own understanding of what they read, not try to guess the teacher's. Thinking is at the center of all reading. The meaning that each individual constructs when reading is dependent, at least in part, on her own knowledge, experiences, and purposes for reading. Two readers may comprehend the same piece of material in quite different ways, but that doesn't mean that one reader is right and the other wrong. Comprehension is relative, not absolute.

• The instructional environment must promote risk taking. Proficient readers are active; they speculate. They think about what they know and what they are likely to encounter while they read. If their predictions are not confirmed, they may continue reading, remaining alert to clues that will help them alter their ideas and make sense of the material, or reread for missed clues and make alternative predictions. Making predictions, or educated guesses, and then evaluating them are essential aspects of reading. Making a guess means taking a chance, and readers are unlikely to take chances in an environment that stresses being "right" or where their ideas are ridiculed or dismissed. Rather, we must show students that we care about their reactions to what they read, regardless of how divergent or unconventional those reactions may be.

• In classrooms, learning is a social process. Obviously, students must interact with text to enhance their abilities as comprehenders. Interacting with others is equally important. The instructional environment should foster group inquiry and problem solving by giving students opportunities to clarify their thinking and understand the thinking of others. Instructionally, two or three heads working together are almost always better than one.

• Readers need opportunities to respond to what they have read. Moreover, children need options for responding to reading and choice among those options. Response options should be plentiful and varied. Students may wish to talk with others, write down their thoughts or feelings, develop written or oral narratives that explore or extend various aspects of their reading, engage in creative drama or art activities, participate in reader's theater . . . and the list can go on and on. By making time for response, sharing a variety of response activities with children, and encouraging students to respond to reading in personally meaningful ways, we show students that "reading/thinking continues after the book is closed" (Goodman & Watson, 1977, p. 869). Equally important, we show children that their personal responses to reading are important and their thinking is valued by others.

These instructional priorities reflect our current understanding of the reading process. We know that reading is the process of constructing meaning and that readers accomplish this by using what's in their heads as well as what's on the page. We also know that children will learn best what we give them opportunities to learn. To develop proficiency, children who have difficulty reading need consistent and plentiful opportunities to behave successfully as readers.

Each of the instructional activities described in this chapter and Chapter 8 reflects our instructional priorities. In this chapter we present activities that work especially well with narrative materials. By *narrative* we mean any text organized as a story. They may be fictitious or imaginary stories, such as those in fiction, fables or tales, and many poems, or true stories, such as those in biographies, autobiographies, or memoirs.

The first section of this chapter describes strategies that support students before reading, and the second deals with strategies that support comprehension while students are reading. The third section presents many after-reading options that allow students to share their responses and thinking with each other. Chapter 8 is devoted to similar strategies that help students comprehend expository text.

Supporting Comprehension before Reading

To understand something they read, readers need some knowledge of the topic. This is certainly true for informational texts and can be true for narrative or story material as well. Knowledge of concepts in the reading and familiarity with the author and his writing style as well as characters, settings, and problems presented in the text can help any reader develop a thorough understanding of the material. Thus, it is essential for teachers to ensure that students have some familiarity with the content and nature of the text before actually reading it. Many students who find reading difficult have limited knowledge of the topics they encounter in their reading. A few minutes spent to develop interest and background before reading can greatly benefit students' understanding of the text.

Of course, one way to ensure that students have some background about a topic is for them to choose materials that they are already interested in. For this reason, knowledge of students' interests is very important. But it is not always possible to match students with familiar topics. In these cases, teachers need to help students develop some initial understanding of the topic that will help them negotiate the reading in a meaningful and satisfying way. Here are several easy approaches that teachers and students can use to develop background and interest.

 ## Jackdaws

Teachers are notorious collectors. One person's junk is often a teacher's treasure. Jackdaws are collections of artifacts built around a particular book topic or theme. Often the objects that teachers include in their jackdaws have surfaced at garage sales or thrift stores. By bringing in real or facsimile artifacts connected in some way to a book about to be read and talking about them with students, teachers help create interest and background that carry students through texts they otherwise find difficult. Figure 7.1 lists the types of items that may go into a jackdaw.

As students become familiar with the concept of jackdaws, they can add to the teacher's jackdaw, which is then displayed in a mini-museum for all students to see, touch, and ponder. More ambitious students can create their own jackdaws as a response activity to a text they have read. What a creative and interesting way for students to demonstrate understanding of a text!

Just what is a jackdaw? A jackdaw is a collection of interesting artifacts that provides information about a particular subject, period, or idea. The term comes from the British name for a bird, similar to the American grackle, that picks up brightly colored, interesting, and attractive objects and carries them off to its nest. For children, jackdaws are particularly useful for building background and interest in books, stories, and other texts.

Artifacts can be collected from a variety of sources in a variety of ways to aid the understanding of particular portions of books. The elements of a jackdaw are synergistic. Each individual artifact may only add a little to a student's background or understanding. Yet when taken as a whole, the jackdaw can create a comprehensive background and make a book come alive.

When making jackdaws, teachers may wish to consider what sorts of things might add to a deeper understanding of a text. The number and types of items are limited only by one's imagination and creativity. They might include the following:

1. Clothes of the type worn by particular characters in a book—catalog pictures, paper dolls, collages, old photos, and so on.
2. Songs or music from a period or event depicted in a book—sheet music, recordings, demonstrations, titles, or musical instruments.
3. A news article from the period, real or a facsimile.
4. Photographs from the time period or geographical area depicted in the book.
5. Household items from the period depicted in the book.
6. A time line depicting the occurrence of events in a book (may also include real-world events not mentioned in the book).
7. A map showing any journey that the main characters make.
8. Recipes and food dishes typical of the time period in the book.
9. Selected poems that reflect the theme of the book.
10. A glossary of interesting or peculiar words in the book.
11. Dioramas that illustrate particular scenes from the story.
12. A biographical sketch of the book's author.
13. A list of other related books (by story, theme, characters, and so on) that students can read to extend their literacy experience.

After the teacher introduces jackdaws, students may wish to add to existing collections or create their own jackdaws in response to their reading..

Figure 7.1
Jackdaws.

For the past several years, Tim's sixth-grade class has explored the Great Depression in the United States. One of the core books is Irene Hunt's *No Promises in the Wind*. Tim says:

I found that this can be a difficult book for many students as they don't have a very good understanding of what it was like to live through such desperate times as the Depression. Several years ago my mother-in-law was going through some of her old things. I noticed she had many items from the Depression—an old camera, some clothing made from sack cloth, old records, an iron that was heated by sitting on the stove, some letters from her brothers who had to leave home to look for work, and many other things. I thought to myself, "What a wonderful way to introduce my students to the Depression!"

With her permission I took the items in and shared them with my students prior to reading the book. I was amazed at how just touching and talking about these items created an instant interest in students and gave them enough background to read the book successfully. Even our discussions of the book seemed more lively as a result of the jackdaw. It wasn't long before students were talking with their parents and grandparents and bringing in their own items related to the Depression.

Tim has used jackdaws with a number of books and themes concerning American history, including the Civil War and the Vietnam era. In addition, he frequently uses jackdaws for stories that take place in different parts of the country and the world. "I guess Show and Tell has a place in the upper grades," he says.

Related Readings

Just reading one story or text about a topic can create sufficient interest and background for further reading. This is why thematic readings and units of study are such a powerful approach to learning. As students' understanding of a topic deepens through reading, their expanded background allows them to read more complex and sophisticated texts successfully.

Students can read the books themselves, or the teacher can read a book aloud to establish background for further reading that students will do on their own. The readings can include all kinds of texts—from books and stories, to poetry, to magazine and newspaper articles. Kathy, a primary-grade teacher of children who have reading difficulties, has developed a reading unit that includes Cinderella stories from various cultures. She has found that one story sets the stage for the next. She even includes Judith Viorst's poem "And then the prince knelt down and tried to put the glass slipper on Cinderella's foot" (from *If I Were in Charge of the World and Other Worries*). "This really gets the talk started," she says.

Reading books by a particular author is also a great way to familiarize students with a writer's style. Books by William Steig, for example, contain many common elements, such as magic, animals that assume human roles, rich vocabulary, a subtle sense of humor, and much alliteration. Developing these understandings about Steig can help any reader tackle his next book.

Series books are particularly potent because they combine one author's style with common characters, settings, and similar story lines. Reading one book in a series creates a rich background for reading, understanding, and enjoying other stories in the same series. Readers are saved from having to establish familiarity with general author and content variables. Instead, they can devote their energy to making sense of the story at hand. Richek and McTague (1988) have developed a sensible reading program for children who have difficulty learning to read that is built around the notion of series books. (See Chapter 10 for a description of this program.) In Appendix D we list some popular series books.

Other Media and Activities

Artifacts and related readings are not the only way to develop interest and background for reading. Guest speakers from the local community (perhaps parents who are experts in particular areas) can excite students about a topic that they will later explore in reading. Before his students read Jane Yolen's *The Devil's Arithmetic,* James, a fifth-grade teacher, invited a Holocaust survivor to speak with the class. Her moving story created an interest that sped many students through the book and into several other books about the Holocaust.

Field trips and movies or videotapes (commercially produced or developed by the teacher or others) can develop interest and background for reading. In his class's study of slavery and the Civil War, Tim arranged for a field trip to a preserved station on the Underground Railroad. Before reading Paul Fleischman's *Bull Run* and performing it later as a reader's theater, Tim showed the class selected segments from the PBS television series "The Civil War." He says, "I think sometimes we assume that students have a good background on a topic when they really don't. Then we're disappointed when they have a poor understanding and don't enjoy a story we thought would knock their socks off. I really think that a key to successful reading experiences, including comprehension and enjoyment, is making sure that students have a solid background in the topic they are to encounter."

Story Mapping

When driving in an unfamiliar city, it is often helpful to have a map at your side. By studying the map before driving, you can familiarize yourself with important intersections, street names, and landmarks that will help you negotiate your way through unfamiliar streets and neighborhoods. Similarly, introducing students to a story by sharing a map of a text they are about to read can help familiarize them with the major characters and events they will encounter in their reading. A story map (or story board) is simply a visual display of the major characters, settings, and events arranged in story order (see Figure 7.2). It can depict the complete story or provide only enough information to get readers going on a text. As a postreading activity, students can also create their own maps or complete partial maps.

Bob, a teacher who works with upper-elementary students who have difficulty reading, puts it this way:

> Sometimes I ask students to read stories that are quite complex. I know that the story can be confusing for them. For these times I will often sketch out a map for them to show them how the story develops and point out some of the diversions that may get them off track. I think many of my kids are helped a lot by the maps. Often, they go up to the map that's on a wall chart and study it as they read. It helps them make sense out of the story.

Role Playing

Another way to build background and interest is to act out in class some of the important issues or conflicts before actually reading the story. By personally connecting with

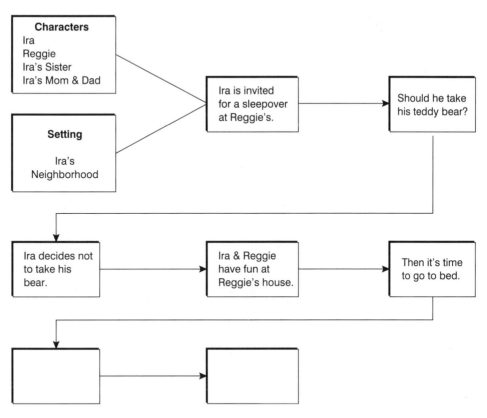

Figure 7.2
Story map for Bernard Waber's *Ira Sleeps Over.*

the story in this way, students are able to get inside the issues and characters that form the story. Before Jane read *Say It* by Charlotte Zolotow to her students, her second graders went out to the playground. She asked students to walk in pairs pretending to be mother and daughter or father and son. Then she challenged them to think of ways to say that they loved or were angry with the other person without using the words *love, angry, mad,* or other words that directly expressed those feelings. Later, the students talked about how they did. Jane recalls, "It was a challenging task and many students had difficulty with it. But it got all of us thinking about the subtle ways we can communicate with each other, it made our reading of *Say It* that much more personal and meaningful, and it led to an excellent discussion when I finished reading the story."

Supporting Comprehension during Reading

To plan comprehension instruction, we must first understand how comprehension happens. Meaning construction (comprehension) depends on several types of prior knowledge as well

Instructional support should provide students with a framework for thinking about text and sharing ideas with others.

as active thought. To read we must understand the features of written language as a form of communication. We make use of our underlying knowledge of graphophonology (sound-symbol relationships), syntax (word order), and semantics (vocabulary and meaning). Furthermore, reading involves thinking and predicting, which are based in part on experiential and conceptual background. In other words, reading is an active thinking process dependent upon the reader's thoughts, language, and experiences as well as the text.

Situational pragmatics, or the context in which we read, also influences comprehension. Obviously, external contextual influences such as lighting or distractions can affect comprehension, as can other, more subtle contextual factors. One of these is purpose, which we use to determine if we have comprehended adequately. In classrooms, students' perceptions of the instructional environment, including the kinds of interactions encouraged, are equally important. To support meaning construction, communication should be open during text discussions. Free and voluntary exchange of ideas should be the goal so that students can try out their ideas and modify them after they hear what others have to say. This sort of context makes it possible for students to "exert a group effort at understanding—enable them, that is, to arrive at conclusions that they could not have reached alone and without that support" (Barnes, Britton, & Rosen, 1971, pp. 97–98).

Directed Reading-Thinking Activity

Instructional support during reading should provide students with a framework for thinking about the text and sharing ideas with others. The Directed Reading-Thinking

Activity (DR-TA) fits this criterion (Stauffer, 1980), as do Think-Pair-Share, Character Sketches, Linguistic Roulette, and imagery, which we describe later in the chapter. DR-TA is a holistic, problem-solving discussion strategy designed to improve students' reading-thinking skills and maximize their learning. Lessons evolve through cycles in which students generate hypotheses and subsequently validate, reject, or modify them.

First, students make predictions about story content based on the title of the selection (and, if appropriate, initial illustrations) and prior knowledge. Students then read silently to predetermined stopping points. Discussions follow, which the teacher facilitates by asking students to indicate whether their predictions were confirmed and encouraging them to support their ideas. Next, students refine their original predictions and/or make new ones. This cycle of predicting; reading to confirm, modify, or reject; providing support from the text; and making further predictions continues until the entire selection has been read.

To prepare for a DR-TA, the teacher decides where students will stop for discussion. Divisions between episodes in a story often work well. Preparation may also involve becoming comfortable with DR-TA questions, which are quite different from more traditional comprehension questions. For example, the teacher initiates discussion by asking, "What do you think this will be about?" He then may ask for elaboration or clarification, asking, "Why?" or "What makes you say that?" After students have read the first portion of the text, the teacher may ask, "Did anything surprise you?" or "Did things happen like you thought they would?" or "Were you right?" Such clarification or elaboration questions encourage students to evaluate their earlier ideas in light of information in the text. Finally, the teacher asks students to think ahead: "What will happen next? Why?" Students then read, and the discussion cycle begins again.

Bonnie conducted a DR-TA with a group of eighth graders, and we reproduce several excerpts here. The students were reading and discussing the short story "All the Years of Her Life" (Callaghan, 1935), which tells what happens when a mother learns that her son has been caught shoplifting.

Bonnie:	*What do you think this story's going to be about?*
Lucy:	Somebody's life. . . .
Joseph:	A diary. It'll be a diary about her life. . . .
Lucy:	She's going to be older.
Bonnie:	*Why do you say that?*
Lucy:	Well it's a story about her life.
Heather:	It says, "All the Years." . . .
Lucy:	So that means she's going to be like older. . . .
Bonnie:	*Some other predictions? . . .*
Joseph:	Someone's problems
Bonnie:	*Why do you say that?*
Joseph:	I don't know. You can just tell by her life. And usually people have problems.

[Students read. Later in the lesson the conversation continues.]

Bonnie:	*Well, what do you think will happen next?*
Joseph:	I don't think they're going to go get a cop.
Bonnie:	*No? Why not?*
Joseph:	Why not? I just don't think that. Uh, with the mother's attitude, the way she came in, I think that it might have changed the owner's mind.

Lucy:	Yeah, you know, with a mother like this maybe the kid'll turn out OK.
Bonnie:	*Is there any sign of that in the story?*
Lucy:	Yeah. Well, he couldn't believe the attitude that his mom came in with. Maybe that might change his opinion about her.
Heather:	I think that he's more likely to get a cop if she came in nice like that. That's what I would do.
Andrew:	Yeah, because he thinks that she's probably not going to do anything to him, or punish him for what he did. . . .
Heather:	The store manager thinks that the mother sort of planned for him to take something. . . .
Bonnie:	*What do the rest of you think?*
Joseph:	Well, maybe the store manager let him off the hook because he'll probably punish himself enough. . . .
Bonnie:	*Tell some more about that.*
Joseph:	Guilt.
Heather:	Yeah, the way he'll feel about himself from now on.
Lucy:	And he probably won't do it again.
Bonnie:	*OK.*
Andrew:	Well, the kid's already scared as it is.

Did you notice how little Bonnie said? In a DR-TA, students do most of the talking. Did you notice that she did not provide important ideas or generalizations for students? Her goals were to encourage thinking and facilitate group interaction rather than manipulate students' thinking or test their recall. The instructional context signaled that students' ideas were valued—that they should explain their ideas so others could understand their reasoning and listen to and talk with each other. In short, students were intellectually involved with text concepts.

The DR-TA is a staple in Bonnie's classroom. "We probably do DR-TAs more often than any other while-they-read strategy," she says.

> The kids love it. They enjoy telling us all what they think, and they seem to find others' ideas fascinating. These discussions really support kids' reading, especially when we have different hypotheses going as they read. Maybe it's because we stop to talk while they read, maybe it's the personal commitment they make or the curiosity that develops so naturally, or maybe it's because kids know we'll want to know where their ideas are coming from—for whatever reason, the DR-TA is really a powerful reading strategy!

Think-Pair-Share

Like the DR-TA, Think-Pair-Share provides opportunities for students to talk about a story as they read it. To prepare for the activity, students find partners. The teacher identifies stopping points for discussion and shares these with students, who can make light pencil marks in their texts to remember where to stop.

Students read to the first stopping point and then pause to think about the reading. They might consider such issues as what they found interesting or puzzling; they often make brief notes about their thoughts. After each partner has completed this thinking, the pairs talk with one another using their notes to remind them of the points they wish to make. Finally, the larger group shares, focusing on interesting issues that arose during the partner discussions. Depending on students' interest and need, these discussions may be brief or lengthy. When the first Think-Pair-Share cycle is complete, students read the next portion of the story and begin the cycle again.

Think-Pair-Share is an extremely adaptable organizational structure for conducting classroom discussions. For example, it can also be used as an after-reading activity and works well with expository text. Harold, who uses the strategy frequently in his work with students with disabilities, sees two major benefits:

> My students often need support as they are reading a story. If we use Think-Pair-Share a couple of times while they read, the thinking and talking allows everyone to be successful. I also like the fact that individuals think things through for themselves (and often write their ideas down) before discussing them with partners. They don't "shoot from the hip." This activity encourages individual response to reading, which I believe is important to helping kids learn, and the writing beforehand makes the partner discussions more lively.

Character Sketches

In Character Sketches, students use the Think-Pair-Share structure to focus their attention on character development. At the first stopping point in their reading (or listening), students jot down words and phrases to describe one or two major characters. This becomes information that they share, first with their partners and then with the larger group. At each successive stop, students return to their notes about the characters, modifying them based on the new insights they have developed through reading. A character who initially seemed selfish or unfeeling, for example, may be revealed as shy or grieving. After modifying their lists, students again talk with partners and the entire group. The Think-Pair-Share cycle continues until students have completed the story.

At the conclusion of the activity, students have notes that reflect their descriptions of major characters. These can be used for a discussion of how authors develop characters or a variety of other follow-up activities. Students also have an increased understanding of the story because characters typically reveal their personalities through what they say and do.

Linguistic Roulette

This small-group discussion technique was developed by Jerry Harste. After reading a portion of a story, each student skims through it again looking for a single sentence that she finds interesting, important, puzzling, or special in some other way. This sentence is written on paper.

Discussion begins when all members of the group have read and selected their sentences. Each student reads his sentence aloud and invites group response. Students often explain why they selected their sentences, which can give rise to interesting comprehension discussions. After all group members have shared, students read the next portion of the story, and the cycle is repeated.

Linguistic Roulette fosters comprehension in several ways. First, stopping periodically to talk with peers supports comprehension. Moreover, students must think again about the story to select their sentences for discussion. Hearing others' sentences and participating in the small-group discussions sometimes encourages consideration of alternate perspectives.

Karen provides resource-room support for intermediate-grade children with learning disabilities. "To tell the truth," she says, "I was pretty suspicious about Linguistic Roulette at first. I wondered how anything that *easy* could really work." But Karen was curious, so she took a risk and tried it. "And, let me tell you, I eavesdropped on those first discussions. What a surprise! I found that my students were perfectly capable of discussing a story independently and that they were really proud that they could do so without me. In fact, the Linguistic Roulette discussions are usually freer and more wide-ranging than they are when I'm part of the group. I like the way it provides a framework for kids—because they know what they need to do, they can manage the discussion on their own."

Imagery

Narratives lend themselves to rich images that readers create as they read. The text is rather like a blueprint that readers flesh out by adding their own background, understandings, and experiences. The result is a mental image that is unique to the individual reader yet enables him to get a clearer picture or understanding of the story. The images that individuals create reflect their own interpretations, which may explain why people usually like the book version of a story better than the movie version in which a director imposes her own images on the audience.

Good readers may take for granted this ability to create internal images as they read. It seems so easy and natural. But many readers who have difficulty with reading do not spontaneously create text-related images. Some scholars have argued that the dominance of television in our society has kept children from creating mental images. As a result, many readers have difficulty using this strategy for comprehending stories.

To nurture this ability in most children, teachers simply need to remind them to form images as they read and then talk about their images after reading. For other readers, however, teachers may need to ask them to draw pictures that represent the content of their reading and then talk about the pictures. Later, the teacher can ask students to create the pictures in their head while reading rather than put them on paper.

Title I teacher Janet told us that many of her students seem to have difficulty creating images of texts. "I found it helpful to ask them specifically to create images of certain stories and poems that lend themselves to images as they read and then to talk about them. This seems to help their retention of the stories. Also, after reading a story I'll sometimes bring a videotaped version and we'll watch part of it. Then we'll talk about how our own images compare with the tape. It makes for a lively discussion."

Text discussions during reading can enhance comprehension if the instructional environment fosters sharing, group inquiry, and problem solving. All the activities we have described encourage students to read actively and thoughtfully. Over time, such instruction will help them learn that they can (indeed, must) construct meaning as they read.

Extending Comprehension after Reading

Discussions during reading should promote thoughtful consideration of the text and individual and group efforts at understanding. Instruction after reading should encourage continued interaction with text content. The Group Mapping Activity, (Write and Share)[2], Agree or Disagree? Why?, Bleich's Heuristic, Sketch to Stretch, compare-contrast charts, reader's theater, and response journals are all effective techniques for encouraging students to continue thinking widely and deeply about what they've read and integrating the text information into their own cognitive structures. The teacher's role in all these activities is to promote sharing, encourage and model critical thought, and moderate discussions. The students' roles require reading, thinking, solving problems, making decisions, and interacting with the text and each other.

Group Mapping Activity

The Group Mapping Activity (Davidson, 1982) promotes individual response to reading and provides a framework for discussion. After reading, students create maps, which are then shared with and explained to others. Classmates may ask questions or make comments, which generally prompts continued discussion of the text.

A map is a diagram or symbolic representation of the reader's personal response to text. Young readers often make pictures when asked to map; older readers tend to use lines, arrows, or other symbols to represent their response. A few words may be used to label portions of a map, but mapping is primarily a nonverbal activity. The first time that students map, the teacher can help them understand the concept by offering directions: "Put your ideas about the story in a diagram. You can sketch if you want to or use circles, boxes, or arrows. Try to show your ideas without using too many words. Don't worry about a 'right' way to map; there isn't one." This detailed explanation won't be necessary after students' initial encounter with mapping. When they see the variety of responses, their concern about being right quickly diminishes.

Students' maps need not be detailed or perfect; in fact, making a map should take only a few minutes. Mapping allows the reader to synthesize his response to the text. But its real purpose is to provide a framework for the discussion that follows, which typically allows students to develop further insights into what they have read and realize that text interpretations often differ. The Group Mapping Activity helps readers recall and retain text information while providing them with a means to respond personally to what they have read.

Anna began using the Group Mapping Activity some time ago. When she learned about it, she said, "I knew it was *made* for my second graders. They love to draw, and many are still beginning writers, so they often have more to say than they have patience to write." Anna has been pleased with children's responses: "The diversity of responses is truly amazing! Children show genuine interest in each other's maps, and the discussions that accompany sharing are fascinating. I feel certain that the kids' understanding is enhanced."

(Write and Share)[2]

Responses to literature may vary among readers, and comprehension is enhanced by considering others' ideas as well as developing one's own. (Write and Share)[2] is a comprehension strategy that fosters response by incorporating both these opportunities (Davidson, 1987). Students write twice and share twice (thus the name) in response to text they have read.

In groups of three to five students, children first read the same text. Then students write, quickly jotting down words and phrases that represent their responses to the text. Teachers often tell students not to worry about putting their ideas into sentences but rather to make quick notes for their own use only. This helps students attend to their ideas rather than the mechanics of writing. The first small-group discussion follows, with each student sharing his notes and all students reacting to the ideas presented.

When the first sharing session is concluded, students again write, this time developing their thoughts into prose, using the story, their own initial notes, and the shared responses as the basis for this second writing. Finally, students share this writing with each other and discuss both the text and their reactions to it. To encourage further response, the teacher may ask volunteers to read their final pieces to the whole group. Another alternative is to ask each small group to select one piece to be shared with the larger group.

The initial note taking allows students to capture their individual responses before sharing them with others. With the first discussion, the note taking serves as a kind of prewriting activity as students generate and organize their ideas about their reading. Of course, hearing and discussing others' ideas during both sharing sessions often enables students to see and appreciate different interpretations and responses to the same text as well as deepen their own understanding. In short, this easy-to-implement activity has a variety of powerful effects on students as comprehenders.

Agree or Disagree? Why?

In this small-group discussion activity, students talk about statements that are related to what they have read or heard. To prepare for the activity, the teacher writes several statements that reflect issues that may yield differences of opinion. For example, the following statements might accompany the first chapter of E. B. White's *Charlotte's Web:*

- Fern's parents showed that they loved her.
- Animals should be treated like people.
- Sometimes adults have to do cruel things.
- Mr. Arable should have killed the runt.

Small groups assemble after students have read or listened to the story (or chapter). Group members discuss each statement, trying to decide if they agree or disagree with it and making notes about their reasons. When the small groups have completed their discussions, the teacher may wish to convene the larger group to facilitate further discussion of the story.

Carol frequently uses Agree or Disagree? Why?, especially when she reads aloud to her primary Title I students. "Sometimes the books kids read independently are rather straightforward," she says, "but those I read aloud hardly ever are. I tend to select read alouds that encourage children to think about life's complexities. Agree or Disagree? Why? provides a framework for them to share their thinking about some of these ideas. It's also a perfect way to extend the read-aloud experience for kids."

Bleich's Heuristic

David Bleich (1978) has long argued that individual, subjective responses to literature have worth and power. His heuristic, or framework, provides a structure within which students develop individual responses and see how they may be connected to both the text and their own knowledge and experiences.

Bleich's Heuristic simply asks students to think about their response to the text in two ways—affectively and associatively. Affective response is prompted by questions such as these: "How did you feel about this story?" and "What's your reaction/response to this reading?" Questions can also promote associative thinking, in which students consider connections among their responses, their own experiences, and the text: "How did you come up with this reaction?" "What did the author do to create your response?" "Why did you respond like that?" and "What's the most important word in this piece? Why do you think so?"

Students can respond to these questions by talking or writing; both writing and talking, as in Think-Pair-Share, also works well. Wayne, who has tried all these variations with his intermediate students, advises flexibility but cautions that sharing is essential.

I first learned about this as a writing activity, so that's the way I introduced it to the kids. It was OK, I guess, but I noticed that students were naturally talking with each other about what they had written. So then I tried just tossing the questions out as discussion starters. We all talked about our responses, even me. And that was OK, too, but it seemed like some of my more hesitant students got kind of bowled over by others who had firm ideas. So I have also asked kids to write their answers to the questions or at least jot some ideas down before the group convenes to share. That, too, is OK. I guess my advice to others would be to try it all three ways and evaluate students' responses. For me and my students, the sharing is really important. It's a powerful activity, though, so it's hard to go wrong.

Sketch to Stretch

Earlier in this chapter we mentioned that creating mental images can aid comprehension by giving students a vehicle for integrating their own information about a story or topic with the information provided by the author. Sketch to Stretch is an interesting elaboration of imaging.

Working in small groups, individual students draw a picture of a favorite or memorable event or scene from a story that they have read. Then students show their illustrations to the group. Rather than describing and explaining the picture, however, each student invites her classmates to provide their own interpretation of the drawing: "What is this a picture of?" and "What did the illustrator think was important about the story? Why?" After others give their interpretations, the illustrator is free to share her own thoughts on the drawing.

Sketch to Stretch encourages students to create images on paper and then use them as the basis for interpretive discussion of the story. Thus, all students participate in high-level thinking and discussion.

Compare-and-Contrast Charts

An important aspect of comprehension is the ability to make thoughtful comparisons across texts, between events within stories, and across other aspects of stories that students read. For many students making comparisons can be a daunting task, and neither textbooks nor teachers always explain the process sufficiently.

One vehicle for allowing students to make good comparisons involves what we call Compare-and-Contrast Charts (CCC). The foundation for this activity is rather generic. We've seen versions of it before in many other activities, including distinctive-features activities or feature-analysis charts (described in Chapter 8).

The CCC activity begins with the creation of a grid, either on a large sheet of chart paper to be displayed for the entire class or on individual sheets of paper. Along one axis of the chart are listed the items to be compared (for example, books by Tomie DePaola, Cinderella stories, biographies, or characters in William Steig stories). On the other axis students brainstorm key characteristics that distinguish at least one item from another (see Figure 7.3). Students then work in pairs or groups to fill out the remainder of the chart. Completed charts provide the information that allows students to compare and contrast the items listed. Students can use their charts in further discussion or as a way to organize their writing.

"These really do work," says Toni, an elementary reading specialist. "I use this with children from first through sixth grade. With the younger ones we make the charts simpler—fewer things to be compared and fewer characteristics against which to compare them. And in some cases students dictate their thoughts to me and I write them in the appropriate boxes. But over time I see really noticeable gains in my students' ability to analyze and compare two or more stories or other items."

Reader's Theater

Virtually any narrative can become a script. Reader's theater, which involves the rehearsed reading of a script for an audience, is an enjoyable and beneficial way for students to

Books	Country for Setting	Main Characters: How Are They Special?	Our Feelings
Fin M'Coul	Ireland	Fin—he's a giant	It's a funny story. Fin acts like a baby.
Strega Nona	Italy	Strega Nona— Grandma witch. She has magic powers	Funny. Big Anthony makes a mess with Strega Nona's magic
Now One Foot, Now the Other	U.S.?	Bob—his grandfather	Kind of happy. The boy has to help his grandpa.
Nana Upstairs and Nana Downstairs	U.S.?	Nanas—they are grand- mothers	It's sad. Nana Upstairs dies.

Figure 7.3
Compare-and-Contrast Chart: Tomie DePaola books.

respond to their reading. Unlike actors in conventional dramas, who portray action on stage, performers in reader's theater use only their voices and facial expressions to convey meaning. The action is left to the imaginations of the audience. Thus, reader's theater can be a powerful comprehension activity for the performers, who must comprehend to convey meaning to others, and the audience, who must comprehend to understand the script. In addition, because the actors rehearse their parts several times before performing them, and meaning is conveyed primarily through the quality of the expression embedded in the reading, reader's theater is an excellent fluency development activity.

Published scripts can be used for reader's theater, but we advise using student-authored scripts because this offers additional comprehension and discussion opportunities and script preparation is a wonderful collaborative writing activity. To prepare a script, children first need to select a story. Short books in which the text (not the illustrations) carry the plot and that feature lots of dialogue and have several characters make good choices. Poems also frequently work well. After choosing the text, students must read it several times and decide on the characters and the need for a narrator. The next step is to draft the script, which can be written by the whole group or individual children who take responsibility for parts. Some groups choose to stay close to the authors' words, but others embellish the plots or change them in other ways that please the participants. Groups typically reread the finished product one or more times before beginning to rehearse their individual parts.

No staging, costumes, or props are required for reader's theater. Performers usually sit or stand in a row facing the audience. No lines need to be memorized; instead, performers generally keep their scripts in their hands so that they can follow along and read their own parts at the right times. Many teachers appreciate the simplicity of this approach. Joel, a sixth-grade teacher, says:

> With reader's theater, doing a script doesn't have to be that big a deal. Before I learned about it, we used to do several plays each year. What a hassle! It seemed like all we did for weeks was work on the plays—painting scenery, arranging for costumes, all that stuff. And although the children seemed to enjoy it, I always worried a bit about whether we were using classroom time wisely. Now we do lots of reader's theater performances, which don't take that much preparation time, and only one or two plays each year. The kids benefit even more, I think, and I don't worry so about time taken away from reading.

Response Journals

Writing is another powerful tool for reacting to and extending one's thinking about reading. (It's so powerful that we devote Chapter 9 to it.) Many teachers encourage students to keep response journals so that they have a special place for capturing reactions and thoughts related to the books they have read. Journal entries can be either open or closed. An open entry is just that: Students can write whatever they want about what they have read. Closed entries are designed to focus students' thinking in particular ways. A teacher who wants to encourage summarization, for example, might ask students to write brief plot summaries. Similarly, a prompt such as "Write about your favorite part of the book so far. Tell us why you like that part so much" encourages evaluative response. Both open and closed entries support students' efforts to construct meaning as they read.

Kate's fourth graders are active journal writers. "Children's ideas provide us with an unending supply of topics for small-group or whole-class instruction," she says. Kate also uses response journals as a way to link reading and writing. "If we're working on great details or ways to 'show, not tell,' I frequently ask children to use their response journals to jot down snippets of language that grab them from the books they are reading. We collect all of these, put them on the board, and talk about what makes them so special so that we can use them in our own writing."

As you might guess from Kate's comments, response journal entries, as well as the other strategies surveyed in this book, can be used in several ways. That's what makes them so powerful. The teacher may read and respond to entries, or students may trade journals among themselves to read and respond to what a peer has written. Peer response works best, of course, if both students have read (or are reading) the same book. Sometimes teachers invite discussion by encouraging students to read journal entries aloud so that classmates can talk further about the issues or ideas raised. Closed journal entries can become the basis for mini-lessons on particular areas of focus. For example, students can share their summaries and then talk about what makes a good summary. A final option is for students to keep response journals for their own purposes, a record of their thinking during reading rather than a product to share with others.

Instruction to Promote Comprehension

Comprehension is like model building. Readers construct text interpretation or their own model of the text by relying upon many raw materials: the content and linguistic information provided by the author, their own knowledge and experiences, and their understanding of how written language works. All this happens in a social, environmental, and instructional context that is critical in determining both what and how students comprehend. The overall environment for instruction and the activities and techniques employed should reflect knowledge of these factors and influences. Moffett and Wagner (1992) synthesize them quite well:

> People read for diverse reasons and in diverse ways—casually to sift, studiedly to recall, raptly to become spellbound. The more schools open up the repertory of authentic discourse, the more apparent this becomes. Thus reader response is a factor of reader purpose and the kind of discourse. But response and purpose go back to choice. (p. 142)

We began this chapter by raising several key questions about how to encourage students to integrate text information with prior knowledge and interact thoughtfully with the text and each other. When students are involved in real reading situations in environments that promote thinking, taking risks, and sharing, these questions answer themselves.

Chapter 8

Comprehension Development with Expository Text

Our goal for all students is to enhance their growth as independent, purposeful readers and learners. In Chapter 7 we presented ideas for fostering students' comprehension of narrative or storylike materials. In this chapter we raise questions, offer information, and describe strategies that will help students make sense of expository or textbook material.

Like those best suited for narrative material, instructional strategies for ensuring students' comprehension of expository text must incorporate understandings about readers' interactions with text and students' interactions with the teacher and each other. Toward that end, we offer several guidelines for developing effective instruction:

• Learning will be enhanced if readers' schemata (background knowledge about a topic) are activated and engaged before reading. That is, students need opportunities to become aware of what they already know about text content and to think about it before they begin reading. They also need opportunities to consider what they don't know but would like to know about a topic.

• As with narrative material, predictions about text content must be encouraged. Good readers think backward and forward when reading; that is, they draw conclusions about what they have read and make predictions about what they're likely to encounter based on prior knowledge as well as information in the text. Like scientists, proficient readers constantly entertain hypotheses about the content communicated in the text.

• The instructional environment should help students learn to comprehend actively and purposefully and evaluate their own efforts as readers and learners. Teachers can support students' growth by providing frameworks for sharing, discussion, and exploration and modeling literate, inquiring, and learned behavior themselves.

• Activities that foster cooperative involvement and joint problem solving enhance learning. The instructional environment must foster taking risks and sharing ideas, and students must know that their thinking is valued.

Instruction based on these criteria can help readers grow in their ability to comprehend and learn from expository text. The strategies described in this chapter are effective with readers of all age and ability levels. Although most of the strategies can be used with individuals, they work best when small groups of students can share their ideas with one another.

Prereading Activities

Too often, students are simply told to read or are given an artificial reason for reading, such as "read to see how tornadoes are formed." We believe that this sort of guidance neither prepares students effectively for reading nor motivates them to read. Effective prereading activities should invite students to do the following:

- Consider what they already know about what they'll be reading and share these ideas with others.
- Anticipate and make predictions about what they're likely to encounter as they read.
- Develop their own purposes for reading.
- Build curiosity and motivation for reading.

Word sorts, brainstorming activities, anticipation guides, and K-W-L are prereading activities that meet these criteria.

Word Sorts

Open word sorts as described in Chapters 4 and 6 can be an effective prereading activity to prime students for comprehending a text (Gillet & Kita, 1979). The teacher selects about 20 words or phrases from the text selection that students will read. For example, Becky, an intermediate-grade Title I teacher, selected the following words from an article about spiders:

liquid silk	tiny claws	egg sac
four pairs of legs	poison fangs	mandibles
spinnerets	water	trap door
wolf	balloon	tarantula
orb weaver		

After preparing sets of word cards, Becky distributed them to pairs of students and directed the children to "put these into groups that make sense to you. Be ready to explain your reasons." Students examined the words, looking for relationships between and among them. To establish and agree upon categories, students discussed the chosen concepts, shared knowledge with each other, and engaged in hypothesis testing.

When the small groups completed sorting the words into their categories, Becky invited groups to share both the categories and their reasoning. Here's how one group of fourth graders sorted the words:

Things Spiders Have	Where Spiders Live
liquid silk	trap door
tiny claws	water
four pairs of legs	egg sac
poison fangs	

Kinds of Spiders	We Don't Know
tarantula	mandibles
wolf	spinnerets
	balloon
	orb weaver

These students obviously know some things about spiders, but they also recognize what they can learn from the article. Whole-group sharing encouraged further exploration of key concepts and gave Becky information about students' prior knowledge.

After students shared their categories, Becky asked them what they expected to be reading about and why. This summarized the word sort portion of the lesson and encouraged students to make and share predictions. Then the students read, armed with relevant knowledge they had organized and shared in their groups.

Word sort activities give students opportunities to activate and share their prior knowledge about concepts and predict text content. They enhance curiosity and provide natural, meaningful purposes for reading: Students are eager to see if their ideas are accurate.

Brainstorming

Brainstorming activities are identical to word sorts except that students generate the words and phrases rather than have them selected by the teacher. The brainstorming we describe here is similar to the List-Group-Label vocabulary activity presented in Chapter 6. Students can brainstorm in small groups, with each group selecting a recorder, or the teacher can serve as the recorder for the entire group. In either case, the teacher provides a key word or phrase and then asks students for all the words that come to mind when they think about the key word. Students should generate words quickly rather than stop for analysis or evaluation. Another group of Becky's students produced this list of words in response to the key word *spider:* black widow, web, flies, bees, insects, ants, silk, haunted house, gross, neat, plants, basement, desert, round, furry, tarantula, jumping spider, eight legs.

After two or three minutes of brainstorming, the teacher can ask small groups to categorize the words and provide titles for the categories, as they do in an open word sort. Students can use chart paper and markers or an overhead transparency to record their categories so that others can easily see their decisions during the discussion and sharing that follows. Figure 8.1 shows a web that one group of children made with the words they'd brainstormed. After discussion and sharing, students read.

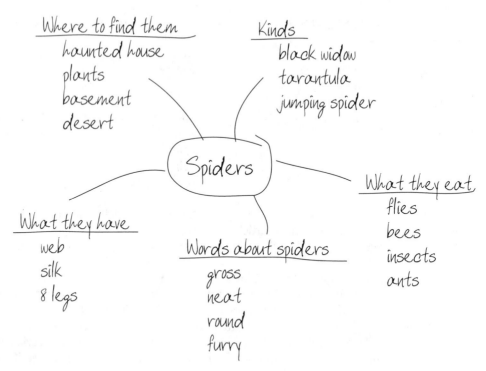

Figure 8.1
"Spiders" web.

Like word sorts, brainstorming is a cooperative activity where students learn from and with each other. Such cooperation fosters successful, purposeful reading among all students, but may be particularly helpful for those who find reading difficult.

Anticipation Guides

A third prereading activity that activates prior knowledge and promotes purposeful reading is the anticipation guide (Herber, 1976; Vacca & Vacca, 1993). It includes sheets that contain written statements for students to think about and discuss before (and often after) they read. The statements are intended to activate prior knowledge and arouse curiosity about issues addressed in the text. A sample anticipation guide, developed for a science article about spiders, appears in Figure 8.2. Note that the directions ask students to indicate those statements with which they agree and be ready to explain their thinking. This process of justifying or explaining their thinking allows students to sharpen and organize what they know about a topic and become aware of what they don't know.

After individuals make decisions about the statements, the teacher leads a discussion so that students can share their ideas and knowledge with each other. The anticipation guide shown in Figure 8.2 directs students to return to the statements after reading the article, again indicating the statements they agree with but now supporting their ideas by referring to pages from the text.

Don provides resource assistance for intermediate-grade students with learning disabilities. He relies frequently on anticipation guides because, he says, "the kids really enjoy them, and I think they help kids' learning. It reassures them to know that they already know something about what they will be reading. Talking about specific issues seems to help them develop a purpose for reading, too." Although Don varies the way he uses anticipation guides, he typically asks pairs of students to complete the guides together. Then, before the group reads the text selection, he asks students to indicate whether they agreed or disagreed with each statement and give reasons for their decisions. Sometimes this discussion proceeds quickly because students arrive at the same decisions for the same reasons. At other

---

Directions: Read each statement about spiders. In the "Before" column, check the ones you agree with. Be ready to explain your thinking.

Before		*After*	*Page(s)*
_____	1. Spiders are insects.	_____	_____
_____	2. Spiders can move in any direction.	_____	_____
_____	3. Spiders have eight eyes and eight legs.	_____	_____
_____	4. Spiders are helpful.	_____	_____
_____	5. Some spiders can float through the air.	_____	_____
_____	6. Spiders use the same webs over and over.	_____	_____
_____	7. The silk in spider webs is stronger than iron.	_____	_____
_____	8. The silk in spider webs has been used in microscopes and telescopes.	_____	_____
_____	9. Spiders won't bite unless they are disturbed.	_____	_____

Directions: Now that you've read about spiders, read the statements again. This time check the statements you agree with in the "After" column. Then in the "Pages" column, write down the page or pages in the book that helped you decide. Again, be ready to explain your thinking.

Figure 8.2
"Spiders" anticipation guide.

times, more lengthy discussions ensue because students' opinions differ or they raise complex issues. After reading, Don generally directs discussion to focus on those areas where students have changed their minds or have additional information to share based on their reading. He says that this postreading discussion allows students to share what they have learned and raise issues for further exploration.

K-W-L

Students complete two portions of the K-W-L chart before reading (Ogle, 1986). This activity gets its name from the label at the top of each column of the chart: what we *know* about the topic, what we *want* to know from reading about the topic, and what we *learned* from reading. Pairs or small groups of students can work independently to complete the K-W-L activity; or the group can work together as a whole, with the teacher serving as recorder.

As with a brainstorming activity, the teacher begins a K-W-L discussion by providing a topic, key word, or phrase related to what students are about to read. They share what they already know about the topic and pose questions that they want to have answered or issues they hope to learn more about. Notes are made in the *K* and *W* columns of the chart. After students have read the text, they complete the third column by recording what they have learned. This may include answers to questions, information related to issues, or other information that students find important or interesting. Students can use information from their K-W-L charts for writing, such as writing a summary, or to guide additional inquiry.

Betsy frequently uses K-W-L charts with her Title I students. She says that the children enjoy sharing their knowledge before they read and these discussions often offer her some effective incidental teaching opportunities: "Sometimes the ideas really come pouring out! After everyone has shared, we need to decide how to record children's ideas on the chart. So I say, 'OK, how should I write this down?' and the students have to think back through the discussion and summarize and synthesize it so that we can decide what to record." Betsy also notes that sometimes children's questions about the topic (from the *W* column) aren't answered by the text selection. "This is good in a way," she says. "If the kids are really curious, we find other resource books—a great reason for a trip to the library!"

Building Background Knowledge

Word sorts, brainstorming, anticipation guides, and K-W-L charts are all effective ways to invite students to think about general topics related to their reading and to recall and organize what they already know about those topics. In other words, these activities help students activate their background knowledge. As a result of the social context in which these activities take place (students talking to and sharing with each other), they may also build some background knowledge. That is, they may make some new discoveries and learn more about the topic by conversing with their classmates. In many cases, such prereading activities provide plenty of support for subsequent reading.

Sometimes, however, students may need additional support. In cases where content is very new, very important, abstract in nature, or loaded with unfamiliar terms, the teacher may wish to help students *build* background knowledge—that is, learn some new things about the topic before they read rather than simply help them *activate* what they already know.

Activities to build background knowledge can involve reading or listening to additional texts. For example, trade books, newspaper articles, and magazine articles are often effective supplements to textbook selections. Two characteristics of these types of texts make them especially effective for helping students build background knowledge: They tend to offer more elaboration or detail than textbook selections and are often storylike. These features can heighten interest and make information easy to remember, thus allowing students to learn new information that can, in turn, support their textbook reading.

Nonreading activities are equally effective ways to build background knowledge. Jackdaws, as described in Chapter 7, can provide vehicles for exploring background and learning. As students examine and talk about the items included in the jackdaws, teachers have natural opportunities to share relevant information. Experiments and demonstrations also work well, as do media or audiovisual presentations.

Activities to build background knowledge take time—a precious commodity in most classrooms. Although we have no magic rule for deciding whether it's worthwhile to spend the time, attention to three questions may help in instructional planning:

How important is this information?
How abstract is the text that students will read?
How much support will they need in order to learn what they need to learn?

When information is important or abstract or students need extra support to read successfully, it probably makes sense to include some background-building activities.

All these prereading activities share common elements that make them successful. Each provides a framework and reason for students to consider what they already know (and what they don't know) about text content. Each also promotes sharing so that students learn from and with each other. Finally, each activity encourages students to hypothesize about the reading selection based on what they know, what others have said, and (in the case of open word sorts and anticipation guides) the information provided by the teacher. These factors combine to create readers who are really ready to read actively, purposefully, and enthusiastically.

Activities to Support Students during Reading

Text discussions during and after reading have long been recognized as effective means of enhancing students' comprehension and learning. We certainly agree, but offer a caution: Discussions must be planned and implemented with careful consideration of what comprehension is and how discussions can enhance students' individual and collective efforts at comprehending and learning. For example, if teachers ask predominantly low-level, literal questions during discussions, students may attempt to collect individual and unrelated facts as they read rather than think about ideas.

Good questions are certainly a key to effective discussions about text. What makes a question good? First, good discussion questions are *authentic*—that is, they are asked because the asker doesn't know and wants to know the answer. "What do you think about . . . ?" is usually an authentic question because the teacher doesn't know the student's thoughts. In contrast, literal questions are usually not authentic because the teacher already knows the answers and is simply testing to see if the student does too. This is not to say that literal information is unimportant in text discussions, for it certainly is. Rather, the issues are how and why students use literal information. Providing literal or factual support for one's ideas enhances text discussions, as does sharing appropriate prior knowledge. Questions that encourage this type of thinking will yield more effective discussions than those intended to test what students remember.

Authentic questions often provoke thought and motivate higher-level reasoning. These, too, are qualities of good discussions. Students should be encouraged to focus on relevant, important information; to synthesize; and to integrate text information with what they already know. In short, good discussions should foster thoughtful consideration of text and promote group and individual efforts at understanding.

Discussions differ from conversations because they are planned, but in many respects a good discussion should be like a conversation: a social exchange of ideas, information, and opinions. A good environment for discussions should invite (but not demand) verbal participation; in other words, students should feel free to speak or not, as they choose. Furthermore, students should be encouraged to talk with each other rather than filter everything through the teacher. The result of effective text discussions is more than a collection of students' individual meanings and verbal reports; new meaning is constructed as students listen to and talk with each other and make connections between ideas that weren't previously considered.

Effective discussions provide a framework for thinking and sharing about text. The Directed Reading-Thinking Activity, the double-entry or dialectic journal, and Save the Last Word for Me are all strategies that can provide just this sort of framework.

Directed Reading-Thinking Activity

The Directed Reading-Thinking Activity (DR-TA), described in Chapter 7, also works effectively with expository text selections (Stauffer, 1980). As with narrative DR-TAs, discussions evolve through cycles in which students generate hypotheses and subsequently validate, reject, or modify them. Preparation for an expository DR-TA involves selecting something for students to read and deciding where they will stop for discussion. Subheads in articles or textbooks provide natural stopping points.

Here is an excerpt from an expository DR-TA. Jane is supporting a group of eighth-grade students who are reading a chapter in their history books that describes social reforms of the nineteenth century.

Jane:	*What do you think this passage is going to be about from just looking at the heading?*
Katy:	What's a reformer?
Karen:	Yeah.
Jane:	*Who can tell us?*
Matt:	A person who likes to reshape or something.
Jane:	*What would a person be doing if he were trying to reshape?*
Matt:	Change it.
Katy:	Make it better.
Mike:	Try to make it better for people.
Jane:	*Can you give us an example of what you think they wanted to change back at that point?*
Matt:	Slavery.
Mike:	Government.
Jane:	*All right. What else?*
Tony:	Laws.
Jane:	*Read the first two paragraphs only.*

[Students read.]

Jane:	*Were you right about anything?*
Tony:	Yeah.
Matt:	Slavery.
Jane:	*Anything else?*
Karen:	Trying to help people defend themselves and that.
Katy:	What reformers meant.
Jane:	*What do you think it means now?*
Katy:	The same thing. Helping people. . . .
Karen:	A person who makes change.
Matt:	Try to do something better.
Mike:	Try to improve something.

As you can see from the excerpt, the questioning cycle for expository DR-TAs is similar to the cycle for narrative. Jane encouraged prediction, reflection, integrating text and prior knowledge, and so forth. Good prediction questions for an expository DR-TA include "What do you think this will be about?" "What issues will the author address?" "What will we read about next?" and "Where is the author going with this?"

After students have read a portion of the text, the teacher can ask these types of questions: "Were your predictions on target?" "Did anything surprise you?" "Have you changed your mind about anything based on what you've read?" or "Now what do you think?" Either before or after reading, questions and comments can invite elaboration or clarification: "Why?" "What makes you say that?" "Tell us some more about that," and "Anything else?"

The teacher's talk is not intended to manipulate student thinking or test students' recall; rather, the purpose is to activate student thought, encourage the use of prior knowledge, and facilitate group interaction. This sort of teacher involvement signals to students that their ideas are valued, that they should justify their opinions so that others can understand their reasoning, that they should listen to and talk with each other, and that the responsibility for learning is theirs.

Dialectic or Double-entry Journal

Dorothy Watson calls this activity dialectic journal, and Ann Berthoff calls it double-entry journal. Both conceive of it in basically the same way: a during-reading strategy for students to identify important information from expository text, share these ideas with others, and develop their own opinions about what they have read. The strategy involves several stages:

• **Stage 1:**   As students read a portion of an article, chapter, or other piece of expository text, they make notes about what they think is important. Notes can be made on separate paper or in a journal, as the title for the strategy suggests; or students can use pencils to underline important information in the text itself.

• **Stage 2:**   Small groups (three to five students) share what they have identified as important. As students listen to others' ideas, they may revise their own notes, add or erase underlines, and so on. Stages 1 and 2 continue as students complete the text.

• **Stage 3:**   Having decided on important information from the text, students now make notes about their own opinions about what they have read. They consider issues such as what they agree or disagree with, how the information might be useful, how new information fits in with what they already knew, and so forth.

• **Stage 4:**   Students share their individual opinions with others in their small groups. Groups discuss individual opinions, synthesize discussion, and may prepare written or oral summaries or lists to share with the entire class.

Because expository text often contains a great deal of new information, it can be particularly challenging for students to decide what's important enough to remember. The dialectic or double-entry journal strategy offers students support as they learn to make these decisions.

Save the Last Word for Me

This activity, developed by Carolyn Burke, is also designed to provide support for students as they read challenging material. As with the dialectic or double-entry journal, students first read a portion of a text and write individually. Then they discuss the reading in small groups.

Here's how it works. Students make notes about whatever they wish as they read each portion of a text. They might note important information, copy a critical sentence, record things they don't understand, or jot down unfamiliar vocabulary; each student decides what to write. Discussion begins after all members of the small group have completed reading the portion of the text. One by one, students introduce an idea from their notes for group discussion. Others in the group may respond to the idea, answer the question, or provide their own definitions for vocabulary words. Conversations take many directions. After all others have offered their thoughts, the student who introduced the topic has the "last word": she may offer an opinion or summarize the discussion. Then the next student in the group offers another topic, and the discussion begins again. After each group member has started a discussion, students then read and make notes about the next portion of the text.

Ted teaches middle school students who find reading difficult. He relies on all three of these during-reading strategies because "the kids need the support that the strategies can provide." Ted uses several criteria to decide which activity to use. "Probably the most important factor in my planning is the difficulty of the text," he says. "I think the DR-TA is the most supportive strategy, so that's the one we use if I think the reading might be tough for the kids. I also think about variety, though. It's more fun for all of us if we vary the routine. And after we've done these things a few times, I sometimes ask students which strategy they want to use. I really don't worry about students' choices because I know all three help them understand what they read."

Ted finds that his students "read for their own purposes or for purposes that arise as part of the discussions. Either way, they care about what they read, and that's half the battle, as far as I'm concerned. Besides that, the discussions themselves foster learning." Students must think carefully while they read and listen carefully during discussions. As a result, according to Ted, "they learn content information. But they also learn that reading is an active, problem-solving process." Text discussions during reading can enhance comprehension and learning if the instructional environment fosters group inquiry, risk taking, and problem solving.

Postreading Activities

Good postreading activities should give students continued opportunities for dynamic interaction with the text and among themselves. Sometimes prereading activities can be revisited after students have read. For example, open word sorts are effective for refining and extending concepts after reading. Students can reorganize the words and phrases based on their reading and then discuss the changes that they made. Brainstorming can also be effective after students have read, this time as a means of integrating new information with prior knowledge. And students can record what they learned as a result of reading and discussion in the L (What We Learned) column of their K-W-L charts. Several other postreading activities that foster continued interaction with text are described in this section.

Distinctive-features Activity

Often, one goal for expository reading is to help students think about similarities and differences between and among related concepts. In such instances, distinctive-features

FEATURES	SPIDERS			
	Tarantulas	Trap-door Spiders	Wolf Spiders	Water Spiders
Size				
General areas where found				
Habitat				
Prey				
How prey is captured				

Figure 8.3
"Spiders" distinctive-features chart.

activities can be effective postreading lessons. Figure 8.3 shows a distinctive-features chart that Becky and her students developed for their science lesson about spiders.

After students read, Becky asked, "What kinds of spiders did we read about?" The children's answers were recorded on the chalkboard and ultimately became one dimension of the chart. Then Becky asked for the features of spiders described in the text: "What were some things that we learned about all of these spiders?" This information became the other dimension of the chart. Students returned to the text to verify their recollections and make any necessary changes before the final version of the chart was constructed.

Students then worked in pairs to complete the chart. They talked with their partners, reread if necessary, and decided what to write in each cell of the chart. After pairs had completed their charts, Becky reconvened the whole group and asked some questions to focus on similarities and differences: "How are all these spiders alike?" and "How are trap-door spiders and wolf spiders alike? How are they different?" Later, the charts were put on display for all to see and examine.

Distinctive-features activities provide frameworks for organizing and categorizing concept information as well as synthesizing and making notes about what students have read. In addition, the completed charts are useful for later review and study.

Herringbone

The herringbone activity also uses a chart to help students summarize and synthesize what they have read (see Figure 8.4). Students read and then work with partners to complete the chart. Together they must decide on answers to each of the detail questions on the chart. This frequently involves rereading but always involves discussion as students identify a variety of potential answers to each question and settle on the most important. Finally, they combine these details to develop a main-idea summary statement for the entire passage.

Like several of the other activities described in this chapter, the herringbone chart provides a supportive framework for students to sort through the information provided in expository text and make their own decisions about what is important. Completing these charts also helps students think about the main idea, significant details, and the relationships among them.

Guided Reading Procedure

An adaptation of Manzo's (1975) Guided Reading Procedure (GRP) is yet another effective postreading activity, particularly when promoting recall or helping students decide on and organize important information from the text are instructional goals. The strategy involves reading, brainstorming, and making decisions about key information.

After students have read a text selection, the teacher asks them to recall everything they can remember from the text. Recalled ideas are shared in brainstorming fashion, and the teacher records all this information on the chalkboard. Next, the teacher provides a purpose for further work with the ideas. For example, students might be told that they will write a summary paragraph or prepare an outline of the text using only information on the chalkboard.

With this purpose in mind, students return to the text selection, this time thinking about what needs to be added, corrected, or deleted from the information that they recalled. After a few minutes, the teacher reconvenes the discussion, asking for changes

Figure 8.4
Herringbone chart.

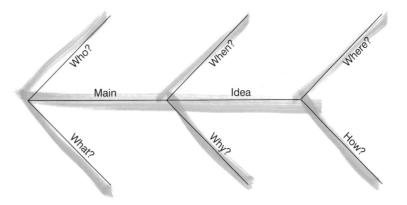

to the information on the chalkboard and reasons for such changes. For example, the teacher might say, "OK. You think we should erase _____ from our list. Why? What do the rest of you think? Should we erase _____ from our list? Why?"

This discussion is usually quite lively. To convince others of their ideas, students must rely on information from the text and their own reasoning ability. The purpose for the final list often enters into the discussion, too. For example, a student might say, "Yes, well I think that *is* important, but we're supposed to be writing a summary. I think that's too detailed to go into a summary paragraph." Majority opinion should be the criterion for making changes. Finally, students write the summary paragraph or prepare the outline using the revised information from the selection.

Note that the teacher never makes recommendations about the information on the chalkboard. Doing so would undermine one of the major benefits of the activity: helping students learn to make decisions for themselves about what is important in their reading.

A similar procedure can be useful for helping students prepare written summaries of nonreading experiences in the classroom, such as conducting a science experiment, viewing a movie, or listening to a guest speaker. The outlines that students prepare in this manner can be valuable additions to the content area study, particularly for readers who have difficulty reading their textbooks successfully.

Maria occasionally uses this adaptation of the Guided Reading Procedure in her work with intermediate-grade students. "It seems like the older they get, the more important summarizing and synthesizing becomes," she comments.

> Years ago, I tried to help by giving kids outlines. Then I tried to teach them to outline. Nothing worked. This GRP takes some time, but it really helps my students learn how to find what's important in their reading. They soon learn that what's "important" depends on why they're reading and what they need to do with the information. What's important for preparing an outline, for example, may not be the same as what's important for writing a short summary.

Maria also notes that this adaptation of the Guided Reading Procedure results in students' learning the content of the text selection. "I bet that's because they read and reread. I like that aspect of the activity, too." Both the recall and decision-making portions of the activity provide opportunities for students to develop and extend their thinking about the information in the text.

Response Activities

Response activities (see Chapter 7) are effective ways for students to summarize, synthesize, and react to expository text or content-area learning. For example, many of the writing activities described in Chapter 9 provide students with opportunities to extend their thinking about text concepts. These can be as brief and informal as writing in a learning log or as extended and formal as preparing a class newspaper or magazine.

Artistic representations such as murals, pictures, sculpture, or dioramas may be appropriate response activities in some instances. Skits or role-playing activities can also

Artistic representation may be appropriate response activities in some cases.

be useful. Lorri, who uses integrated thematic units in her classes, frequently encourages this sort of response as a culminating activity. "It's always an option," she says. "Some students are naturally drawn to these more creative ways of responding, and others have the opportunity to look at things somewhat differently. Trying to role-play characters or situations from history, for example, really gives you a different slant on what you've learned."

Lorri and her students occasionally enjoy a day of celebration after they have spent some time exploring a theme or issue. "We take part of a day to sort of sit back and reflect on what we've learned. We invite parents and grandparents to join us. The kids present their skits, explain their newspapers, or whatever. The children enjoy these days, and they're a great way to involve the folks from home in what we do in school. There's value to the sort of summary-thinking that leads students to their culminating projects, too, I think. And it sure makes a natural transition for us in our curriculum."

Principles for Effective Comprehension Instruction

Did aspects of these strategies seem similar? We hope so. They share assumptions about what students should do and what teachers should do in order for comprehension instruction with expository text to be effective. Students should read, think, solve problems, make decisions, and interact with the text and each other. Teachers should facilitate the process of comprehension attainment rather than direct it or test whether or not students can remember what they've read.

The instructional framework reflected by each of the activities has been termed the Teacher-Student Generated Lesson (Davidson, 1986). This curricular framework takes "into account the social nature of reading and its relationship to comprehension, thinking, and learning" (p. 89). Teacher-Student Generated Lessons are based on four premises:

- Learning is a social process.
- Students need maximum opportunities to use the language associated with the content area.
- Learners need to be actively involved.
- Students and the teacher construct meaning through interaction with each other and the text.

Lessons based on these principles will benefit all students, of course, but they are especially helpful for students experiencing difficulty with reading. Students who find reading difficult need support; they also need to maintain control over the thinking and learning processes. Teacher-student generated lessons provide both.

Comprehension is the goal of reading. Before reading, readers need to activate their prior knowledge, make predictions, and formulate purposes for reading. Discussions during reading should provoke thoughtful consideration of ideas in the text and promote individual and group efforts at understanding and learning. Finally, postreading instruction should encourage continued interaction with text content and among students. The teacher's role in all these activities is to promote sharing, encourage critical thought, and moderate discussions. The students' roles, on the other hand, require reading, thinking, solving problems, making decisions, interacting with the text and each other, and learning.

Chapter 9

Writing Development

J ason and Amy were playing house. Amy, the mom, was getting ready for work and leaving instructions for Jason, the dad, who was going to watch the baby. She scribbled on a tablet, then tore up the page and began again. When asked what she was doing, she replied, "I have to put more down. I forgot that Jason doesn't know how to make eggs." Both Amy and Jason were three years old.

What does Amy know about written language? Quite a bit, actually. She knows that writing serves a purpose, in this case to communicate information about caring for the baby. She also knows that we write for an audience, that writing is meant to be read. She revised her note because "Jason doesn't know how to make eggs." Like many other children, three-year-old Amy has learned a great deal about written language. Yet she has had no instruction, and she is neither a reader nor a writer in the conventional sense. As with other aspects of language learning, some children learn about concepts of print earlier or more easily than others. Youngsters who have not yet developed notions about the form of written language need opportunities to do so. Until they do, reading and writing instruction will be frustrating and confusing for them. In short, they will find reading and writing difficult.

We have written this book to help teachers help these children. In other chapters, we describe instructional strategies for reading that focus children's attention on important aspects of written language. Although such reading instruction is helpful, it is not enough. Frequent opportunities to write are also essential to support the development of understandings about written language.

Writers learn about both writing and reading. Young writers learn about the conventions of print. Writers of all ages learn how to think like authors, which helps them as they read what other authors have written. Moreover, writers learn the importance of using just the right word or sentence to communicate their intended meaning. This way of thinking about words and sentences also applies to reading. Thus, a strong focus on writing is an important component in programs for students who find reading difficult.

We will not offer a comprehensive discussion of writing programs in this chapter; that's enough material for another book. But we do have some thoughts about why and how writing can inform reading as well as some suggestions about supporting writers and classroom activities that seem to enhance the reading-writing connection. First, however, we look at what children learn about written language, why readers should write, and how teachers can discover what writers know about the way that written language works.

Learning about Written Language

As young children learn to read and write, they begin to think about written language as a system and hypothesize about how it works. They learn about the way to use books, for example, and they learn that lines of print run from left to right and lines on a page run from top to bottom.

Children also develop concepts about units of written language. One critical understanding is that print carries meaning. An eager toddler may grab for a book that is being read to him, cover up the print, and look puzzled when the reader has to stop. Within a year or two, the same child may ask, "What does it say on this page?" or "Where does it say that?" Such comments demonstrate that the child has discovered that reading involves print. Related to this is the understanding that the print stays the same from one reading to the next.

In addition, children learn about the conventions of print—about the way in which written language represents meaning. Developing a concept of *word* as a unit of written language is particularly important, and this is no small task. First, the child must be able to think about language as a system, to separate the form of language from its function. Then she must be able to impose psychological segmentation on a steady stream of oral speech. In other words, the child must learn to separate, think about, and become aware of individual words within spoken language. Finally, the child must use her knowledge of oral speech to discover that words are also units of written language. In addition to the basic concept of written word, the child must learn about the convention of unmarked space before and after words and that the beginning of the word is on the left and the end is on the right. Further, the child must develop similar understandings of concepts such as *sentence, line,* and other features related to written language.

As children write (not copy), they reinforce their own understandings about how letters and letter combinations represent sounds in language. Thus, writing supports students' phonics and word recognition development. Learning about written language doesn't stop as students get older. They may explore the common characteristics of a particular form of writing, such as mysteries or newspaper articles, or become interested in different types of poems, perhaps haiku or sonnets. Students of all ages may become fascinated by the way in which authors use language to communicate with others. In fact, people who are readers and writers continue learning about written language throughout their lives.

Learning about written language, like other aspects of language learning, is accomplished gradually and informally through many opportunities to hear, think about, and talk about written language. All children, especially those who find reading and writing difficult, need time and exposure to writing to develop these understandings. The learning process for developing concepts about written language is the same as for any other language learning: hypothesis generation and testing. For example, simply telling a child that words have spaces around them cannot guarantee understanding of the concept. In essence, children must invent their own concepts and then test them as they interact with print and other readers and writers.

Certainly, children can learn a great deal about the conventions of written language through reading instruction. Accordingly, most teachers focus some instruction for beginning readers on the physical aspects of print. Much of this instruction is informal. When children watch something being read, such as a language-experience text or a big book, they gain knowledge about the conventions of print. Likewise, saying words while writing them during dictation is helpful. Some teachers even provide running commentary about the conventions of print as they take dictation. For instance, while they write, they may say, "OK, that's the end of the sentence, so I'll put a period here. This new sentence will need a capital letter." Over time, such informal and incidental learning pays dividends in terms of children's understandings.

As children become readers, they must learn how written language works. To mature as readers, they need opportunities to explore the complexities of written language. Much of this learning can be accomplished through the sort of reading instruction described elsewhere in this book. But a strong writing component can and should complement reading instruction.

Why Should Readers Write?

What do children learn through writing that applies to their reading? They learn a great deal. Children who write frequently learn how writing works and come to understand what authors do and why. "Children confirm that written text makes sense because, in producing their own writing, they have had to make their ideas into sense for others" (Department of Education, 1985, p. 79). Through their own writing, children learn about the writing cycle (what writers do) and the writing process (the thinking that may occur at all stages of the cycle). These understandings help children "see" the author behind what they read and perhaps understand his purposes and processes. In one study Silvers (1986) noticed that a group of third graders read more and differently as they grew to believe in themselves as writers. The amount of free reading increased, and children's comments about books were more frequent and more critical. In other words, they read as authors to see how other authors had written. Graves and Stuart (1985) say it well: "Just as children who grew up on a farm know where milk comes from, children who write know where writing comes from" (p. 119).

Opportunities to write also foster understanding about writing itself. Yetta Goodman (1985a) suggests that children must solve three sets of problems about how writing works. *Functional* principles develop as children solve the problem of how writing is used and the purposes and significance that it serves for themselves and others. *Relational* principles develop as children solve the problem of what written language comes to mean—of how written words, oral words, and the concepts that they represent are related. *Linguistic* principles develop as children determine how written language is organized in order for writers to share meanings with readers.

As children write, they learn about these physical and mechanical aspects of written language; this, too, applies to their reading. Writing can help children crystallize their concepts of *word* and *sentence*. In addition, inventing spelling provides valuable practice with the sound-to-letter system. Moreover, young writers learn that the beginning-to-ending sequences of sounds in words relate, although not exactly, to the left-to-right sequences of letters in words. Writers must attend to other aspects of directionality as well, such as words in a line and lines on a page. Children must solve all these problems to develop as literate persons, and all are solved most easily and naturally when they read and write often and purposefully.

A final answer to the question "why should readers write?" is more practical: Lots of writing yields lots of material to be read. Like all authors, young authors read and reread drafts in progress. They also read their finished products, both for their own pleasure and to share with others. And, of course, children like to read what their classmates have written. An active writing program, then, complements a reading program by providing a wealth of reading material in addition to helping children develop concepts about authorship and writing that form a foundation for reading development.

Discovering What Children Know about Writing

Planning a writing program is easier and the resultant program more effective if we know a bit about children's current understandings about the way in which writing works. In this

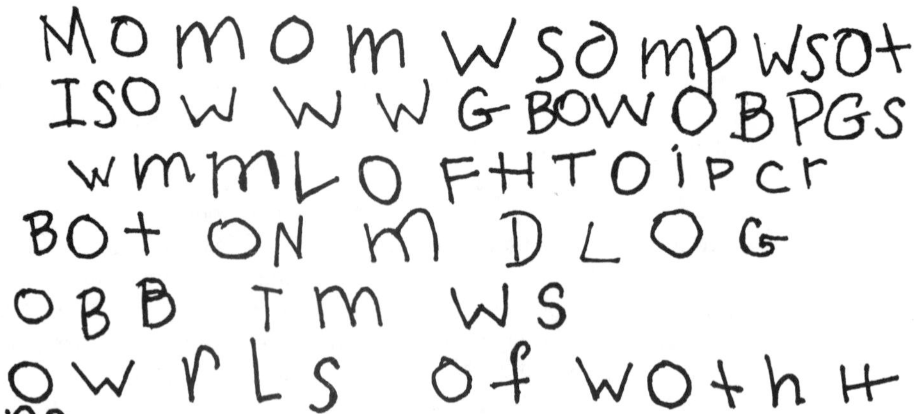

Me and my mom were sitting on the couch talking about birthday presents because my brother is going to have a birthday in two more weeks.

Figure 9.1
Entry from Mary's September journal.

my mom sad Totobr
I am gom get my
o n r m at Totobr

My mom said October. I am gonna get my own room at October.

Figure 9.2
Entry from Mary's January journal.

section we describe two ways to gain these insights about children as writers. We can learn about children's concepts of print and current hypotheses about the writing system by examining their unaided writing. Talking with children about their writing is also important, especially if we wish to explore their ideas about the functions of writing. Finally, we can explore children's graphophonic knowledge (what they know about sound-symbol relationships) by examining their invented spellings. Look at Figures 9.1, 9.2, and 9.3, for example. They are pages from Mary's first-grade journal. Mary had a difficult time with reading during much of that year. As you analyze her journal entries, try to determine how her concepts of print are revealed in her writing, what she knows about the sound-symbol system, and how these understandings changed during the year.

Figure 9.1 accompanied a picture of two people sitting on a couch. Mary wrote to explain and elaborate upon the picture she had drawn, showing that she knows the difference between drawing and writing. She also knows that writing can communicate meaning and how lines of print are arranged on the page. Mary's teacher watched as she wrote and noticed that she wrote in left-to-right and top-to-bottom fashion. All these aspects of Mary's concepts about print are evident in her writing.

Mary's writing also reveals concepts that are still developing. Although she knows how to make letters, she doesn't yet know how to make them work for her. In fact, had the teacher not recorded what Mary said when she read her writing, we wouldn't be able to understand her message. Further, she doesn't yet use word boundaries in her writing, which suggests that her concept of word is still developing.

Mary's January journal entry (Figure 9.2) demonstrates growth in her understanding of print concepts. Her writing can be read fairly easily, and she has begun to leave spaces between words. By May (Figure 9.3), this concept of word is even stronger; space boundaries around words are clearly evident. Thus, we can see that Mary has developed important concepts about print during her first-grade year. What she knows is visible in her writing.

Children's unaided writing also reveals their graphophonic knowledge. Examining Mary's journal entries from this perspective reveals her growing understanding of sound-symbol relationships. Many of the words she spells are invented, but these inventions are not ran-

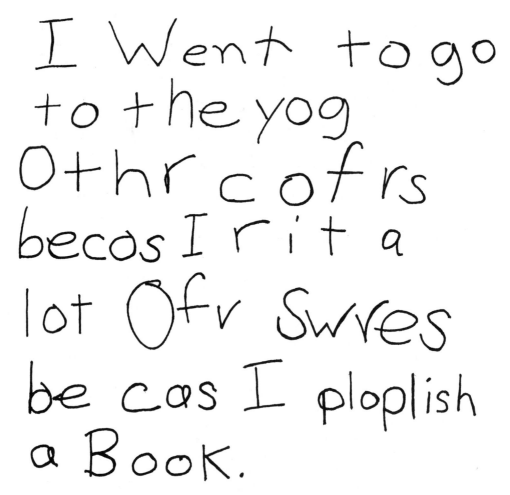

Figure 9.3
Entry from Mary's May journal.

dom. They are governed by her current hypotheses about how oral language and written language are related, which influences her ability to use phonics as an aid to identifying words.

Scholars have been exploring the characteristics of young children's spelling since the early 1970s, when Charles Read's (1971) landmark work established the predictability of young children's spelling errors and the developmental progression of growth in spelling. In brief, this research has helped us understand how spelling develops: from random, incomprehensible strings of letters (and sometimes other symbols) to spellings that evidence some understanding of sound-symbol relationships to conventional spelling. Thus, important word knowledge is revealed through invented spellings.

Looking at children's writing in this way underscores the hard work that goes on when they write. Their writing, including their invented spellings, reflects their ideas about how written language works. Because we use our ideas about how written language works when we read, we can learn a great deal about children as readers by examining what they write.

Talking with children about their writing and listening in as they talk to each other about writing are also valuable ways to develop insights into children as writers. Talk is often necessary to discover what beginning writers mean to say. For example, had Mary's teacher not asked her to read her early journal entry (Figure 9.1), we would not have been able to figure out what Mary was writing about. Other kinds of conversations are equally informative. In general, questions should be open ended and aimed at discovering what the writer is doing, why, and how a teacher (or someone else) can provide help. In Chapter 12 we offer more advice about interviewing children.

Supporting Writers: General Principles

Understanding how insights about written language develop, the role of writing in a program for children who find reading difficult, and how to discover what children know about written language are all necessary to the development of an effective writing program. In this section we consider some general principles that apply across writing programs and specific writing activities. The best writing teachers we know use these principles to support active and involved writers in their classrooms.

Classroom Atmosphere: Lots of Writing

Perhaps the most important aspect of support for student writers is the classroom atmosphere itself. Children must learn to believe in themselves as writers, to believe that they can write and that what they have to say is worthwhile. One way to help these

Talk is often necessary to discover what young writers mean to say.

beliefs develop is simply to invite children to write every day, from their very first day in your classroom or program.

Young children usually come to school expecting to learn to read and write. For them, invitations generally lead them to try. Older children, however, may hesitate when invited to write. Previous experiences in school may have taught them that they cannot write, that they are not writers, that writing is difficult or boring, or other negative lessons. The teacher's patience and persistence are critical in order for these negative lessons to be unlearned; so continue to invite, to praise attempts, and to establish the expectations that everyone can write and everyone will.

First efforts from all writers, especially young ones, may be drawings rather than writing; but letters and words soon appear. Those who study young children's writing have explored the relationship between drawing and writing. Marie Clay (1986) summarizes two possibilities: "Some people have explained the drawing as the thinking up of ideas which will later occur in sentences. Others have seen it as an aide memoire holding the ideas in mind while the child struggles with the message she is writing" (p. 765). Donald Graves and his colleagues found that children's drawings became smaller and less detailed as children learned to let words do their work. Some children's drawings even became abstract, more like mental notes than illustrations for an audience (Sowers, 1985). Whatever its purpose, drawing seems to facilitate writing for many children. So persistent teacher invitations to write, along with patience as children draw or develop the courage to try again, are essential features of the classroom atmosphere.

Talk about Writing

Opportunities to talk and listen are equally important. Graves (1983) has detailed several ways in which children use oral language when writing. They sometimes plan their writing by talking to themselves or others. They may also read parts of drafts to themselves, as if to get a running start on what should come next. Some children compose aloud and translate their speech into writing rather than use the thought-to-writing process most adult writers employ. Others play with prosodics such as rhythm or intonation. Children may also talk themselves through writing by making procedural comments such as "There! Now I need to write 'The End.'"

Of course, children read drafts of their work to others, either to help solve problems they've encountered or to get more general feedback. This use of oral language may be particularly important for those who find reading and writing difficult. Reading a draft aloud to an interested audience shows the child that his writing has value and demonstrates the communicative power of writing and the link between reading and writing. Talking about revision possibilities also helps children understand and examine their options, which aids them in critically analyzing their own writing (Hanser, 1986). Those who respond to children's writing learn to listen carefully and ask good, helpful questions. Of course, all this learning relates to reading as well. In fact, the concepts and procedures used in writing conferences can easily be applied to discussions about books written by authors outside the classroom.

Support, Encouragement, and Acceptance

Children need teacher support to develop as writers. Some of this support is mundane, such as having necessary supplies readily available. But other aspects of support, such as encouraging spelling efforts, may be a bit more problematic for some teachers. Accepting invented spelling allows children to be true to their own meanings and precise in their language because they can say what they want to say, not just what they know how to spell. In addition, children need opportunities to manipulate words and discover spelling principles so that phonological relationships become clear to them. In essence, children test their hypotheses about the way the alphabet works by contrasting the words they spell with the same words used in books that others have written (Gentry & Henderson, 1980).

Teachers' responses to early efforts are crucial to children's continued experimentation with print. Anne Haas Dyson (1984) suggests the following:

> The most helpful response to early writing efforts [is] to accept whatever writing the
> child produces, respond to any written message, answer the child's emerging questions,
> and through sensitive questioning, focus the child's attention on specific print features,
> thus promoting the development of more sophisticated encoding strategies. (p. 270)

Teachers can foster growth in spelling by encouraging independence and accepting the inventions that independence produces. Rather than directly answering a child's question about how to spell a word, the teacher can encourage the child to say the word. Then the teacher may ask, "What sound do you hear at the beginning? What letter would that be? Good. Write it down. Now say the word again. What sound do you hear at the end?" and so on. This strategy encourages children to develop independence as spellers. Listening for sounds and then representing them with letters supports children's efforts at phonemic segmentation, or separating words into their component sounds. In this way children's first recognizable efforts at spelling will bear strong resemblance to the sounds they hear as they articulate words. Later, as children become readers, visual memory also plays a role in spelling; that is, children may inspect their efforts to see if they "look right."

At some point, particularly if the child's written work will be read by others, standard spelling or traditional orthography becomes an issue. But both teachers and writers should keep issues such as spelling and other surface features of writing in perspective; all involved should understand that the content or ideas expressed through writing are more important than any aspect of form. As children become more conscious of standard spelling, they may express concern about their spelling efforts. Then teachers should help them deal with these concerns. Jane Davidson suggests that teachers should reply to students' queries about "is it right?" with a statement like this: "It's good enough for now. You can read it, and I can read it. We both know what you're saying here. Later, we can change some things, if you'd like, to make them look like they do in other books." This sort of discussion helps lessen concern about spelling at the idea-generation stage of the writing cycle, yet assures writers that their efforts will receive the polish they deserve.

Sometimes writing is for personal expression.

Modeling and Corrections

Two other general principles are important to consider as writing programs are planned: teacher as model and opportunities to connect reading and writing. In a way, these two principles are related, for both provide children with opportunities to learn from more sophisticated writers. Teachers who write when their students do, keep journals, and share their writing with students demonstrate the importance of writing and the way in which it works. Likewise, writers benefit from opportunities to make the reading-writing connection—to use others' writing as a model (see the copy-change activity later in the chapter) or conclude a read-aloud session with a discussion of how the author used language.

Both teacher modeling and activities or discussions that connect reading and writing focus children's attention on the qualities of good writing and the actions and thoughts that skilled writers employ. Frank Smith says that we learn to write by reading and learn to read by writing. We think he's right on both counts.

The atmosphere and attitude that best foster writing (and reading) development are characterized by support and encouragement. We can support children's writing efforts by nurturing their beliefs in themselves as writers. Belief leads to feelings of control and ownership, which in turn allow children to make their own decisions about the content and form of their writing. Having made these decisions, children are in a better position to understand the decisions that other authors have made.

Writing Activities

Most children are eager to express themselves in writing, particularly if they feel that what they have to say is interesting to other people and will be read by them. Children should have daily opportunities for individual and shared writing. Classroom writing activities should also allow them to explore all the ways in which writing can be used.

Those interested in developing a repertoire of writing activities will find many to choose from in other chapters of this book. For example, Chapters 7 and 8, which address comprehension instruction, include descriptions of many reading-writing activities [such as Think-Pair-Share, character sketches, Bleich's Heuristic, (Write and Share)[2], Agree or Disagree? Why?, response journals, webbing or mapping, K-W-L, dialectic (or double-entry) journals, distinctive-features activities, and herringbone charts]. All these activities help students develop as writers in addition to fostering their understanding of what they have read. In this section, we describe several other writing activities. In combination with activities described elsewhere, these approaches will help students develop as writers and see connections between their reading and writing.

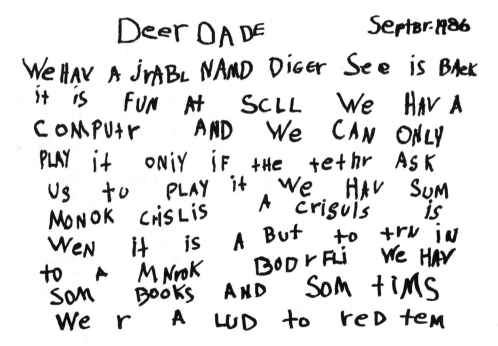

Figure 9.4
Entry in Elizabeth's personal journal.

Personal Journals

Sometimes we write for personal expression. Children can express their thoughts and feelings in personal journals. Many teachers ask children to write in journals daily, either as an independent activity or during a sustained silent writing time (when the teacher also writes in a journal) similar to SSR. The contents of personal journals should not be restricted in any way; children should be able to write whatever they wish. Some children, particularly beginning writers, may decide to draw or write single words or lists of words. Others may recount important events or write stories. One enthusiastic first grader used her journal to write a letter to her father about school (see Figure 9.4).

Gay and Tina work as Title I teachers in the same school. Gay works with primary children, and Tina works with older ones. Both provide several times each week for students to write in their personal journals. Both also write while their students write. "It's sort of like SSR," they say. "We all write at the same time. Often children choose to write in their journals at other times or ask to take them home. That's OK, too, of course."

Gay and Tina write while their students write because they know the power of teacher-as-model. But they see other benefits as well. "We've noticed a dramatic drop in requests for assistance since we started writing with the children," they say. "It's almost as if they don't want to interrupt us. So what happens is that the children become more independent, more willing to guess and try. That surprised us, but we're delighted because so many of our students *need* to learn to try."

Dialogue Journals

Sometimes we write to share information with a reader, as Elizabeth did in her journal entry (Figure 9.4). Dialogue journals, which are essentially notes written back and forth between two writers, provide children with opportunities to sustain written dialogue with other members of the class. Most teachers initiate dialogue journals by responding themselves to children's journal entries. This is a good way to get to know children at the beginning of the year, help them understand how dialogue journals work, and encourage fluent written expression without undue concern for mechanical perfection. Later, the use of dialogue journals can be expanded so that children write notes to friends as well as the teacher. Children are generally eager to read what another student or the teacher has written to them and to write responses.

Jeff provides resource assistance to middle school students with learning disabilities. He and his students rely heavily on both personal and dialogue journals. "The choice is theirs," Jeff says. "They can use their journals in either way. My only rule is that everyone writes." Jeff has noticed that students frequently want feedback from him, especially early in the school year. He likes this because it enables him to get to know his students and establish a trusting relationship with them. "Sometimes what starts out as a personal entry, with a response from me, sort of mutates into a dialogue journal. I have a tendency to ask questions in my written responses to students, and that sometimes encourages them to do the same." As a new group of students becomes comfortable with one another, "they start writing for people besides me. It's kind of funny, in a way. I think it's like teacher-authorized note writing to some of them. And I guess that's exactly what it is! They're so eager to read what someone else has written to them and then to write back."

Learning Logs or Content Area Journals

Sometimes we write to remember—to record thoughts, ideas, or facts for later use. Young writers can also be encouraged to use writing for this purpose. Gloria, who teaches first grade, introduces new units of study in science or social studies by asking small groups of children to talk about what they would like to learn. One child in each group serves as a secretary to record group members' ideas. Figure 9.5 shows one group's report from a discussion that preceded a new science unit about space.

As each group reads the report of its conversation about space to the rest of the class, Gloria prepared a large chart, titled "What We Want to Learn about Space," with enough room beneath each child's contribution to record information discovered during the course of the science unit. Every few days, Gloria and the children reread the chart, discussed what children had learned, and recorded new information where possible.

Children can also write individual accounts of content area lessons, record results of science observations or experiments, or write their own definitions of new concepts or

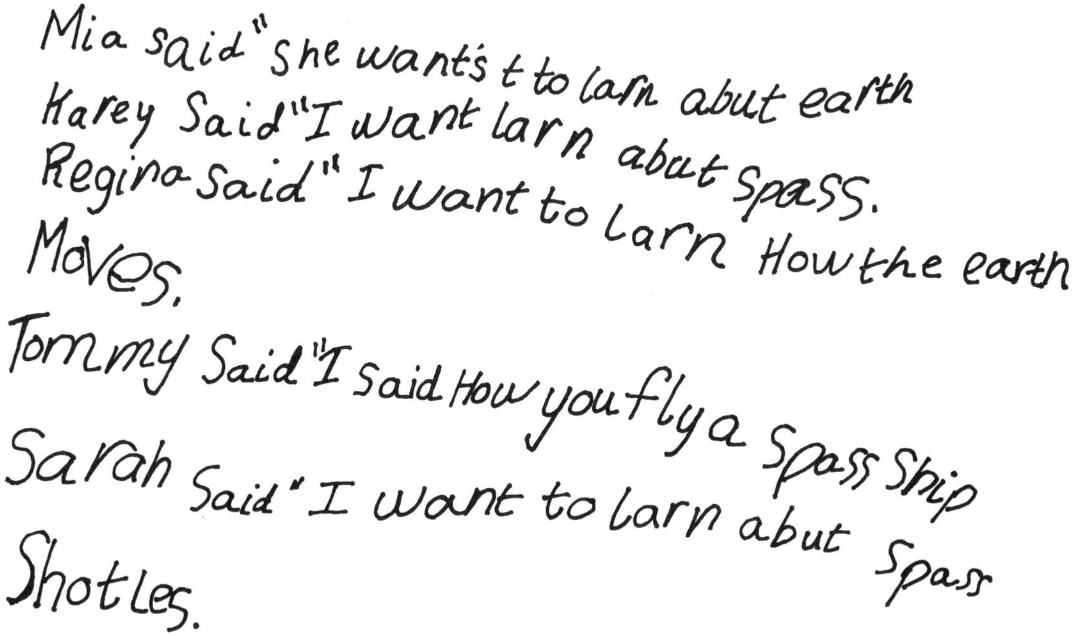

Mia said "she wants t to larn abut earth
Karey Said "I want larn abut spass.
Regina Said " I want to larn How the earth
Moves.
Tommy Said "I said How you fly a Spass Ship
Sarah Said " I want to larn abut Spass
Shotles.

Figure 9.5
Entry from a learning log.

descriptions of new procedures. This sort of writing is similar to the writing that children do in response journals (see Chapter 7). Learning logs or content area journals can be helpful for storing and organizing these writing efforts. Like the other journals we've described, these logs need not be fancy. Small spiral-bound notebooks work well, as do several pieces of paper stapled together and bound with construction paper.

Entries in learning logs may be open or closed (Davidson, 1987). Open entries encourage personal response or reaction because students decide what to write for themselves. Closed entries provide for more structured response, such as note taking, outlining, charting, synthesizing, or comparing. For example, students may be asked to summarize a class demonstration or movie, record their observations about something they are studying, or make notes to remind themselves about a new procedure they have learned.

Fifth-grade teacher Christine Evans has described her students' experiences with learning logs (1984). Her students made three types of log entries during two units of math instruction: definitions of new concepts; explanations of new procedures, such as how to multiply decimals or draw a geometric figure; and trouble shooting, where students analyzed their errors and wrote about why they had made mistakes. Another fifth-grade teacher taught the two math units in the traditional manner. Both classes took publisher-prepared tests before and after each unit. Test results indicated that Evans's students began each unit with less knowledge about the math concepts than the other class. After instruction, however, her students' test scores matched the other group's for one unit and exceeded them by 10 percent for the other. Evans attributes this growth to writing: Learning logs "get students to 'own' knowledge rather than just 'rent' it" (p. 835).

Learning logs can also be places for students to experiment with different discourse forms as they write about content area learning. For example, they might write newspaper accounts of historical happenings and scientific discoveries or letters to the editor about past and current events. They might write first-person accounts of life in other places or at other times. They might write poetry as a means of reacting to or summarizing what they have learned. "Name poems," which use letters of a name or word to begin lines of a poem, can easily be applied to content area concepts. All entries in learning logs should be dated so that students may easily refer back to entries. A child who forgets how to subtract three-digit numbers, for example, can simply look it up in his math log. Likewise, the teacher may use previous log entries as the basis for new ones: "Use your entries from September 18 and September 24 to analyze the. . . . "

Learning logs give children a place to record their thoughts about and reactions to content area instruction. Keeping a log also introduces children to note taking in a natural and functional way. Moreover, the logs become valuable learning resources for students as the school year progresses and thus enhance content learning.

How journals look is not as important as what they do. Personal journals, dialogue journals, and learning logs give children authentic reasons for writing and for reading what they and others have written.

Copy Change

Writing can be a means of creation or a way to express one's imagination. Young writers can create their own stories based on actual or fanciful happenings. Children's literature

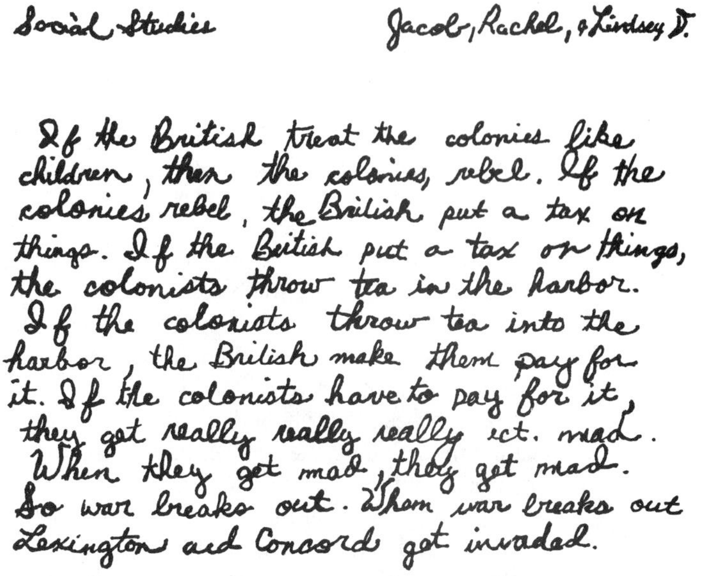

Figure 9.6
Example of a copy-change activity.

> Social Studies   Jacob, Rachel, & Lindsey D.
>
> If the British treat the colonies like children, then the colonies rebel. If the colonies rebel, the British put a tax on things. If the British put a tax on things, the colonists throw tea in the harbor. If the colonists throw tea into the harbor, the British make them pay for it. If the colonists have to pay for it, they get really really really ect. mad. When they get mad, they get mad. So war breaks out. When war breaks out Lexington and Concord get invaded.

can be an effective springboard and scaffold for this type of writing. If tall tales or fairy tales are read or told to children, discussion and subsequent dictation and a class text can focus on key elements or characteristics. Then, using the dictation as a guide, children can write their own tall tales or fairy tales.

Individuals or groups can write their own versions of books, too. This activity is sometimes called copy change because children use the author's copy as a framework for writing but change it to reflect their own ideas. Hesitant writers often need extra support or scaffolding to compose on their own, and the framework or ideas supplied by an exemplary author can provide this support.

Simple poetry works well as the impetus for copy-change activities. Children often find success with short poems in particular, which tend to be less overwhelming than longer pieces or stories. But predictable-pattern books also work well for introducing children to copy change. For example, it's easy to see the pattern that Bill Martin used to develop *Brown Bear, Brown Bear,* and that pattern can be used to dictate or write new versions:

Mr. Jones, Mr. Jones, what do you see?

I see some first graders looking at me.

Copy changes can also be more complex. Figure 9.6 presents an example written by a group of fifth graders who applied the pattern in *If You Give a Mouse a Cookie* to their learning in social studies.

Students can recast a story in the form of a script that can be performed as reader's theater (see Chapter 7). This, too, is a form of copy change because students use a favorite story as a framework for rewriting it in a different form.

Whether they're simple or complex, copy-change activities encourage careful reading or listening so that students can discover and use the author's pattern (Rhodes, 1981):

> As children find that they can use other authors' patterns to generate and shape their own ideas, they often become rather prolific writers. They may borrow a considerable amount from other authors at first, but their writing tends to deviate more from the authors' ideas as they gain control over print and take greater risks. (p. 515).

Thus, the pattern itself may provide a supportive framework for young authors, in much the same way as a poet might use a haiku or sonnet framework. Indeed, copy change and creating scripts from stories are very authentic types of writing. Professional writers often emulate the work of writers they admire, and Hollywood is filled with professional screenplay or script writers

Children need to write both for their own purposes and for others in and beyond the classroom, including the teacher. In fact, sharing writing can be one of the most gratifying aspects of the writing cycle. Figure 9.7 offers several ways for students to share their writing with others. All these activities make the connection between reading and writing strong and explicit for students.

Writing is meant to be read. This, of course, is a strong motivation for writing and a solid rationale for including writing activities in a program designed to strengthen children's reading. Through writing, children learn how written language works; they

---

- Students can make individual books for the classroom library or the school library. Children's books from one classroom can be loaned for children in another classroom to read.
- Students can make class magazines, newspapers, or books. These can be collaborations, where children work together on one cohesive product, or collections, where children contribute their favorite story or poem to a class book. Children can also make class books related to content-area study.
- Students can create bulletin boards or corridor displays of their writing. These, like all other writing for children to read, should be displayed at children's eye level.
- Students can make posters of poetry, jokes, riddles, and so on.
- Photocopies of students' writing can be shared with families and friends.
- Students can write notes or memos to classmates or the teacher. These can be "mailed" and delivered daily.
- Students can enact or present their writing through drama, puppetry, and so on.
- Students can read their writing aloud to classmates during writing conferences, to classmates during daily sharing time, to students in other classrooms, or to the school community via the intercom.

Figure 9.7
Sharing writing.

develop and deepen understandings about the conventions of print, the ways in which stories and other text forms work, and graphophonic knowledge. Moreover, by becoming authors, students learn to think like authors. They learn to think about purpose and audience and to analyze the author's craft. They discover that authors have options. All of this helps students understand that both reading and writing involve the exploration of language and the construction of meaning.

Chapter 10

Putting It All Together: Making Reading Programs That Work

I n the preceding chapters we presented a set of instructional strategies aimed at overcoming difficulties that children often encounter in their reading development. These strategies can assist students who are just beginning to experience difficulty and can also be effective with children for whom reading development has been significantly disrupted.

But effective corrective or remedial instruction is more than just the sum of these various strategies. It is not enough to use them; teachers must also consider how they fit together to form a coherent and effective instructional package. Effective corrective instruction means looking at the big picture and designing complete programs for children that make the best use of their time in helping them achieve the goal of proficient reading.

If you have read this whole book, you know that we believe firmly that teachers are in the best position to make instructional decisions for students who find reading difficult. There are many reasons for this belief, but perhaps one is more important than the others: We must teach in ways that reflect our beliefs about literacy learning. Students should also be actively involved in setting the direction of instruction. Packaged curricula, teacher's manuals, and other instructional resources can be good for finding ideas or provoking thought (indeed, that's why we wrote this book), but teachers and students together create curriculum and instruction in classrooms.

Teachers' teaching styles differ, as do students' needs and preferences. Moreover, aspects of the instructional environment vary from classroom to classroom. Imagine, for example, 10 Title I teachers teaching the same lesson to 10 groups of children in 10 different classrooms in 10 different schools in 10 different communities. What do you think would actually be the same about all these lessons? Probably very little. Such pragmatic realities are also a rationale for teachers' developing their own curricula: No one knows you, your students, and the specifics of your teaching situation as well as you.

In this chapter we deal with a critical but too often ignored issue: developing instructional systems that work. In essence, we discuss putting the strategies in this book into systems designed for children's specific needs and teachers' style of instruction. We suggest some principles or guidelines for designing corrective instructional packages and provide examples of effective instructional packages that already exist and are based on many of the principles we outline. We also discuss how individual teachers can design such systems for themselves and their students.

Guidelines for Program Development

This section offers several guidelines for developing a program that will successfully meet the needs of students who find reading difficult. We recommend that you think about these guidelines (and others that may be important to you) within an overall curriculum-development/instructional-planning framework that has four steps:

1. ***Formulate a philosophy.***   We all have philosophies or sets of beliefs about literacy learning, but sometimes we have not articulated them or considered the relationship between our beliefs and our instructional practices. The first step in the curriculum-development framework is to decide what you believe about the reading process, children as language learners, the role of the teacher, the classroom atmosphere, and appropriate materials and activities. We recommend that you write these statements down because you will need them in all other steps of the planning process.

2. ***Develop a few broad instructional goals.***   The goals serve as a foundation for planning instruction. As such, they should reflect your philosophy, describe the general areas within which literacy instruction will occur, and be based on broad notions of children's needs. We have found that too many goals are hard to manage and tend to fragment instruction, so try to limit the number—perhaps no more than five.

3. ***Decide on instructional routines.***   Routines (described in Chapter 2) offer children consistent opportunities to achieve the goals you have established. Moreover, because routines are predictable, they foster children's security and independence in the classroom. When you have made preliminary decisions about routines, look again at your goals. Make sure that the routines, as a whole, will enable children to achieve the goals.

4. ***Develop a plan to evaluate the curriculum.***   You might ask questions such as "How can I determine the extent to which instruction reflects my philosophy? How will I know that instruction really *is* providing students with opportunities to achieve the goals? How can I find areas that need fine-tuning?" Many of the ideas in Chapter 12 can be used for evaluating both curriculum and children.

As we noted earlier in this chapter, we believe that instructional planning is part of teachers' professional responsibility. Many teachers with whom we have worked find the four-step framework helpful for thinking about the planning process and ensuring that what happens in the classroom reflects their best thinking about children and literacy learning. The framework is rather general; it is even useful for planning "regular" classroom instruction. Several guidelines for program development that apply more specifically to the issue of helping children who find reading difficult are presented in the following sections of this chapter.

Focusing the Program

Reading programs for children who have difficulty learning to read should aim to help readers overcome difficulties in specific areas of reading and thereby improve their overall reading performance. Thus, to be truly effective, programs should address the specific problems manifested and observed in the reader and promote purposeful, authentic, and satisfying reading experiences.

If the reader manifests difficulty in reading fluency, providing the child with experiences in vocabulary development will not ameliorate the problem at hand. Indeed, the child may have a superior vocabulary; thus, providing supplemental instruction in vocabulary may have minimal positive results. If fluency is the problem, then we must design activities aimed at strengthening that essential aspect of reading.

The same is true for every difficulty—attitude toward reading, comprehension, vocabulary, word recognition. Please note that when we argue that instruction needs to be aimed at the area of difficulty manifested in the child, we define the area of difficulty rather widely. We do not mean specific skill areas such as "fluency in multiple-phrase sentences" or "recognition of the =ed ending in words." We feel that difficulties in specific skills generalize to difficulties throughout that particular aspect of reading. Thus, corrective instruction should be aimed at the more generalized area of concern.

Developing a focused program also requires some attention to what children are doing as readers, observing behaviors and attitudes that can facilitate their literacy growth and those likely to impede progress. In other words, teachers must determine what strategies nonproductive readers use so that they can plan instruction to meet their needs. Here are three suggestions to guide this process:

1. ***Watch for patterns of behavior across situations and times.*** During any day, children read lots of materials for lots of reasons in lots of instructional situations. Drawing conclusions based on one type of reading situation ignores the complexity and diversity of reading demands.

Effective instructional programs rely on a good understanding of children and their reading.

2. ***Rely on information from informal observations and conversations.***   To develop an instructional plan to support children, we need to understand how they operate within instructional settings. Therefore, standardized-test results are rarely helpful for this type of instructional planning. For example, children who score poorly on the comprehension subtest of a standardized reading test may indeed have difficulties. (Most often, of course, we already know this before the test is administered.) To help them, however, we need to understand how they approach typical reading tasks and situations. It's not enough to know *that* they have problems in reading; we need to understand the *whys* and *hows*.

3. ***Focus on the whole reader.***   Especially with children who find reading difficult, we have a tendency to look for problems. These are important, to be sure, but we must look equally carefully at what children *can* do as readers. This focus on strengths is important psychologically for both teacher and students; moreover, instruction can frequently be planned to use strengths as a platform or scaffold for addressing weaknesses.

Children's attitudes about reading and perceptions of the reading process and their roles as readers also deserve attention. We know that people who enjoy reading usually read and consequently have many opportunities to grow as readers. Moreover, children use their perceptions of the reading process to guide their actions while reading and evaluate the success of their efforts.

Massed and Spaced Practice or Activity

Whatever the reader's difficulty, practice within that area, and plenty of it, is usually required to overcome the difficulty. Significant chunks of time need to be devoted to the area in which the reader is experiencing difficulty to achieve significant and lasting progress. It is not good enough to work on the area for a few minutes. We need to direct the reader's attention to the difficulty using a variety of activities, contexts, and reading passages.

In line with our holistic approach to correction, we define areas of difficulty rather broadly in this book. If, for example, a reader is having difficulty with word recognition, instruction should be aimed at providing the reader with a variety of activities, strategies, and practice in learning to recognize or decode words quickly and efficiently; the reader also needs opportunities to apply that knowledge in real reading situations.

A more traditional and limited approach might isolate specific areas of difficulty or skills needed for word recognition, such as the *pl* consonant blend or vowel diphthongs or the *=ing* ending. Such instruction would focus almost entirely on these skill areas and be in the form of worksheets that isolate the skill at the expense of applying it in real reading situations. We feel that these limited approaches do not give the reader broad enough experience to practice the full range of skills and strategies needed to recognize all words efficiently. Moreover, they do not provide sufficient breadth to allow the reader to apply the practiced skill or strategy in the larger context of authentic reading.

This leads us to a related issue: the nature of material used for instruction and practice. Throughout this book, we have pointed to the value of using authentic reading material that children find interesting. Additionally, the reading material should be rather easy for children, especially as we begin to focus their attention on some aspect of the reading process that is new or difficult for them. Thus, we advise selecting material carefully to increase the likelihood of success and decrease the possibility of frustration.

Consistency over Time

It is important that the reader receive consistent instruction over the long term. Massed and long-term instruction and practice are the best assurance that the reader will permanently overcome the difficulty. Moreover, developing a consistent instructional routine that includes authentic reading experiences as well as instructional activity in the area of difficulty makes lessons predictable for students and the teacher. This results in a degree of student independence, more efficient use of time, and greater on-task behavior.

Some may argue that developing a consistent routine will result in lessons that students find uninteresting. This need not be the case. Within the general lesson framework that includes work on the area of difficulty and authentic reading experiences, teachers have the freedom to vary the instructional activities (several activities can be devoted to any one difficulty area, as preceding chapters show), texts to be read and who makes the choices, how the text reading might occur (silent, oral, choral, paired), and the surrounding context for the instruction (such as where the instructional activity takes place: individually, in pairs, or with a group). There are so many variables available that all lessons should be fresh, engaging, and interesting.

Proficient, Professional Instructors

We are firm believers that highly qualified instructors provide the best instruction, especially with students who have difficulty reading. Indeed, an international study of reading found that student achievement in reading was positively associated with the level of teacher training (Elley, 1992).

Staying professionally current is part of every teacher's responsibility, but we think it is particularly critical for those attempting to assist children who find reading difficult. We learn more about readers and reading each year, and much of this new knowledge has direct instructional application. By maintaining memberships in professional organizations, reading and discussing literacy-related journals, attending professional meetings, and interacting informally with colleagues, we can plan instruction based on best practice and state-of-the-art knowledge.

Moreover, those who select a particular program for reading instruction, such as the ones described later in this chapter, must understand the philosophy, purposes, and procedures of the program and be proficient in its implementation. This may involve initial professional development through reading or in-service education, frequent opportunities to talk with colleagues who also use the program, and ongoing in-service education on the program.

*Staying professionally current is
every teacher's responsibility.*

Effective Instructional Programs

Reading Recovery

One of the best-known corrective reading instructional programs is Reading Recovery (Pinnell, 1989; Pinnell, Fried, & Estice, 1990). Reading Recovery is an individual tutoring program in which a highly trained tutor works with a first-grade child experiencing difficulty in reading for 30 minutes each day. This work takes place in addition to the child's regular classroom reading instruction.

Limited to first graders, the program operates under the assumption that the best way to correct reading problems is to treat them early and intensively. The older a student becomes, the more entrenched reading problems become. Thus, instruction to ameliorate reading difficulties becomes progressively more time-consuming and less effective.

Each Reading Recovery lesson is based on a series of brief activities aimed primarily at improving word recognition and reading fluency. The activities are consistent from day to day; the routine is very predictable. Students know what they will do in every session. With such consistency the tutoring sessions are intensive and involve little wasted time.

In the first part of the lesson, students read familiar stories they have read previously. The teacher then does a diagnostic check by keeping a running record of the child's oral reading of a newer text, one that was introduced in the previous day's lesson. Next, the child and teacher engage in letter recognition and manipulation activities. Then the child dictates a sentence that the teacher records and rereads aloud, after which the child is guided in writing it himself. After practicing reading and writing the sentence, the teacher rewrites it on a strip of paper, cuts it into individual words, and asks the child to reconstruct the message. The words are taken home for further practice and play.

Finally, the teacher introduces a new book that the child can learn to read successfully. The child and teacher explore the book; the teacher introduces new concepts, language patterns, or words to the child as necessary. After the introduction, the child attempts the book on his own with the teacher guiding appropriate strategy use when the text becomes too difficult.

First graders remain in Reading Recovery until they are able to read at about the average level of students at their grade level in their school. This usually requires several weeks of instruction. Research on Reading Recovery suggests that it is a highly effective program in advancing students to more normal levels of reading and that, compared to other corrective reading programs, Reading Recovery graduates are less likely to need continued reading assistance throughout their elementary years.

Tutors who specialize in Reading Recovery are certified teachers who engage in a year-long program of intensive education in Reading Recovery. The education program consists of studying the reading process of young children and methods of instruction and practicing, observing, and critiquing Reading Recovery instruction throughout the training period.

Cunningham, Hall, and Defee's Approach

Cunningham, Hall, and Defee (1991) describe a first-grade program that could easily be adapted to a variety of instructional settings and employed with any readers who need assistance in developing proficiency in word recognition. In this unnamed approach students engage in daily literacy instruction through four 30-minute time blocks, each featuring a distinct aspect of literacy.

The "writing block" consists of a five-minute mini-lesson in which the teacher demonstrates and talks about a piece of her own writing with the students. Writing conventions and strategies are modeled and discussed daily. Next, the child writes independently, getting assistance and feedback from others and eventually publishing the work. At the end of the block, the group discusses its progress and shares completed work.

In the "basal block" the teacher engages students in direct and traditional instruction around a reading textbook and supplementary materials. During part of this period students read the stories from the text with a partner.

In the "real-books block" the teacher reads a book to students. Then students read self-selected books on their own (including books published by fellow students in the writing block). Students are also encouraged to talk about their reading with other students.

The final time block, "working with words," includes a Word Wall and Making Words activities. The emphasis of this period is to develop students' word recognition or decoding abilities. The Word Wall is a bulletin board to which students and teacher add about five words each week. These common words are written on cards so that they can be arranged in alphabetical order. Students practice the words each day. Making Words is a word-building activity in which students manipulate a limited set of letters to make a variety of words. Both activities are described in detail in Chapter 4.

The focus of this approach is to develop students' facility with word recognition while allowing them to apply their new-found knowledge to real reading and writing situations. Cunningham, Hall, and Defee report that, with this approach, nearly 90 percent of first-grade students made exceptional or acceptable progress over a year's instruction.

Although we do not necessarily advocate the uninformed application of this approach for any group of beginning readers or students encountering problems in word recognition, we do feel that several aspects are worthy of notice and adaptation by teachers who face similar circumstances. First, children receive specific and extended instruction in the area requiring attention. Further, they immediately apply the learning to real and guided reading and writing situations. In addition, the consistent and predictable daily blocks of instruction enable students to know what they will be doing. They do not have to waste instructional time learning new routines. We also like the active engagement of readers in choosing books, writing on their own, and making their own words.

A program like this works because students are engaged in real reading, real writing, and real problem solving through effective word recognition activities. Moreover, this good instruction is massed in a significant time period and is consistently applied on a daily basis.

Success for All

The Success for All program is aimed at children in grades pre-K through 3 (Slavin, Madden, Karweit, Dolan, & Wasik, 1992). It has been implemented in an inner-city elementary school with great success, bringing all children up to grade-level achievement in reading and other basic skills. The program is designed around special tutors who are certified teachers with experience in Title I, special education, or primary-grade reading instruction. Tutors work individually for 20-minute sessions each day during a 60-minute social studies period. Instruction focuses on what the students encounter in their regular reading curriculum. Each tutor is able to work with 11 students individually per day.

During the 90-minute regular reading period, the tutors work within the classroom and serve as additional reading teachers. Thus, tutors provide additional on-line support to regular reading instruction and learn about the regular curriculum content in order to coordinate and reinforce their individual tutoring with the regular classroom instruction.

In regular instruction, students in grades 1–3 are regrouped according to reading achievement across grades so that each class has about 15 students, all reading at the same level. This arrangement allows teachers to teach the whole class; increases time available for direct instruction; and largely eliminates the need for workbooks, photocopies, and other independent, "make-work," follow-up activities.

The reading instruction for beginning readers includes time for sharing and discussing children's literature to develop comprehension and vocabulary, oral reading of big books, letter and sound instruction, repeated oral reading of phonetically regular minibooks, composing, and instruction in specific comprehension skills including story structure. Older children (grades 2–3) also hear and discuss literature and engage in cooperative learning of story structure through prediction, summarization, vocabulary, decoding, and story-related writing using a basal textbook series. Students are expected to read material of their own choosing for 20 minutes each night at home. This reading is discussed in regular "Book Club" sessions in school. Every eight weeks, students' reading progress is assessed. These results determine which students will receive tutoring in the upcoming weeks.

A family-support team made up of social workers and a parental liaison provides parenting education services and encourages home support of children's school learning. The team also intervenes when there are indications that students are not working up to their potential. Teachers and tutors receive two days of in-service training at the beginning of the school year to learn about implementing the program. Throughout the school year they receive regular in-service instruction on relevant topics.

Several aspects of Success for All seem worthy of mention. These include tutors' consistent and massed instruction for students most in need of instruction, ongoing student assessment, coordination with the regular reading curriculum to ensure consistency and maximize practice within a particular content or skill area, maximizing teacher-student contact through the efficient use of tutors and the regrouping process, connection between home and school, and attempts to maximize students' voluntary reading. Together, these elements ensure intensive and meaningful instruction that leads to strong gains in reading achievement.

The Curious George Strategy

The Curious George Strategy (Richek & McTague, 1988) is aimed at helping students in the primary grades develop fluency and comprehension in their reading. It is based on the use of a particular type of children's book—series books—with the idea that authentic literature is more interesting to students than the dull, dry materials that students who have difficulty reading are often required to read. Moreover, the use of series books, such as *Curious George* (H. A. and Margaret Rey), *Clifford the Big Red Dog* (Norman Bridwell), and *Harry the Dirty Dog* (Gene Zion), allows students to gain background knowledge about characters, setting, plot, and author's style, which can set the stage for comprehension and fluent reading.

The Curious George Strategy is implemented as a weekly cycle in which one book is covered per week during 30-minute group sessions. On the first day the teacher introduces a series book and reads it to the students. Then the teacher and students reread the first third of the book chorally or in some other joint way. Next, each child chooses five favorite words from the story for future study and reference. Students are given individual copies of the book and asked to read the book at home and practice their words.

On the second day of the weekly cycle students begin by sharing their word cards with each other. Next, the second third of the book is read together. Finally, students choose five new words to practice on their own and are asked to read the book at home. Day 3 repeats the day 2 session using the final third of the book.

Day 4 culminates the cycle. Children dictate their own version of the Curious George story to the teacher, who writes it in a large blank book. This language-experience activity sets the stage for other writing activities that follow. On day 5, students can engage in other group and individual literacy-expansion activities.

In the following weeks students read other Curious George books with their teacher and later move on to other series books. Fluency and comprehension continue to improve as students' familiarity with the author, plot, characters, and words increase.

Evaluation of this strategy showed that students' comprehension and oral reading fluency improved significantly over a comparison group using more traditional corrective instruction. In addition, teachers and parents noted improvements in students' attitudes toward reading and their writing ability.

Often students, especially younger ones without much experience in the real world or with stories, are asked to read material for which they have little interest or background. As a result, they struggle in their reading as they attempt to make sense of the text. That struggle often leads to further difficulty and frustration. In addition to the consistency and focus of this program, the Curious George Strategy acknowledges students' need to become familiar with what they are reading in order to experience success in reading and understanding the text.

Fluency Development Lesson

Although we detailed the Fluency Development Lesson (FDL) in Chapter 5, we feel that it's worth mentioning again as an example of developing a lesson format that meets the needs of students and is applied in a systematic and consistent manner. Rasinski, Padak, Linek, and Sturtevant (1994) created the FDL to address the needs of primary-grade students who seemed to lack the fluency skills that would enable them to read texts easily, effectively, and efficiently. We took what we felt were important aspects of fluency instruction and put them together into an instructional package that was quick and easy for teachers to implement and students to accomplish. Among these principles were the use of highly predictable texts; the notions of modeling, support, and assistance during initial readings of the passage; multiple readings of the text; focus on individual words of choice and word patterns; and opportunities for students to respond meaningfully to the passage and perform it for a wider audience.

First, teachers read a short, predictable text to students. Then students read and reread the text, with initially high levels of support that gradually diminish as children become more familiar and fluent with the passage. At the end of each lesson students have the opportunity to read the passage to the class or other groups of children or adults in the school.

The FDL was developed as a daily instructional activity that supplemented students' regular instruction. We found that, over the course of a year, students receiving the FDL instruction made significant gains in reading when compared to a group of children who also received supplemental instruction but in a more traditional manner (Rasinski et al., 1994).

Just Do It

A recent advertising campaign for a popular brand of sports apparel uses the phrase "just do it" to suggest that now is the time to use the company's shoes and get into shape. No more thinking about it, no more procrastination—the time is now. We think the phrase also applies to developing reading programs for children who find reading difficult. We've shared with you our thoughts and philosophy about effective teaching strategies for corrective reading, the elements of effective programs for helping children overcome reading problems, and examples of programs developed by and for teachers that have proven effective with young readers. Now is the time to "just do it." Develop a program that works for you and is responsive to the needs of your students.

The five programs we described in this chapter do not cover all the effective programs that exist in the field. Nor are they meant to be prescriptive. That is, just because these programs work does not mean that they should be followed blindly. We describe the programs only to demonstrate the wide variety that exists and point out their many common characteristics, such as focus and consistency.

In a review of programs for first graders who are experiencing difficulty in learning to read, Pikulski (1994) identifies several critical instructional elements:

- Extra or supplemental reading instruction should be closely coordinated with regular classroom instruction.
- Children benefit from additional instructional time.
- Simple texts, especially those employing predictable and natural language patterns, ensure success.
- Meaningful opportunities to reread foster fluency development.
- Instruction should be focused when children need help.
- Writing activities foster reading growth.
- Close cooperation between school and home is beneficial.

Pikulski also urges careful monitoring of children's progress and encourages teachers to find professional support.

We believe that most of these suggestions apply to reading instruction for children of any age. By employing these guidelines and the principles we outline in this chapter and incorporating many of the instructional strategies we describe in this book, teachers can develop effective programs that respond to their own situations.

Ownership is one of the concepts that has come to characterize effective literacy instruction. Student achievement increases when students have some ownership over their own learning. They have ownership when they can choose what they need and want to read, how they can respond to their reading, and with whom they can read. We feel that the same notion applies when it comes to teachers' designing their own instruction. When teachers have ownership over their instruction, when they can determine their own methods and procedures, they will have more of themselves and their ideas invested in the program and greater reason to make instruction work. Thus, we urge teachers who work with children having difficulty in reading to identify for themselves the principles of instruction that are key to successful intervention, develop realistic and workable programs for themselves and their students, and then just do it.

Chapter 11

Involving Parents in Children's Reading

Throughout this book we have argued that a central part of any reading program is maximizing the amount of time that students actually read connected text. As we have emphasized, there is a strong, direct association between students' progress in reading and the amount of real reading they do. Yet the unfortunate truth is that most students do very little reading either in or out of school. One study reported that, on average, fifth-grade students in a midwestern school read books less than five minutes per day when they were out of school (Anderson, Wilson, & Fielding, 1988). Other research has reported similar results at different grade levels.

Given the relative absence of children's authentic reading experiences, we wonder why more children don't have difficulty reading. We also wonder just how much better all readers, especially less proficient ones, might become if their volume of contextual reading could be increased. Because students currently engage in such a small amount of real reading, it would take a small increase to double or even triple the amount of time they devote to reading. This is certainly a worthy goal for all school reading programs.

One area with tremendous potential for affecting student reading progress is the home. Elementary students spend most of their time at home, yet they do little reading there. Thus, home and parental involvement in reading are truly untapped sources for increasing the sheer amount that students read, which in turn will increase their proficiency in reading.

Parental involvement can significantly influence children's learning. There have been several extensive reviews of research on the impact of parental involvement on children's academic achievement in general and reading achievement in particular. These reviews have found that parents can play a major role in children's academic success. Ann Henderson (1988), for example, concluded that parental involvement leads to improvements in student achievement, grades, test scores, and overall academic performance. Moreover, she concluded that parental involvement has the secondary but significant effect of improving community perception of school effectiveness and positively influencing the attitudes that families and educators have about one another. Results from the National Assessment of Educational Progress indicate that students who were regularly involved with their families in literacy-related activities had higher levels of reading achievement than students who were not. Similarly, an international study of reading instruction found that the "degree of parental cooperation" was the most potent of 56 significant characteristics of schools most successful in teaching reading (Postlethwaite & Ross, 1992).

Unfortunately, few schools or teachers make ongoing or consistent efforts to involve parents in children's reading. Many teachers have had unsuccessful and unrewarding experiences when working with parents. Others feel they don't have time or energy for such a program when they seldom get release time, remuneration, or recognition. Still other teachers feel uncomfortable around parents who may question methods of instruction and assessment. Most schools and teachers that do sponsor parental involvement programs in reading tend to offer one-shot affairs such as talks by local experts in reading, "make it and take it" workshops, pre-packaged commercial programs, or short-term incentive programs. These approaches have little effect on students' reading or their attitudes toward it. Still, when parental involvement in reading is actively supported by teachers and schools, takes place over the long term, promotes simple yet enjoyable involvement, and offers parents ongoing communication and support from teachers, there is every reason to believe that it can make a significant and positive impact on students' reading. In fact, parental involvement can become a superb complement to the instruction that students receive in school.

In this chapter we discuss several important characteristics of parental involvement in reading programs that work. Using these characteristics as guidelines, teachers and schools can design their own parental involvement programs that meet their specific needs. The characteristics can also be used to design assessment instruments to evaluate existing programs.

Use Proven and Effective Strategies

Too often, the educational activities that teachers ask parents to do with their children have questionable value for improving academic performance. Drawing and coloring pictures or cutting out photographs from magazines may not be, in and of themselves, poor activity choices. But they may not be the best use of parents' and children's time together at home. The amount of time that parents can devote to working with their children is often limited. Therefore, teachers and schools should ensure that suggested at-home activities are based upon proven and appropriate methods for achieving academic success in reading. Many of the methods and strategies we described in earlier chapters can be readily adapted for home use.

Provide Training, Communication, and Support

Most parents do not share teachers' level of instructional expertise. They need good and understandable training that includes demonstrations and opportunities for discussion and questions. Training should be provided by someone who is enthusiastic about and committed to parental involvement. Continuing communication and support in a number of forms should be offered so that parents get timely feedback to their questions and concerns. This support can be in the form of a regular informative newsletter, monthly training and support sessions in the school, encouraging and taking phone calls from parents, sending home informative articles from professional journals that might interest parents, and creating a parent lounge/library in the school where parents and teachers can chat and find professional resources. Ongoing support demonstrates to parents that they are not alone in working with their children. Other people care.

Real Reading

The research on real reading is quite clear. One of the best things that parents of all ages can do for children of any age is to read to them. Research tells us that parents and teachers who read to their children regularly tend to have children with larger vocabularies and better comprehension. Similarly, when parents read with their children or listen to their children read, children grow as readers. Reading material should be relatively easy or include enough support from parents that children can read with ease. These simple activities—read to, read with, and listen to children—are powerful ways to promote student growth in reading.

Make Activities Easy and Consistent

Parents tell us that parental involvement activities don't work if they are too complex, take inordinate amounts of time, or change from day to day or week to week. They say it's hard to develop a routine of working with their children under these conditions. Even in the best of situations, parents' time is limited. With all their other obligations they must carefully ration their home time and energy.

Therefore, the instructional activities that teachers send home for parents need to reflect this situation. Activities should be simple and not time consuming. Because parents are unlikely to be familiar with elaborate instructional schemes, it is best to focus on simple, successful activities with some variation to keep interest high. Such activities make it easier for parents and children to develop predictable, time-efficient routines. These, in turn, increase the likelihood that the at-home activities will be conducted regularly and successfully.

Make Reading Fun

For parents and children to persist in academic tasks over the long term, the activities must be enjoyable for everyone. First, have parents and children read authentic and exemplary reading material. Second, ensure that parents can successfully implement the

Parent-child reading activities should involve authentic reading and be enjoyable for all.

activities with their children and children can successfully complete them. Third, infuse a sense of informality and playfulness into the activities. Parents and children need to have fun as they play with written language. Fourth, encourage parents to be enthusiastic, provide positive encouragement, and support their children's attempts to read. Finally, allow children some control over the activity. For example, parents can allow children to choose the material to be read in an activity. If the reading is followed by some word games, children can choose the games as well as the words to include. We think that the best type of parental involvement activities are those in which parents and children share ownership.

Provide Texts and Other Instructional Materials for Parents

Some parental involvement plans fail because parents lack adequate materials, the time or resources to acquire them, or knowledge of where to acquire appropriate materials.

Even with explicit directions about materials acquisition, many parents will fail to get the right materials at the right time. The easiest solution is to provide parents and children with the materials. When the materials are present—whether they are books, poems, diaries, or games—parents are more likely to remember to do the activities with their children. The materials themselves remind parents to get the job done.

Provide Ways to Document Home Activities

Having parents document their activity with their children permits teachers and schools to monitor parent-child involvement and evaluate the degree to which the program is successful in achieving its goal. More important, perhaps, documentation gives parents tacit encouragement and reminds them to continue reading with their children.

Usually, documentation can be accomplished with a log sheet on which parents record their work with their children over a specified period of time. Parents tell us that they post the sheet in a prominent place to remind them to do the activity. At the end of the time period the log sheets are returned to the school (see Figure 11.1).

Be Consistent over the Long Term

Don't plan major changes or disruptions in the instructional activities and procedures for parents and children. Rather, allow families to develop a level of comfort with activities known to be effective. Create variety by changing the texts and the ways in which parents and children respond to what they read.

With these principles or guidelines in mind, teachers or school administrators can design programs for parental involvement in reading that effectively supplement the instruction that students receive in school. When home and school collaborate to provide enjoyable and authentic reading experiences, students benefit because they have multiple daily opportunities to grow as readers.

Successful Parental Involvement Programs

Communication

Communication is key to any successful educational program, including at-home reading programs. Teachers need to keep parents apprised of children's growth in reading, describe classroom activities, and suggest at-home literacy activities. While communication between classroom and home can occur in several ways, we think that written com-

FAST START READING LOG

_____ Name   SEPTEMBER–OCTOBER _____ Month

_____ School   *Please return this log to your child's
                                          teacher at the end of the month.

Date	Time spent on Lesson	Name of New Passage Introduced	Other Reading Activities
9-28			
9-29			
9-30			
10-1			
10-2			
10-3			
10-4			
10-5			
10-6			
10-7			
10-8			
10-9			
10-10			
10-11			
10-12			
10-13			
10-14			
10-15			
10-16			
10-17			
10-18			
10-19			
10-20			
10-21			
10-22			
10-23			
10-24			
10-25			
10-26			
10-27			
10-28			
10-29			
10-30			

Figure 11.1
Home Reading log.

176

munication, particularly in the form of a regular newsletter, is especially effective. By its nature, written communication is permanent. Parents can read and reread newsletters and post them in a place that allows easy access and referral.

We know many Title I and classroom reading teachers who send home monthly or semimonthly newsletters to parents. The better letters include information on what the children have done in school and what they will be encountering shortly. Teachers also include articles that describe ways in which parents can help their children, lists or brief reviews of appropriate and exemplary books for children, and descriptions of specific literacy-related games and activities that parents can share with their children.

Some newsletters include articles that children write and photographs of children at work. These offer added incentives for parents and children to read the newsletters, and preparing the articles gives children added practice in reading and writing. For example, the Title I program in a school near us publishes a newsletter made up largely of articles written by students enrolled in the program (see Figure 11.2). The teacher reports that student work makes parents look forward to upcoming issues. "Once I have their eyes and ears, I can share with them some of the things they can do at home to promote their children's learning."

Newsletters should be personal and informative. The personal is best achieved by including student work or descriptions of individual students' accomplishments. The informative is achieved by including information that will help parents help their children read. Book lists, instructional ideas and strategies, answers to questions that parents frequently ask, news about upcoming meetings and speakers, and practical tips will help many parents better meet the reading needs and interests of their children.

Teachers should also ensure that their newsletters avoid talking down to parents. Many parents complain that they feel intimidated or are made to feel inadequate at their children's schools. Newsletters should be informal and conversational, highlighting the notion of partnerships between home and school. (See Appendix K for an example of an introductory letter to parents.)

Incentive Programs

We discussed some incentive programs in Chapter 3 as approaches to improving students' attitudes and motivation to read. The home is a great place to help nurture student reading, and incentive programs may offer a good connection between home and school.

Pizza Hut's Book It is a well-known incentive program designed to promote recreational reading. In the program students read books on their own and receive certificates for pizzas if they meet certain teacher-established goals for the amount of reading they do.

Book It is a nationwide program, but local incentive programs can also be devised. One that we are familiar with is called the Reading Millionaires project (O'Masta & Wolf, 1991). The staff at Diablo Elementary School in the Panama Region Department of Defense Schools wanted to increase students' out-of-school reading, so they devised a schoolwide incentive program. They set a goal for students: reading for a million minutes by the end of the school year. An informational flier and newsletters about the program were sent to parents, who were asked to play an integral part in the project. Par-

READING

Right to Read Week
March 1 - 6

A POTPOURRI
OF READING

A Parent's Response

As a parent of a child in Chapter I reading, I have taken the opportunity to check out some of the reading material Mrs. Smith has available for parents. One of the books I have read is titled "Parent Tricks-Of-The-Trade" by Kathleen Touw. This book is a combination of Heloise Helpful Hints and Dr. Spock. There are many ideas on everything from trying to stop a crying baby, travel tips with children, party activities, to recipes, to making play dough, just to name a few. If you are a parent open to new ideas or suggestions on these topics and others, I would recommend you read this book. "Parent Tricks-of-the-Trade" is a very informative book.

Sincerely

Cheryl

Mom & Johnathan

AUTHOR, AUTHOR!

Author Amy D will present an evening program for Chapter I students and their parents on March 1st. Students and parents will have an opportunity to do creative writing together.

Books written by Amy include "Me and My Friends," "The Ghost Man," "The Squirrel's Dinner," "No Homes," and others.

Figure 11.2
Reading Newsletter

The Moral of the Story is . . .

The farmer and the little boy think that nothing ever happens in the stories of *Hill of Fire* and *The Boy Who Cried Wolf.* The farmer and the little boy were bored. In the *Hill of Fire* there was a big explosion. In *The Boy Who Cried Wolf* the wolf came to eat the sheep for lunch. The people in the village got away to safety but the wolf ate the boy's sheep. I liked *The Boy Who Cried Wolf* the best because it was funny and the boy tricked the fisherman and the hunters.

by Rosa

Nobody believed the boy when he cried "wolf." The hunters and the fisherman believed him at first but after they were tricked and there really was a wolf, the sheep were eaten.

by Robert

I will never tell a lie so that I won't get in trouble because it is not fun.

Heidi

It is better to tell the truth because people will believe what you say when you tell the truth.

by Jo

Figure 11.2, continued

179

A POTPOURRI OF READING

FUN READING

I Love A Story

Mouse Soup by Jacob S.

The mouse was reading a book under a tree. A wolf was behind a tree and caught the mouse and brought it home. The wolf put the mouse in a cage to save for supper. The mouse told the wolf four stories. The wolf believed the stories and got into trouble. The mouse got away.

The story was make-believe. The wolf should not have listened to the mouse.

George and Martha

The best part of the story was story number three. The Tub. George peeked in on Martha. It was funny.

By Brian

Dreams
Hold fast to dreams
For if dreams die
Life is a broken-winged bird
That cannot fly.
Hold fast to dreams
for when dreams go
Life is a barren field
Covered with snow.

Langston Hughes

Poetry Surprise

I like to go sledding in the middle of winter.
Going down the hill at the cemetery, I hit the big snow ramp.
Elbows hitting the ground, I go up in the air—the best part.

> Sijo —This verse pattern was developed in Korea. Its structure has three lines with 14 to 16 syllables to each line.
>
> by Mathew

Figure 11.2, concluded

180

Communication is a key component of any effective home-school reading program.

ents monitored children's reading at home, encouraged home reading, read to their children, and completed periodic reading logs that indicated the number of minutes that children had read. Pages from books that parents read to children also counted.

A display chart was set up in the school to show progress toward the reading goal. Teachers and the school principal constantly encouraged the children to read at home. In the end, the goal was achieved, students felt a sense of community accomplishment, student reading at home increased and remained high throughout the school year, and parents felt better about helping their children in reading.

Paired Reading

Paired Reading is a reading-support program that we described in Chapter 5. Although less able students can be matched with more proficient classmates, older students, teachers, parent volunteers, or other reasonably proficient readers, the program was initially intended for parents who were working with their children (Topping, 1987). In Paired Reading, parent and child sit side by side and read one text aloud together. (The child chooses the text.) The reading is done at a comfortable rate for the child, and either the parent or child points to the text as they read to draw both readers' attention to the print. In places where children feel comfortable reading alone, they signal parents nonverbally (perhaps with a nudge of an elbow). Parents stop reading aloud but continue to follow the reading and begin to read again if necessary. When children come to words they don't know and are unable to decode after a reasonable period, the parents simply say the words and the reading continues. Parents work with their children 5–10 minutes daily.

In England, where Paired Reading was first developed as a parental involvement program, research indicates that it is a powerful method for improving students' reading.

Researchers there have reported that students engaged in Paired Reading have made gains in word recognition and comprehension 3 to 5 times above normal. That's an impressive achievement, especially given the small amount of time involved in the program.

Several schools in North America have incorporated Paired Reading as a parental involvement program. At Robinson School, an inner-city school, parents are invited to learn about Paired Reading at the beginning of each year. Because Robinson has used the program for several years, parents know about it and are anxious to get involved. The gymnasium is full when the Title I teachers Sandra, Gail, and Nancy introduce Paired Reading in an hour-long training session that includes a live demonstration, a video-taped description and demonstration, and an explanation of how the program works at Robinson. Parents try out Paired Reading with their children during this training session while the teachers provide feedback. Parents learn that students are given books of their own choosing to bring home. They also learn that parents are asked to work daily with their children; maintain a monthly log of their Paired Reading; and should contact Sandra, Gail, or Nancy if they have questions about how Paired Reading works. Parents receive a packet of information about the program for future reference. They sign a contract in which they agree to do Paired Reading with their children throughout the school year. The contracts, along with photographs of the children and parents taken at this session, are displayed on a bulletin board in a prominent location in the school.

Sandra, Nancy, and Gail have found Paired Reading to be one parental involvement program that actually works. Nancy says, "It works because parents know how they can help their children in a way that's easy, fun, and doesn't take the whole evening." Jackie, another veteran Title I teacher in the same school district, gives Paired Reading an enthusiastic and unconditional thumbs up: "Paired Reading and Reading Recovery are the best things to have happened in the remedial reading programs" (Rasinski & Fredericks, 1991, p. 515).

Fast Start in Reading

Fast Start is a program we developed at Kent State University for involving parents of young readers (kindergarten through grade 2) and students who find reading difficult. In Fast Start parents read short, highly predictable passages with their children. We have found that rhyming poetry, nursery rhymes, jokes and riddles for children, and short vignettes work very well. Each day parents and their children spend about 15 minutes on one of the passages. What we ask parents to do is very specific and based upon effective instructional principles.

1. The parent reads the passage to the child, and they talk about its content.
2. Parent and child read the passage together until the child feels that she can read it alone.
3. The parent listens to the child read and gives encouragement, support, and praise.
4. Parent and child choose a word or two from the passage, write them on index cards, add them to their word bank, and engage in word play and word bank activities. (See Chapter 4 for a description of making and using word banks and word sorts.)

Fast Start begins with an hour-long training session at the beginning of the school year. School personnel invite parents to attend training sessions. Several sessions are offered at each school, morning and evening, so that parents can choose which session to attend. We have found that, because of this active encouragement and flexible scheduling, parents do attend the meetings. Normally we have 85–100 percent participation in the training/introductory sessions. Parents leave the sessions with informational packets, enough passages for one month, and log forms on which they record their work with their children. Each month from October through May, teachers send home new sets of readings and new log sheets. They also write and distribute a newsletter in which common questions and concerns about the program are answered, the program is reexplained, other activities related to reading are described, and grade-appropriate books for children are listed. Figures 11.3 and 11.4 show examples of Fast Start materials.

Parent participation in Fast Start has been exceptionally high, and student growth in reading is apparent. In as little as one month we have detected noticeable and significant improvement in students' reading and word recognition when compared with students who were not part of the Fast Start program but were receiving extra tutoring in reading.

The program is relatively inexpensive and time efficient. The major cost is duplication, and the major time commitment for teachers is in the initial training sessions. Fast Start has demonstrated to us that parents really do want to help their children in reading. In many cases they just don't know what to do or what materials and programs to choose. When schools get parents involved in a systematic way, using effective methods of instruction and providing support, materials, and communication, children will make substantial and significant progress as readers.

Backpack Programs

Providing books, materials, and activities is critical to successful parent involvement. Backpack programs, in which students bring the materials and activities home with them, capitalize on this characteristic. Ray Reutzel and Parker Fawson (1990) describe a program they used in their own classrooms to promote writing (see Figures 11.5 and 11.6).

Reutzel and Fawson call their program Traveling Tales. In this approach teachers develop a backpack that contains materials for writing, from various types of paper, to rulers and paper clips, to a letter of introduction and direction for parents. The letter explains the program and invites parents to write a story with their children. It provides details for parents and children about the various stages of the writing process. When the writing is complete, parents come to school with their child so that they can share the story. Then the backpack is sent home with the next child. Reutzel and Fawson found that parents were eager for specific guidance in working with their children and valued close working relationships with school personnel.

Although the Reutzel and Fawson model focuses on writing, such an approach can be readily adapted for reading at any elementary grade level. Teachers need to decide what sort of activity to invite parents and children to do together, gather materials that will allow parents and children to complete the activity successfully at home, provide appropriate direc-

Fast Start in Reading
Newsletter #1
Timothy Rasinski
Kent State University

Welcome to the **Fast Start in Reading** program. **Fast Start** is a simple yet effective way for parents to help their first grade children get off to a fast start in reading. Together with the instruction in reading your child receives in school, the Fast Start program helps to lay a solid foundation for continual growth and enjoyment in reading for your child. Parents are important and in Fast Start parents are asked to work with their children a few minutes each day in a way that is enjoyable for both parents and children.

Fast Start employs short, highly readable passages that children will learn easily. Familiar rhymes, poetry, and other fun-to-read short passages form the core of materials that parents and children read in Fast Start.

The key activities in Fast Start are actually quite simple and easy to follow. We ask that you follow these four steps in every lesson.

1)   Read the passage to your child.
2)   Read the passage with your child.
3)   Listen to your child read to you.
4)   Choose and practice words from the passage.

This four step procedure has been found to be extremely effective, in conjunction with regular classroom instruction, in helping children learn to read at an accelerated pace and diminishing the need for corrective or remedial instruction. Children who have been in the Fast Start program for as little as 4 weeks have demonstrated marked improvements in their reading as measured by various reading tests.

General Plan for Fast Start

In the Fast Start program, parents are asked to work with their children for about 10 minutes per day, every day. We realize that it isn't possible to work every single day with your child. Nevertheless, we want to set this as a goal and hope that all parents involved in Fast Start will be able to work with their first-grade child as much as possible.

We ask that you work with your child every day for about 10 minutes. The schedule for introducing new passages is as follows:

Monday: Introduce and read new reading passage or rhyme.
Tuesday: Introduce and read a second new passage.
Wednesday: Review and reread passages from Monday and Tuesday.
Thursday: Introduce and read a third new passage.
Friday: Introduce and read a fourth new passage.
Saturday and Sunday: Review passages introduced during the week.

We hope you will be able to keep as close to this schedule as possible throughout the year. Although you are asked to work each day with your child, the amount of time you need to devote to the Fast Start readings is only about 10 minutes. Remember, one of the most important aspects of this program–one that accounts for children's great progress in reading–is the consistent, daily interaction between parent and child in reading.

In addition to doing the Fast Start program with your child throughout the school year, it is important that parents encourage and invite their children into reading in other ways as well. These other ways include reading interesting books to your child every day, making regular visits to the library to allow your child to choose books, having plenty of books and other reading materials around your home for you child to read, allowing your child to write by keeping a journal or diary, composing letters and notes to others, writing his or her own stories, providing your child with interesting experiences and discussing them with your child, and allowing your child to dictate stories to you that you then write down and read together. Above all, make sure your child knows that **you think reading is important and fun.** The best way to share your enthusiasm is to read to your child every day and talk about what you read together.

Figure 11.3
Fast Start in Reading Newsletter.

tions for the activity to parents, and develop a management system that will allow every family to have access to the backpack for enough time to complete the activity.

Many teachers have found backpack programs to be a great way to introduce parents to more extensive parental involvement activities. But even if this is the only type of parental involvement that a teacher or school offers, everyone benefits. Parents are provided with solid and enjoyable reading and writing activities as well as appropriate directions and materials. And children read and write in the warm, supportive environment of their home with their parents.

While parental involvement may not be a cure-all for every difficulty that children encounter in reading, we know that it does make a difference—in some cases, a huge difference. Whether you are a classroom teacher or a special reading teacher, we strongly recommend that you try and try again to involve parents actively in children's literacy development. The potential benefits are simply too great to ignore.

Daily Fast Start Lesson

Parents: Please
1) Read the rhyme to your child
2) Read it with your child
3) Listen to your child read
4) Word play—write interesting words from the rhyme on this sheet; expand to other related words (dock—sock, rock, block)

Hickory, dickory, dock,
The mouse ran up the clock.
The clock struck one,
The mouse ran down,
Hickory, dickory, dock.

Figure 11.4
Daily Fast Start Lesson.

Dear Parent(s),

Home writing activities are a great way to improve your child's reading and writing development. Traveling Tales is a backpack that includes a variety of writing materials for you to use with your child. We encourage you to work together with your child to create a story that we can share and enjoy at school.

Your child has been given this backpack for two nights. If you need more time, please call us at 672-2836.

We hope these guidelines will help you have a successful and enjoyable Traveling Tales experience with you child.

1. With your child brainstorm a list of ideas or topics for writing. Ask questions that will invite your child to express ideas, interests, feelings, etc., about which he or she may wish to write. Stories about personal experiences (factual or fictional), information stories that tell of an area that your child finds interesting, stories about family members or others, and stories of science or history are great topics.

2. Next, help your child decide which of the writing materials included in the Traveling Tales backpack he or she will need to use to create the story. Suggest that the story may take several different forms. Some ideas include: (a) poetry, (b) fold-out book, (c) a play or skit, (d) puppet play, (e) dialogue, (f) pocket book, (g) backward book, and (h) shape book.

3. Help your child plan the story before beginning writing. You may wish to write down some of the ideas your child expresses for him or her to use in writing the first draft.

4. Remember, your child's first draft is a rough draft. It is all right for it to contain misspellings, poor handwriting, and incomplete ideas. Be available to answer questions as your child works on the first draft. Be careful to encourage him or her to keep writing and not worry about spelling, punctuation, etc. Ask your child just to do his or her best. Both of you can work on correctness later. Now is the time to develop ideas for writing.

5. Once the first draft is done, try to involve others at home by asking them to listen to it read aloud. Reading one's writing aloud helps writers determine the sense of the message. Be sure to tell those who listen to be encouraging rather than critical, and ask questions about ideas that were unclear or were poorly developed. Questions help a writer think about his or her writing without feeling bad.

6. Write out questions and suggestions made by the home audience. Talk with your child about how a second draft could use these suggestions to make the story easier to understand or more interesting. Remember to be supportive and encouraging! Offer your help, but encourage your child to make his or her best own efforts first.

7. After the second draft is completed, your child may want to read his or her writing to the family again for their response. If not, it is time to edit the writing. Now is the time to correct spellings, punctuation, etc. Praise your child for his or her attempts and tell your child that you want to help make his or her writing the best it can be. Show your child which words are misspelled and explain why. Do the same with punctuation and capitalization.

8. With the editing complete, the writing is ready to be revised for the final time. When writing the final draft, encourage your child to use neat handwriting. Feel free to help your child at any point during final revisions.

9. Once finished, encourage your family to listen to the final story and respond positively. This practice will help instill confidence in your child as he or she shares his or her writing at school.

10. We invite you to come to school with your child, if possible, to share the writing you have done together. Your child will appreciate the support and we would enjoy talking with you.

Thank you for your help. We appreciate your involvement. If you are unable to come to school with your child, please call us or send a note with your child. We will be glad to call back or visit with you. Thanks again for your support. We hope you enjoy writing with your child!

Sincerely,
Ms. Robinson

Figure 11.5
Traveling Tales instructions.

Source: Adapted from Reutzel, D. R., & Fawson, P. C. (1990). Traveling Tales: Connecting parents and children through writing. *Reading Teacher, 44,* 222–227.

Materials for the Traveling Tales Backpack

Instructions and ideas in a notebook	Small stapler
Plain unlined paper	Staples
Lined paper	Brass fasteners
Construction paper—multiple colors	Card stock
Drawing paper	Hole punch
Poster paper	Yarn
Crayons	Wallpaper for book covers
Watercolors	Glue stick
Water-base markers	Tape
Colored pencils	Paperclips
Pencils	Ruler
Felt-tip pens	Letter stencils
Scissors	Examples of other books done by students and parents

Figure 11.6
Contents of the Traveling Tales backpack.
Source: Adapted from Reutzel, D. R., & Fawson, P. C. (1990). Traveling Tales: Connecting parents and children through writing. *Reading Teacher, 44,* 222-227.

Chapter 12

Determining Instructional Needs: Observing Readers in Action

Sally Burtch's elementary school decided to create a pre-first-grade class for students thought to be at-risk for success in first grade. Sally volunteered to teach the class. During the summer before the new program began, Sally gathered available information about the children who would be in the class: their readiness test scores and brief anecdotal notes from their kindergarten teachers. As Sally examined the children's records, she realized that she had a problem—she didn't really know any of her students as readers or people. She worried about creating a classroom environment that would respond to children's needs because she had no clear ideas about what those needs might be.

As she reflected on this problem, Sally considered what kind of information she needed about the children and how best to gather it. She didn't believe that test scores would provide all the answers because "when we contrive a reading or writing task, setting the topic and the purposes for reading or writing, what we observe may bear little resemblance to students' natural reading and writing behavior" (Rhodes & Dudley-Marling, 1988, p. 36). Instead, Sally decided that she wanted information about children as readers in naturally occurring classroom reading situations.

The kindergarten teachers' anecdotal notes provided some of this information. Nevertheless, although she valued her colleagues' opinions, Sally knew that her classroom would be different than theirs and that classroom contexts influence children's actions as readers. She also knew that her students would change over the summer.

Sally finally decided to create a reading portfolio for each student. An artist's portfolio is a sample of work collected to demonstrate the artist's breadth, depth, and flexibility. Likewise, a reader's portfolio is a sample of information about the reader. During the first few weeks of school, Sally began to develop reading portfolios for each child by observing, talking, and collecting reading and writing samples. During choice time, for example, she watched to see who would choose to read or write. During read-aloud time, she noted who paid attention and appeared to enjoy the story. She talked with children to discover their interest in books; these conversations also allowed her to evaluate their oral language development. She combined the insights she developed with other available information, such as the kindergarten teacher's notes and standardized test scores. In this way, she gained an in-depth and valuable perspective about each student as a reader and a person, which helped her develop a literacy program responsive to children's needs and interests.

Sally's situation was a bit atypical; after all, she was planning a new program. In many ways, however, her problem is one we all face. We need ways to find out about students as readers—what kinds of instructional opportunities to provide for them, what progress they are making, and what that progress means in terms of future instruction. These are important issues for all students but are particularly critical for children who find reading difficult.

We believe that observing at-risk readers in action is a valuable way to find out about them as readers. In earlier chapters, we described reading as the process of constructing meaning. We also detailed several factors that influence reading, such as background knowledge, perceived purpose, instructional expectations, and type of materials or activities. All these factors vary among children, of course. But even for one child, they may vary throughout the school day or from one day to the next. This variation provides a strong rationale for observing at-risk readers in action.

In this chapter we develop that rationale. Then we describe several informal, classroom-based techniques and strategies for learning about children who find reading difficult. We also provide concrete suggestions for implementing each technique. Our overall goal is to present several systematic assessment and evaluation strategies that can serve as alternatives or additions to formal and informal tests. Rich descriptions of children involved in the day-to-day business of being readers can yield useful instructional insights.

The Classroom As Setting, the Reader As Informant

More and more often, teachers are turning to informal, in-process assessment and evaluation techniques to help them understand at-risk readers. This shift is partly due to advances in our understandings about the processes of reading and learning to read. We know that the reading process is fluid and flexible rather than static. We also know that children become readers in a variety of ways, with different learning tempos, and by using different strategies and styles when interacting with text.

For these reasons, many teachers and reading researchers (for example, Harp, 1994; Rhodes & Shanklin, 1993; Valencia & Pearson, 1987) question the assumptions that underlie standardized tests. They ask, "If the reading process is fluid and growth in reading ability idiosyncratic, how can a single measure designed to compare students with each other (or to some prescribed set of expectations) provide useful instructional information?" Like many others seeking to understand at-risk readers, we think the answer is simple: Standardized tests alone cannot do the job. They don't help teachers understand and assist children who find reading difficult.

Fortunately, alternatives are available. In developing many of the techniques and strategies described in this chapter, we have borrowed ideas from naturalistic inquiry and qualitative research methods. The goal of naturalistic inquiry is to understand something in the way that those involved in the activity do. Thus, our goal is to understand reading from the child's perspective. To achieve this goal, we need an evaluation plan.

A first step in developing the plan involves deciding where assessment should take place and what kinds of reading tasks children should complete as part of the assessment. We recommend that assessment and evaluation take place *in* the classroom rather than outside it. Moreover, assessment should focus on authentic (classroom-like) reading activities rather than artificial ones. Ideally, assessment and evaluation should be natural parts of the continuous learning process in classrooms. Indeed, good assessment methods maximize instruction and involve children in real reading activities.

Next, we must decide whose opinions to seek. Because he is an active participant in the classroom who knows students and activities better than anyone else, a knowledgeable teacher may be the best evaluator. But the teacher shouldn't be the only evaluator; at-risk readers should have some say in evaluating their own growth. In fact, students' ideas and opinions are crucial information in any assessment or evaluation. Self-evaluation can benefit both students and the teacher. Yetta Goodman (1989) explains the process and the benefits:

> Students help by keeping records about their own learning experiences and meeting with the teacher in conferences to evaluate what they have accomplished and what goals they hope to achieve, planning with the teacher how these are to be met. In this manner, the teacher helps kids learn about themselves and their capabilities. Simultaneously teachers reflect on their own development as they see their practices and plans reflected in their students' responses to learning. (p. 13)

These ideas make good conceptual sense, and they also allay some of our concerns about conventional evaluation techniques. But acknowledging the good sense of the ideas is not enough. We must also find ways to implement them. Assessment and evaluation plans aimed at creating reading portfolios for children who find reading difficult can provide a framework for successful implementation.

The Value of Portfolio Assessment

Portfolios can document what at-risk readers think and do in situations involving reading. Teachers who use portfolios do not intend to test and measure students. Rather, they want to inquire—to look "more closely at the thought, language, and skill children bring to their . . . attempts to read" (Chittendon & Courtney, 1989, p. 108). They formulate questions about at-risk readers and look to naturally occurring events in their classrooms to provide answers. They value the insights and interpretations that emerge from this process and realize that parents, children's previous teachers, and even friends can also be good sources of information about a child.

To implement portfolio assessment successfully takes some initial planning, as the overview in Figure 12.1 shows. First, we must generate questions to be answered. These questions may relate to broad curricular goals or hunches about at-risk readers based on

Figure 12.1
An overview of assessment.

- **Generate questions based on the following:**
  Broad curricular goals
  Observations
  Hunches
- **Decide upon forms of evidence:**
  Observation
  Interaction
  Analysis
- **Develop a systematic and comprehensive plan for gathering information from and with the following sources:**
  Students
  Parents
  Other teachers
  Peers
  Yourself
- **Analyze information:**
  Look for patterns
  Form hypotheses

preliminary observations. Questions may be very general: "What does Janey know about reading? What evidence is there that she is developing as a reader?" Or they may be more specific: "In what areas is Mikey experiencing difficulty in reading?" "What does Ricky do when he encounters an unknown word?" Either way, theoretical understandings about reading and learning are critical. Just as a reading portfolio provides the physical framework for assessment and evaluation, the teacher's theoretical beliefs about reading and learning to read provide the conceptual framework.

Questions provide a focus for deciding upon the contents of the portfolio. The next step in planning involves deciding what kind of evidence belongs in the portfolio and how that evidence should be obtained. A student's reading portfolio might contain anecdotal notes and records of observations, conversations, and interviews; checklists or charts kept by the teacher or the student; and performance samples documenting reading behaviors and abilities. We describe each of these information-collecting techniques later in the chapter.

Whatever the focus and content of portfolios, the plan for gathering information must be systematic and comprehensive. Yetta Goodman (1989) suggests three different student-teacher situations or relationships that are particularly helpful when gathering information for portfolios. The first, *observation,* simply means watching what at-risk readers are doing. Students may be reading alone or working with each other. In either case, the teacher is not directly involved but only observes. The second, *instructional interaction,* may be the most powerful form of evaluation because teachers can probe or talk with students in depth. In the third situation, *analysis,* the teacher elicits information from the student for purposes of evaluation. For example, a teacher might ask a student to read a portion of a book aloud to check word-identification strategies.

Observation, interaction, and analysis are useful ways to collect evidence to be included in a reading portfolio. Each can occur formally; for example, teachers might plan specific times or activities for observation. Each can also occur informally and incidentally as teachers and students naturally come into contact during a school day. They can even occur simultaneously: Observing an interesting situation might lead to interaction and analysis as the teacher seeks to understand the student more completely.

Standardized tests are often described in terms of their validity and reliability. The value of portfolio assessment can be determined by thinking about the same concepts. An assessment or evaluation is valid if it offers a true picture of the issue under study. Certainly, information about at-risk readers in action in natural classroom settings has the potential to offer true pictures of them as readers. Moreover, the reliability or consistency of data in the portfolio can be ensured by developing a systematic and comprehensive plan for gathering information. Thus, the diagnostic insights that emerge through analysis and interpretation can yield valid and reliable conclusions about readers at-risk.

The Importance of Observation

The best situations for assessing or evaluating at-risk readers' attitudes, thoughts, and behaviors are not separate from day-to-day instruction but integral parts of it. This view of the relationship between assessment and instruction suggests the importance of observation as a tool for understanding at-risk readers. Opportunities for observation are abundant. Over the course of any day, teachers can observe students as readers in a wide variety of instructional situations, from free-choice activities, through informal and incidental encounters with reading, to more formal instructional situations. Thus, "the teacher's observational database is potentially a broad one" (Chittendon & Courtney, 1989, p. 109). We can learn a great deal about at-risk readers by observing them as they read, write, and respond to instruction.

Yetta Goodman calls this approach "kidwatching." The informal name is purposeful because kidwatching is an informal but systematic process that aims to record at-risk readers' naturally occurring behaviors in reading situations. Effective kidwatchers share a few critical beliefs and skills. First, they believe in observation as a valid and valuable tool for learning about at-risk readers. They also believe that their own judgment is critical as they watch what readers do, listen to what they say, and make decisions about what these observations mean. In other words, kidwatchers are comfortable as professional decision makers. Finally, kidwatchers are skilled observers who use several means of gathering and recording information. In the following sections we explore each of these characteristics in more detail.

Why Kidwatching?

There are at least two good answers to this question—one related to the nature of language use, the other to the nature of language learning. Harste, Woodward, & Burke (1984) describe the social nature of language use: "Language, whether oral or written, is a social event of some complexity. Language did not develop because of the existence of one language user, but of two. If we are to understand language, we must see it as an orchestrated transaction between [at least] two language users which has as its intent to convey meaning" (p. 28). Unlike more formal assessment procedures, kidwatching allows a teacher to record these natural and social language events for later examination and analysis.

Language use and language learning are also situational. Language and concepts grow and develop depending on the settings in which they occur and students' experiences in those settings—including interactions with texts, the teacher, and each other (Goodman, 1985b). Therefore, situations for reading assessment should be as close to genuine instructional situations as possible. By altering reading situations, more formal assessment techniques may give us "very good answers to the wrong questions" (Rhodes & Dudley-Marling, 1988, p. 37). Kidwatching allows teachers to explore what happens when at-risk readers interact with genuine texts for real purposes. Moreover, the information derived from this sort of observation is easier to apply to instructional situations.

Professional Judgment in Making Diagnostic Decisions

Through kidwatching, we can learn about students as readers and develop insights about the impact of instruction on their growth. Professional judgment allows us to translate these observations into instructional improvements. Effective kidwatchers are comfortable making educational decisions. They trust their own professional judgment, even in the face of conflicting information. Unfortunately, many teachers lack this faith in their own judgment.

Sue is one such teacher. Not too long ago, we visited an elementary school for a day. During the lunch hour, we overheard a conversation between Sue and John, two fifth-

Sue and John were chatting about the results of the district-mandated testing program.

grade teachers who were chatting about the results of the district-mandated standard-ized testing they had just received. The conversation went something like this:

Sue: I was really surprised by some of these results.
John: Me too.
Sue: Take Andy, for instance. I thought he was a pretty good reader. It seems like he's always got his nose in a book. And the things he shares during our dis-cussions are usually good—pretty insightful, actually.
John: So?
Sue: Well, the test says he's reading at the 18th percentile. I wonder if I should ask Ms. D [the Title I teacher] to take a look at him.

Why didn't Sue trust her own observations about Andy? Why did she assume that he might need extra help in reading? We don't know her well enough to answer these ques-tions, but we suspect that she has not yet learned to trust her own professional judg-ment.

We also suspect that Sue is not alone. Where do these professional insecurities come from? Some people, such as Jerry Harste (1989), believe that researchers, theoreticians, and policymakers have sent negative messages about teachers' professionalism and that we have lost faith in ourselves because of such messages. Another possible cause of our professional uncertainty may be an unexamined belief in the truth of statistical informa-tion such as standardized test scores. Yetta Goodman (1989) notes:

> Because numbers take on an aura of objectivity, which they do not intrinsically deserve,
> statistical data are equated with the development of knowledge and are valued more
> highly than the sense of an informed, committed professional who uses knowledge
> about the students, the community, and the context to make judgments. (p. 6)

Whatever the causes, teachers have traditionally been given little respect as thinkers and decision makers. Therefore, educators who wish to become effective kidwatchers must learn to exercise professional judgment and trust themselves as decision makers. To do so may involve considering, and perhaps altering, two sets of attitudes: attitudes toward themselves and attitudes toward their students.

Teachers who trust their professional judgment are a bit like detectives. They con-stantly and carefully observe, looking for clues that will help them find answers to their questions about students. Like detectives, they base observations on the enormous amount of information they already have about students and the classroom community as well as their interactions with and analyses of students' reading behavior. They are also careful not to jump to conclusions. They continually ask, "What do I think this means? What else might this mean?" As they generate hypotheses about students, they test them out through further observation, interaction, and analysis. Experience with this process helps them learn to trust the results of their efforts.

Evidence of growth is often revealed through students' errors, so teachers' attitudes toward errors are also important. Dictionaries define *error* as "a usually ignorant or unintentional deviation." Wise kidwatchers know better. Although they acknowledge the occasional careless mistake, they view errors as windows to students' current ways of thinking about language. They look for changes in patterns of errors as signs that students are developing as readers.

Brenda, a Title I teacher at the primary level, is a kidwatcher. Early in each school year, she gathers several samples of her students' oral reading behaviors, which she uses to determine how students deal with unknown words—an important developmental hurdle for young readers. Last year, she found that several students were what she called "phonics bound": sounding words out seemed to be their only word identification strategy. Their oral reading errors or miscues tended to look and sound like text words but often changed the author's meaning completely. Some children even made up nonsense words.

Brenda did not assume that these miscues were ignorant or unintentional. Instead, she hypothesized that children were doing what they knew how to do or what they thought they should be doing. So she made a conscious effort to help them broaden their repertoire for identifying words. She emphasized combining context ("what would make sense here?") with what the children already knew about phonics. After several weeks of instruction, Brenda made another informal check of children's word identification strategies. She found evidence of growth in flexible use of strategies. Children were beginning to correct miscues that made no sense or changed the author's meaning.

Several of Brenda's actions and decisions are good examples of professional judgment. First, she understood the importance of gathering data about her Title I students in authentic reading situations. She knew that samples of children's oral reading obtained over several sessions could yield insights about their word identification strategies. Further, she viewed miscues as opportunities to explore how the children were currently organizing things (Goodman, 1985). She saw qualitative differences in errors— that is, patterns of graphophonically similar but nonsense miscues meant something different to her than patterns of self-corrections. In other words, she used her own professional judgment to make diagnostic decisions.

Professional judgment is critical to kidwatching, which in turn is key to effective observation. Professional judgment is at its best when teachers combine their concrete knowledge about the classroom and particular students with their theoretical knowledge about how students learn, what language is, and how language develops. This combination provides a useful framework for observing children who find reading difficult.

Observing Throughout the School Day

Because reading and writing are variable processes, effective kidwatchers are experts at recognizing and interpreting patterns of behavior. They differentiate between recurring behaviors and isolated ones. Patterns become evident when teachers observe over time and in various reading and reading-related activities. Collectively, observations can document at-risk readers' actions and attitudes in a variety of situations and on a variety of days.

This, of course, requires a plan for observation. Merriam (1988) describes general aspects of an event or situation that may be important for an observer to record. She also suggests questions that can help focus the observer's attention.

- **The participants.**   Who's there? What are they doing? How are they working together? Although the at-risk reader's behaviors may be the focal point for observation, it is equally important to note who else is in the general vicinity and what all the participants are doing.

- **Activities and interactions.**   What's going on? What's the sequence of activities? How do people interact with the activity and each other? This is a particularly important aspect of an event or situation to note. Most of us have variable attitudes toward reading; we enjoy some reading activities and dislike others. Our students are no different. When we watch children within the context of particular reading activities, we can often discover the circumstances that promote and detract from positive reading experiences.

- **Frequency and duration.**   How long does the activity last? Does it happen often? These questions can be applied to indicators of student behavior in reading. For example, the teacher might note how frequently an at-risk reader chooses to read during free periods or how long he sustains interest in reading on different days in different situations.

- **Subtle factors.**   What unplanned, spontaneous events occur? What nonverbal signs and signals can be observed? Both these aspects can be revealing. Students who enjoy reading books, for example, may be impatient with disruptions during an SSR period and reluctant to stop reading at the end. Students who enjoy neither reading nor their books may be eager to participate in disruptions and delighted at the end. To understand subtle factors, it may be helpful to talk with a student: "You look puzzled. What's the matter?" Effective kidwatchers are good listeners as well as keen observers.

Attention to all these aspects of classroom reading does not have to be complex or difficult. Observations need not be time consuming; just a few occasional minutes of concentrated effort ought to provide adequate data.

Matt, who offers extra support in the regular classroom for intermediate-grade students with learning disabilities, has been relying on observation for several years. He is particularly interested in watching his students interact with others.

> I watch pretty intensively at the beginning of a school year so I can get a feel for what students might need, and then I do "spot-checks" throughout the year. If I see something that surprises me, either good or bad, I observe more carefully again. It took me a while to get the hang of observing, especially organizing what I'd written, but I am convinced that I now know lots more about my students. And that makes it easier for me to help them, so the time and effort are worth it to me.

Techniques and Strategies

Karen Dalrymple (1989) is a kidwatcher. Here's how she describes the process as it operates in her classroom: "The ability to observe and record student learning, assess that learning, and make decisions about what experiences to offer a student is critical to my teaching. Good records allow easy reporting about an individual student; but they also reflect and store the many observations [a teacher] makes" (p. 115). Good records may take several forms. In this section, we offer advice about specific techniques and strategies that are helpful in observing at-risk readers in action. Information gleaned from any or all of these methods, when added to a student's reading portfolio, adds depth and detail to the picture of the student as a reader.

Anecdotal Notes

One way to learn about a child who finds reading difficult is to keep anecdotal records about informal, unplanned observations and the results of instruction. As all teachers know, classrooms are busy places; without making notes, important incidents can easily be forgotten. Additionally, anecdotal notes can guide instructional planning. We can assess the impact of instruction as we plot students' progress in anecdotal notes and records.

Although any time can be the right time for making anecdotal notes, it's helpful to develop a plan or framework for note taking. Chittendon and Courtney (1989) suggest basing observations on routines in the classroom, those predictable reading or reading-related activities that form the schedule for instruction (see Chapter 2). Using classroom routines as a framework can help teachers make sure that observations will yield a representative sample of how children take advantage of classroom opportunities.

Teachers also need to consider the format for their anecdotal notes and records. Ultimately, this is an individual decision. Each teacher should experiment with formats to determine what will work best for her. There are plenty of options to choose from.

Some teachers keep impressions notebooks where they record general impressions of children (Goodman, 1989) or make brief observations on Post-It notes or large adhesive-backed labels. Later, they expand on their notes and transfer them to students' portfolios. Jacobson (1989) uses a three-column sheet of paper for recording significant anecdotal information in her classroom. The columns are labeled "goals," "observations," and "instructional plans." This format allows her to make both objective ("what do I see or hear?") and subjective ("what do I think this means?") notes, which researchers suggest can yield more useful records (Merriam, 1988; Patton, 1990).

At the Fair Oaks School in Redwood City, California, teachers collaborate to gather and analyze anecdotal information. For example, they occasionally videotape portions of instruction and later view the tapes together to share observations and insights. They also spend time in one another's classrooms and make notes about their observations for later discussion (Bird, 1989). Colleagues, then, can be record-keeping devices, as can videotapes or audiotapes.

Any system or device for recording anecdotal information should first be field-tested to determine the level of specificity to include in notes. Matt, whom we introduced earlier, did this by looking at his notes a couple of weeks after they were taken. In reviewing the notes, he asked himself, "What doesn't make sense any more?" and "What do I want to know more about?" Answers to these questions helped him modify his note-taking strategies to ensure maximum usefulness.

Kidwatchers who are comfortable with their system for recording anecdotal information are convinced of the usefulness of this documentation technique. Teacher Mary

Kitagawa (1989) puts it this way: "In spite of the after-school time they consume, anecdotal records seem to be the most accurate way to document the full picture of students' language development" (p. 108).

Checklists and Charts

Many teachers use checklists or charts to help ensure that their observations of at-risk readers are systematic and organized. For example, they develop charts that reflect curricular goals or specify instructional routines and include blocks of space for recording information about students. As Figures 12.2 and 12.3 show, charts or checklists can be completed by using a coding system or making brief notes.

Betsy, a first-grade teacher, uses both types of charts to provide a systematic focus for observing her students. Because she teaches reading skills only if her students need them, different children attend different mini-lessons on different days. Betsy uses the mini-lesson checklist (Figure 12.2) to record which students attended skill and strategy lessons and evaluate the impact of the lessons on children's reading. For this latter purpose, therefore, she observes carefully during the week after the mini-lesson when children have opportunities to use the new skill or strategy. She then codes the checklist with her conclusions about the children's use of the skill.

The chart in Figure 12.3 is more open-ended. Over the course of several days, Betsy makes brief notes about particular students in the boxes. Later, she elaborates on these notes and files them in students' reading portfolios. She keeps the chart on a clipboard; it is always nearby when she teaches. Betsy also uses the same chart format to explore other aspects of children's behavior and attitudes as readers, such as their engagement with different types of text material or their reactions to different types of activities.

Class Roster	Dates/Types of Mini-lessons			
	9/3 Using Context			
Jenny	NE*			
Peter	D			
Amy	M			
Jimmy	M			
* NE: not evident during the week after the mini-lesson; D: appears to be developing; M: appears to be mastered				

Figure 12.2
Checklist for results of mini-lessons.

Routines	Students				
	Mike	Matthew	Emily	Katy	Mary
SSR					
Sharing SSR books					
Small-group instruction					
Read aloud					
Free choice					
Library visits					

Figure 12.3
Chart for noting influence of instructional routines.

Students can keep checklists or charts about their own reading. They can record insights in reading logs or reading journals and can keep lists of books they have read. Students can also evaluate their own reading habits and behaviors by responding to questions in their logs: "How was my reading today?" and "Why do I think so?" Finally, students can track their progress as strategic readers by maintaining a three-column chart: things I can do well, things I'm working on, and things I plan to learn (Hansen, 1987). Teachers who encourage students to evaluate aspects of their own reading find that this practice has several benefits: Students learn to take control of their reading behavior and become more aware of their growth as readers, and teachers have yet another source of information about students.

Conversations and Interviews

A few summers ago, we worked with Dale, a student who had just completed his first year in middle school. Dale's parents and some of his middle school teachers were concerned about his textbook reading. His parents were perplexed because he'd done all his homework diligently in elementary school. They said that he'd begun the school year with equal diligence but soon stopped reading assignments from his texts. When they asked him why, he always answered, "I don't need to." They feared that the middle school textbooks were too difficult for him.

Terry, Dale's tutor, attempted to determine what aspects of textbook reading were giving Dale trouble. It appeared, however, that the boy was quite capable of reading and studying middle school texts independently. Somewhat exasperated, Terry decided to talk to Dale about the situation. Here's how the conversation went:

Terry:	Your parents are concerned because you didn't read your textbook assignments last year. Did you read them?
Dale:	Well, I did at the beginning of the year, but then I stopped.
Terry:	Why did you stop?
Dale:	I figured, "Why bother?"
Terry:	What made you think that?
Dale:	Well, the teachers always told us all the stuff in the book the next day. I figured it didn't make much sense to do all that reading when they were going to tell us all of it anyway.

As you have probably guessed, this brief conversation was as helpful in understanding Dale's reading behavior as all the informal diagnosis that preceded it. The anecdote underscores the importance of conversations and interviews as ways of gathering information. By asking the right kinds of questions in the right ways and listening carefully to how students respond, teachers can learn about students' actions and attitudes as readers. Sometimes, as with Dale, this information cannot be obtained in any other way.

Other people's perceptions can also be important. Parents and previous teachers, for example, can provide helpful information, as can the regular teacher for children who receive assistance outside the classroom. By talking with students and their "significant educational others," we can add both depth and breadth to our understanding of children as readers.

Behavior during a conversation or interview influences responses. A good interviewer has rapport with the person being interviewed but remains neutral about the content of responses. For example, consider these two questions, each of which might be asked to determine a student's opinion about a book:

"I really liked this book. Didn't you?"
"What did you think about this book?"

The first question offers cues or implicit suggestions about the response the teacher is seeking. To such a question, many students would simply respond yes, regardless of their true feelings. The second question is content-neutral; neither a positive nor a negative response is cued by the question. Neutral questions help create an environment where students know they can share freely. Free sharing is more likely to yield useful, accurate information.

A variety of content-neutral questions can enhance the value of an interview or conversation. Researchers who use interviews as a way to gather information have identified several beneficial types of questions (Merriam, 1988; Patton, 1990). Here are some that work particularly well in attempts to understand at-risk readers:

- **_Experience/behavior questions._**   These questions are aimed at eliciting descriptions that might have been observable had the interviewer been present. Questions might include "What's something you've learned to do in reading?" or "How did it go with this book?" or "What do you do when you come to a word that you don't know? How do you try to figure it out?"

- **_Opinion/value questions._**   These questions can determine what people think and what their goals, intentions, desires, or values are. Such questions include "What's the best book you've read this month? Why did you like it?" and "What would you like to learn so that you can become a better reader?"

- **_Feelings questions._**   These questions are designed to elicit readers' feelings. They include "How do you feel when you run into problems in your reading?" and "Do you like to read? Why?"

- **_Hypothetical/future-oriented questions._**   These are "what if?" questions designed to encourage speculations, including those about the future. Examples include "What if you could choose all the things you read in school? What would you choose?" and "What are your plans for this next month in reading? What do you hope to accomplish?"

- **_Ideal-position questions._**   These questions are related to readers' notions of perfection, such as "What does someone have to do to be a good reader?" or "Who's the best reader you know? What does he do as a reader?"

- **_Interpretive questions._**   These questions generally occur at the end of an interview or conversation. The teacher interprets and summarizes the interview and asks the student to validate the summary: "So would you say that . . . ?" or "You seem to be saying. . . . Is that what you think?"

Questions should guide conversation rather than create a rigid structure.

Conversations and interviews can be planned or spontaneous, focused on a certain aspect of reading or general in their focus. Preparing interview questions beforehand helps ensure that they will be comprehensive, content-neutral, and related to the area of interest. In use, however, questions should guide conversation rather than provide a rigid structure.

Some teachers take notes during interviews. Others prefer to tape-record interviews so that they can actually converse with students. In any event, it's important to prepare written summaries of these conferences about reading and add them to students' reading portfolios.

Performance Samples

Performance samples, as their name suggests, are samples of students' performance as readers. They should also be included in students' reading portfolios. Because performance samples provide tangible evidence, they can complement data gathered through observation and conversations.

Instructional activities can be performance samples included in a student's reading portfolio. For example, reader-response entries from students' reading logs can be evaluated holistically, using procedures similar to holistic evaluation of writing, to explore growth in reading comprehension and response to reading. Writing samples can also document reading-related growth. For example, analyzing a young child's spelling strategies can yield important insights about her graphophonic knowledge. An early piece of writing can also be dictated back to a child. Then the teacher, alone or with the child, can analyze the two pieces looking for evidence of development in spelling and other conventions of written language.

Performance samples can also result from planned, informal reading conferences with students. These are planned conversations between teacher and student that revolve around a book that the student is reading. It's easy for many teachers to accept the theoretical value of basing conferences on real books but less easy, perhaps, to figure out the real-world logistics. For example, what if the student reads a book unfamiliar to the teacher? In such a case, the teacher can evaluate comprehension and response to reading more generically or even read the book at a later time.

Teachers also need to consider how much assistance to give students who encounter problems during the reading conference. We wish to discover what the student can do if left to his own resources. But frustrating students who encounter problems they can't solve independently makes little sense. Our best advice is to wait a second or two and then help if the student still needs it, noting the student's reaction to the assistance. In reviewing records from the conference, the teacher can ask, "Did the student profit from my help? How do I know?"

Reading conferences that last about 10 minutes every month or so should provide sufficient information about at-risk readers, particularly when combined with observational and interview data. Some teachers plan conferences with all their at-risk readers on the same day and then invite an adult helper (parent, grandparent, reading specialist, or the principal) to assist in the classroom on conference days.

Reading conferences offer important opportunities to learn about how at-risk readers interact with text and feel about reading and themselves as readers. Like other kidwatching techniques, the format of the conference can vary according to the teacher's purpose. He might ask the student to read a page or two aloud, for example; or the student and teacher might simply discuss the book. Retelling might be an appropriate activity as well.

Reading conferences can be used to find out about word identification. Teachers can note miscues made during reading on a copy of the text, keep track of them on a separate piece of paper, or tape-record the reading. Ann Marek (1989) tape-records her students' oral reading, prepares a miscue sheet, and selects several miscues to discuss with students. She bases miscue selection on the types of miscues the reader frequently makes. Together Ann and the student listen to the tape and evaluate the miscues in a discussion guided by questions such as these: "Does that one make sense?" or "Why did/didn't you correct that one?"

Should a student decide to reread a book, comparing the two tape-recorded versions can provide evidence of increased fluency or changes in sight vocabulary or word identification strategies. Jacobson (1989) asks students to evaluate changes in their own reading by listening to tapes of the same book made at different times so that they become more aware of their growth as readers.

Figure 12.4 provides a framework for recording information from a reading conference. Completed charts, which offer comprehensive summaries of reading conferences, should be placed in students' reading portfolios.

In this chapter we have described both why and how to observe at-risk readers in action. We have encouraged teachers to be kidwatchers, to observe and talk with at-risk readers to understand their behaviors and attitudes as readers in the context of the classroom. The resulting data should be used to create reading portfolios for students.

A final question about portfolio assessment relates to the quantity of evidence needed. When we talk with teachers about portfolios, they frequently ask, "How much information should I gather?" Our answer: "Enough to answer your questions." We don't mean to be flippant. Rather, our answer underscores the importance of questions that provide focus for evaluation and assessment and the variable nature of reading behaviors and reading growth.

Sally, whom we described at the beginning of the chapter, used many of the ideas we have outlined to create a systematic and comprehensive plan for observing her pre–first-grade students in action. She says:

> I was interested in both a broad look, so I could get to know the kids, and some specific information that could guide instruction. When I tried to summarize all the information I had, I found some unevenness in students' behaviors and attitudes. But then I thought, "Well, we all have reading behaviors; we all have reading attitudes. Why should the kids be any different?"

Sally's goal became to gather data until patterns of strength and interest in different situations became apparent, until her questions about children had been answered. Thus, "enough was enough" for her when patterns became evident.

Student _____

Date   _____

Book   _____

Choice/Background (Why was this book chosen? How familiar does the student seem to be with the book?)

_____

_____

Interests/Attitudes (Does the student seem anxious or relaxed? What evidence is there that the student is interested in the book?)

_____

_____

Understanding (What evidence is there that the student understands the author's message—spontaneous remarks, comprehension monitoring, response to discussion?)

_____

_____

_____

_____

Problem-solving Strategies (How does the student solve problems encountered while reading? How does he or she maintain momentum? What is the student's strategy for identifying unknown words?)

Miscue	Text	Notes

Figure 12.4
Observations from individual reading conferences.

Source: Adapted from Chittendon, E., & Courtney, R. (1989). Assessment of young children's reading: Documentation as an alternative to testing. In D. S. Strickland & L. M. Morrow (Eds.), *Emerging literacy: Young children learn to read and write* (pp. 107–120). Newark, DE: International Reading Association.

To find patterns and answer questions requires an open mind and a reflective posture. As Sally reviewed the contents of her students' reading portfolios, she thought about the evidence of learning using a problem-solving process that involved induction—the parts-to-whole search for patterns of behavior and attitudes. "I really tried to keep an open mind," she remarked. "I didn't want to jump to conclusions. I wanted to find the patterns." She found patterns and used them to form hypotheses about the children. She checked the value of these hypotheses in two ways. First, she reviewed the contents of the portfolio one more time, looking for evidence that did not fit her hypotheses. When she found evidence, she reconsidered her thinking. "Sometimes I changed my mind and sometimes I didn't," she commented. "But it was always worth it to think things through again." If she didn't find conflicting evidence, she checked the hypotheses with further observation. This, too, sometimes led her to modify her conclusions about children.

Good teachers have always acknowledged the potential of observation as a tool for understanding their students. Nevertheless, because of the many demands on teachers' time and thoughts during a school day, observational data have often gone unrecorded. The processes and procedures in this chapter should help teachers develop a workable plan for observing, understanding, and helping students who find reading difficult.

Award-winning Books

Caldecott Award

Since 1938, the Association of Library Service to Children of the American Library Association has annually awarded the Caldecott Medal to the illustrator of the most distinguished picture book published in the United States in the preceding year. The recipient must be a citizen or resident of the United States. The medal was named in tribute to well-known English illustrator Randolph Caldecott (1846–1886).

1995   *Smoky Night* by Eve Bunting, ill. by David Diaz, Harcourt Brace. **Honor Books:** *Swamp Angel* by Anne Issacs, ill. by Paul O. Zelinsky, Dutton; *John Henry* by Julius Lester, ill. by Jerry Pinkney, Dial; *Time Flies* written and ill. by Eric Rohmann, Crown.

1994   *Grandfather's Journey* written and ill. by Allen Say, Houghton Mifflin. **Honor Books:** *In the Small Small Pond* written and ill. by Denise Fleming, Holt; *Owen* written and ill. by Kevin Henkes, Greenwillow; *Peppe the Lamplighter* by Elise Bartone, ill. by Ted Lewin, Lothrop; *Raven: A Trickster Tale* written and ill. by Gerald McDermott, Harcourt Brace; *Yo! Yes?* written and ill. by Chris Raschka, Orchard.

1993   *Mirette on the High Wire* written and ill. by Emily Arnold McCully, Putnam. **Honor Books:** *The Stinky Cheese Man* by Jon Scieszka, ill. by Lane Smith, Viking; *Working Cotton* by Sherley Anne Williams, ill. by Carole Byard, Harcourt Brace; *Seven Blind Mice* written and ill. by Ed Young, Philomel.

1992.   *Tuesday* written and ill. by David Wiesner, Clarion. **Honor Book:** *Tar Beach* written and ill. by Faith Ringgold, Crown

1991   *Black and White* written and ill. by David Macaulay, Houghton Mifflin. **Honor Books:** *"More More More," Said the Baby: 3 Love Stories* written and ill. by Vera B. Williams, Greenwillow; *Puss in Boots* by Charles Perrault, tr. by Malcolm Arthur, ill. by Fred Marcellino, Farrar, Straus.

1990   *A Red Riding-Hood Story* by Lon Po Po, tr. and ill. by Ed Young, Philomel. **Honor Books:** *Bill Peet: An Autobiography* written and ill. by Bill Peet, Houghton Mifflin; *Color Zoo* written and ill. by Lois Ehlert, HarperCollins; *Hershel and the Hanukkah Goblins* by Eric Kimmel, ill. by Trina Schart Hyman, Holiday; *The Talking Eggs* by Robert D. San Souci, ill. by Jerry Pinkney, Dial.

1989   *Song and Dance Man* by Karen Ackerman, ill. by Stephen Gammell, Knopf. **Honor Books:** *Free Fall* written and ill. by David Wiesner, Lothrop; *Goldilocks and the Three Bears* retold and ill.

by James Marshall, Dial; *Mirandy and Brother Wind* by Patricia McKissack, ill. by Jerry Pinkney, Knopf; *The Boy of the Three-Year Nap* by Diane Snyder, ill. by Allen Say, Houghton Mifflin.

1988 *Owl Moon* by Jane Yolen, ill. by John Schoenherr, Philomel. **Honor Book:** *Mufaro's Beautiful Daughters* written and ill. by John Steptoe, Lothrop.

1987 *Hey, Al!* by Arthur Yorinks, ill. by Richard Egielski, Farrar, Straus. **Honor Books:** *The Village of Round and Square Houses* written and ill. by Ann Grifalconi, Little, Brown; *Alphabetics* written and ill. by Suse MacDonald, Bradbury; *Rumpelstiltskin* retold and ill. by Paul O. Zelinsky, Dutton.

1986 *The Polar Express* written and ill. by Chris Van Allsburg, Houghton Mifflin. **Honor Books:** *The Relatives Came* by Cynthia Rylant, ill. by Stephen Gammell, Bradbury; *King Bidgood's in the Bathtub* by Audrey Wood, ill. by Don Wood, Harcourt Brace.

1985 *St. George and the Dragon* retold by Margaret Hodges, ill. by Trina Schart Hyman, Little, Brown. **Honor Books:** *Hansel and Gretel* retold by Rika Lesser, ill. by Paul O. Zelinsky, Dodd, Mead; *Have You Seen My Duckling?* by Nancy Tafuri, Greenwillow; *The Story of Jumping Mouse* by John Steptoe, Lothrop.

1984 *The Glorious Flight: Across the Channel with Louis Blériot* by Alice Provensen and Martin Provensen, Viking. **Honor Books:** *Ten, Nine, Eight* by Molly Bang, Greenwillow; *Little Red Riding Hood* retold and ill. by Trina Schart Hyman, Holiday.

1983 *Shadow* by Blaise Cendrars, tr. and ill. by Marcia Brown, Scribner. **Honor Books:** *When I Was Young in the Mountains* by Cynthia Rylant, ill. by Diane Goode, Dutton; *A Chair for My Mother* by Vera B. Williams, Greenwillow.

1982 *Jumanji* written and ill. by Chris Van Allsburg, Houghton Mifflin. **Honor Books:** *Where the Buffaloes Begin* by Olaf Baker, ill. by Stephen Gammell, Warne; *On Market Street* by Arnold Lobel, ill. by Anita Lobel, Greenwillow; *Outside Over There* by Maurice Sendak, Harper & Row; *A Visit to William Blake's Inn* by Nancy Willard, ill. by Alice Provensen and Martin Provensen, Harcourt Brace.

1981 *Fables* written and ill. by Arnold Lobel, Harper & Row. **Honor Books:** *The Grey Lady and the Strawberry Snatcher* ill. by Molly Bang, Four Winds; *Truck* ill. by Donald Crews, Greenwillow; *Mice Twice* written and ill. by Joseph Low, Atheneum; *The Bremen-Town Musicians* ill. by Ilse Plume, Doubleday.

1980 *Ox-Cart Man* by Donald Hall, ill. by Barbara Cooney, Viking. **Honor Books:** *Ben's Trumpet* written and ill. by Rachel Isadora, Greenwillow; *The Garden of Abdul Gasazi* written and ill. by Chris Van Allsburg, Houghton Mifflin.

1979 *The Girl Who Loved Wild Horses* written and ill. by Paul Goble, Bradbury. **Honor Books:** *Freight Train* written and ill. by Donald Crews, Greenwillow; *The Way to Start a Day* by Byrd Baylor, ill. by Peter Parnall, Scribner.

1978 *Noah's Ark,* ill. by Peter Spier, Doubleday. **Honor Books:** *Castle* written and ill. by David Macaulay, Houghton Mifflin; *It Could Always Be Worse* retold and ill. by Margot Zemach, Farrar, Straus.

1977 *Ashanti to Zulu: African Traditions* by Margaret Musgrove, ill. by Leo Dillon and Diane Dillon, Dial. **Honor Books:** *The Amazing Bone* written and ill. by William Steig, Farrar, Straus; *The Contest* retold and ill. by Nonny Hogrogian, Greenwillow; *Fish for Supper* written and ill. by M. B. Goffstein, Dial; *The Golem* written and ill. by Beverly Brodsky McDermott, Lippincott; *Hawk, I'm Your Brother* by Byrd Baylor, ill. by Peter Parnall, Scribner.

1976 *Why Mosquitoes Buzz in People's Ears* retold by Verna Aardema, ill. by Leo Dillon and Diane Dillon, Dial. **Honor Books:** *The Desert Is Theirs* by Byrd Baylor, ill. by Peter Parnall, Scribner; *Strega Nona* retold and ill. by Tomie dePaola, Prentice Hall.

1975 *Arrow to the Sun* adapted and ill. by Gerald McDermott, Viking. **Honor Book:** *Jambo Means Hello* by Muriel Feelings, ill. by Tom Feelings, Dial.

1974 *Duffy and the Devil* by Harve Zemach, ill. by Margot Zemach, Farrar, Straus. **Honor Books:** *Three Jovial Huntsmen* written and ill. by Susan Jeffers, Bradbury; *Cathedral: The Story of Its Construction* written and ill. by David Macaulay, Houghton Mifflin.

1973 *The Funny Little Woman* retold by Arlene Mosel, ill. by Blair Lent, Dutton. **Honor Books:** *Anansi the Spider* adapted and ill. by Gerald McDermott, Holt; *Hosie's Alphabet* by Hosea, Tobias, and Lisa Baskin, ill. by Leonard Baskin, Viking; *Snow White and the Seven Dwarfs* tr. by Randall Jarrell, ill. by Nancy Ekholm Burkert, Farrar, Straus; *When Clay Sings* by Byrd Baylor, ill. by Tom Bahti, Scribner.

1972 *One Fine Day* written and ill. by Nonny Hogrogian, Macmillan. **Honor Books:** *If All the Seas Were One Sea* written and ill. by Janina Domanska, Macmillan; *Moja Means One: Swahili Counting Book* by Muriel Feelings, ill. by Tom Feelings, Dial; *Hildilid's Night* by Cheli Duran Ryan, ill. by Arnold Lobel, Macmillan.

1971 *A Story, A Story* written and ill. by Gail E. Haley, Atheneum. **Honor Books:** *The Angry Moon* by William Sleator, ill. by Blair Lent, Atlantic/Little; *Frog and Toad Are Friends* written and ill. by Arnold Lobel, Harper & Row; *In the Night Kitchen* written and ill. by Maurice Sendak, Harper & Row.

1970 *Sylvester and the Magic Pebble* written and ill. by William Steig, Windmill. **Honor Books:** *Goggles!* written and ill. by Ezra Jack Keats, Macmillan; *Alexander and the Wind-Up Mouse* written and ill. by Leo Lionni, Pantheon; *Pop Corn and Ma Goodness* by Edna Mitchell Preston, ill. by Robert Andrew Parker, Viking; *Thy Friend, Obadiah* written and ill. by Brinton Turkle, Viking; *The Judge* by Harve Zemach, ill. by Margot Zemach, Farrar, Straus.

1969 *The Fool of the World and the Flying Ship* by Arthur Ransome, ill. by Uri Shulevitz, Farrar, Straus. **Honor Book:** *Why the Sun and the Moon Live in the Sky* by Elphinstone Dayrell, ill. by Blair Lent, Houghton Mifflin.

1968 *Drummer Hoff* by Barbara Emberley, ill. by Ed Emberley, Prentice Hall. **Honor Books:** *Frederick* written and ill. by Leo Lionni, Pantheon; *Seashore Story,* written and ill. by Taro Yashima, Viking; *The Emperor and the Kite* by Jane Yolen, ill. by Ed Young, World.

1967 *Sam, Bangs & Moonshine* written and ill. by Evaline Ness, Holt. **Honor Book:** *One Wide River to Cross* by Barbara Emberley, ill. by Ed Emberley, Prentice Hall.

1966 *Always Room for One More* by Sorche Nic Leodhas, ill. by Nonny Hogrogian, Holt. **Honor Books:** *Hide and Seek Fog* by Alvin Tresselt, ill. by Roger Duvoisin, Lothrop; *Just Me* written and ill. by Marie Hall Ets, Viking; *Tom Tit Tot* written and ill. by Evaline Ness, Scribner.

1965 *May I Bring a Friend?* by Beatrice Schenk de Regniers, ill. by Beni Montresor, Atheneum. **Honor Books:** *Rain Makes Applesauce* by Julian Scheer, ill. by Marvin Bileck, Holiday; *The Wave* by Margaret Hodges, ill. by Blair Lent, Houghton Mifflin; *A Pocketful of Cricket* by Rebecca Caudill, ill. by Evaline Ness, Holt.

1964   *Where the Wild Things Are* written and ill. by Maurice Sendak, Harper & Row. **Honor Books:** *Swimmy* written and ill. by Leo Lionni, Pantheon; *All in the Morning Early* by Sorche Nic Leodhas, ill. by Evaline Ness, Holt; *Mother Goose and Nursery Rhymes* ill. by Philip Reed, Atheneum.

1963   *The Snowy Day* written and ill. by Ezra Jack Keats, Viking. **Honor Books:** *The Sun Is a Golden Earring* by Natalie M. Belting, ill. by Bernarda Bryson, Holt; *Mr. Rabbit and the Lovely Present* by Charlotte Zolotow, ill. by Maurice Sendak, Harper & Row.

1962   *Once a Mouse . . .* written and ill. by Marcia Brown, Scribner. **Honor Books:** *The Fox Went Out on a Chilly Night* written and ill. by Peter Spier, Doubleday; *Little Bear's Visit* by Else Holmelund Minarik, ill. by Maurice Sendak, Harper & Row; *The Day We Saw the Sun Come Up* by Alice E. Goudey, ill. by Adrienne Adams, Scribner.

1961   *Baboushka and the Three Kings* by Ruth Robbins, ill. by Nicolas Sidjakov, Parnassus. **Honor Book:** *Inch by Inch* written and ill. by Leo Lionni, Obolensky.

1960   *Nine Days to Christmas* by Marie Hall Ets and Aurora Labastida, ill. by Marie Hall Ets, Viking. **Honor Books:** *Houses from the Sea* by Alice E. Goudey, ill. by Adrienne Adams, Scribner; *The Moon Jumpers* by Janice May Udry, ill. by Maurice Sendak, Harper .

1959   *Chanticleer and the Fox* adapted from Chaucer, ill. by Barbara Cooney, Crowell. **Honor Books:** *The House That Jack Built* written and ill. by Antonio Frasconi, Harcourt Brace; *What Do You Say, Dear?* by Sesyle Joslin, ill. by Maurice Sendak, Scott; *Umbrella* written and ill. by Taro Yashima, Viking.

1958   *Time of Wonder* written and ill. by Robert McCloskey, Viking. **Honor Books:** *Fly High, Fly Low* written and ill. by Donald Freeman, Viking; *Anatole and the Cat* by Eve Titus, ill. by Paul Galdone, McGraw-Hill.

1957   *A Tree Is Nice* by Janice May Udry, ill. by Marc Simont, Harper. **Honor Books:** *Mr. Penny's Race Horse* written and ill. by Marie Hall Ets, Viking; *I Is One* written and ill. by Tasha Tudor, Walck; *Anatole* by Eve Titus, ill. by Paul Galdone, McGraw-Hill; *Gillespie and the Guards* by Benjamin Elkin, ill. by James Daugherty, Viking; *Lion* written and ill. by William Pène du Bois, Viking.

1956   *Frog Went A–Courtin'* ed. by John Langstaff, ill. by Feodor Rojankovsky, Harcourt Brace. **Honor Books:** *Play with Me* written and ill. by Marie Hall Ets, Viking; *Crow Boy* written and ill. by Taro Yashima, Viking.

1955   *Cinderella, or the Little Glass Slipper* by Charles Perrault, tr. and ill. by Marcia Brown, Scribner. **Honor Books:** *Book of Nursery and Mother Goose Rhymes* ill. by Marguerite de Angeli, Doubleday; *Wheel on the Chimney* by Margaret Wise Brown, ill. by Tibor Gergely, Lippincott; *The Thanksgiving Story* by Alice Dalgliesh, ill. by Helen Sewell, Scribner.

1954   *Madeline's Rescue* written and ill. by Ludwig Bemelmans, Viking. **Honor Books:** *Journey Cake, Ho!* by Ruth Sawyer, ill. by Robert McCloskey, Viking; *When Will the World Be Mine?* by Miriam Schlein, ill. by Jean Charlot, Scott; *The Steadfast Tin Soldier* by Hans Christian Andersen, ill. by Marcia Brown, Scribner; *A Very Special House* by Ruth Krauss, ill. by Maurice Sendak, Harper; *Green Eyes* written and ill. by A. Birnbaum, Capitol.

1953   *The Biggest Bear* written and ill. by Lynd Ward, Houghton Mifflin. **Honor Books:** *Puss in Boots* by Charles Perrault, ill. and tr. by Marcia Brown, Scribner; *One Morning in Maine* written and ill. by Robert McCloskey, Viking; *Ape in a Cape* written and ill. by Fritz Eichenberg, Harcourt; *The Storm Book* by Charlotte Zolotow, ill. by Margaret Bloy Graham, Harper & Row; *Five Little Monkeys* written and ill. by Juliet Kepes, Houghton Mifflin.

1952   *Finders Keepers* by Will, ill. by Nicolas, Harcourt Brace. **Honor Books:** *Mr. T. W. Anthony Woo* written and ill. by Marie Hall Ets, Viking; *Skipper John's Cook* written and ill. by Marcia Brown, Scribner; *All Falling Down* by Gene Zion, ill. by Margaret Bloy Graham, Harper; *Bear Party* written and ill. by Willian Pène du Bois, Viking; *Feather Mountain* written and ill. by Elizabeth Olds, Houghton Mifflin.

1951   *The Egg Tree* written and ill. by Katherine Milhous, Scribner. **Honor Books:** *Dick Whittington and His Cat* written and ill. by Marcia Brown, Scribner; *The Two Reds* by Will, ill. by Nicolas, Harcourt Brace; *If I Ran the Zoo* written and ill. by Dr. Seuss, Random House; *The Most Wonderful Doll in the World* by Phyllis McGinley, ill. by Helen Stone, Lippincott; *T-Bone, the Baby Sitter* written and ill. by Clare Newberry, Harper.

1950   *Song of the Swallows* written and ill. by Leo Politi, Scribner. **Honor Books:** *America's Ethan Allen* by Stewart Holbrook, ill. by Lynd Ward, Houghton Mifflin; *The Wild Birthday Cake* by Lavinia Davis, ill. by Hildegard Woodward, Doubleday; *The Happy Day* by Ruth Krauss, ill. by Marc Simont, Harper; *Bartholomew and the Oobleck* written and ill. by Dr. Seuss, Random House; *Henry Fisherman* written and ill. by Marcia Brown, Scribner.

1949   *The Big Snow* written and ill. by Berta Hader and Elmer Hader, Macmillan. **Honor Books:** *Blueberries for Sal* written and ill. by Robert McCloskey, Viking; *All Around the Town* by Phyllis McGinley, ill. by Helen Stone, Lippincott; *Juanita* written and ill. by Leo Politi, Scribner; *Fish in the Air* written and ill. by Kurt Wiese, Viking.

1948   *White Snow, Bright Snow* by Alvin Tresselt, ill. by Roger Duvoisin, Lothrop. **Honor Books:** *Stone Soup* written and ill. by Marcia Brown, Scribner; *McElligot's Pool* written and ill. by Dr. Seuss, Random House; *Bambino the Clown* written and ill. by George Schreiber, Viking; *Roger and the Fox* by Lavinia Davis, ill. by Hildegard Woodward, Doubleday; *Song of Robin Hood* ed. by Anne Malcolmson, ill. by Virginia Lee Burton, Houghton Mifflin.

1947   *The Little Island* by Golden MacDonald, ill. by Leonard Weisgard, Doubleday. **Honor Books:** *Rain Drop Splash* by Alvin Tresselt, ill. by Leonard Weisgard, Lothrop; *Boats on the River* by Marjorie Flack, ill. by Jay Hyde Barnum, Viking; *Timothy Turtle* by Al Graham, ill. by Tony Palazzo, Viking; *Pedro, the Angel of Olvera Street* written and ill. by Leo Politi, Scribner; *Sing in Praise: A Collection of the Best Loved Hymns* by Opal Wheeler, ill. by Marjorie Torrey, Dutton.

1946   *The Rooster Crows . . .* (traditional Mother Goose) ill. by Maud Petersham and Miska Petersham, Macmillan. **Honor Books:** *Little Lost Lamb* by Golden MacDonald, ill. by Leonard Weisgard, Doubleday; *Sing Mother Goose* by Opal Wheeler, ill. by Marjorie Torrey, Dutton; *My Mother Is the Most Beautiful Woman in the World* by Becky Reyher, ill. by Ruth Gannett, Lothrop; *You Can Write Chinese* written and ill. by Kurt Wiese, Viking.

1945   *Prayer for a Child* by Rachel Field, ill. by Elizabeth Orton Jones, Macmillan. **Honor Books:** *Mother Goose* ill. by Tasha Tudor, Walck; *In the Forest* written and ill. by Marie Hall Ets, Viking; *Yonie Wondernose* written and ill. by Marguerite de Angeli, Doubleday; *The Christmas Anna Angel* by Ruth Sawyer, ill. by Kate Seredy, Viking.

1944   *Many Moons* by James Thurger, ill. by Louis Slobodkin, Harcourt Brace. **Honor Books:** *Small Rain: Verses from the Bible* selected by Jessie Orton Jones, ill. by Elizabeth Orton Jones, Viking; *Pierre Pigeon* by Lee Kingman, ill. by Arnold E. Bare, Houghton Mifflin; *The Mighty Hunter* written and ill. by Berta Hader and Elmer Hader, Macmillan; *A Child's Good Night Book* by Margaret Wise Brown, ill. by Jean Charlot, Scott; *Good Luck Horse* by Chic-Yi Chan, ill. by Plao Chan, Whittlesey.

1943   *The Little House* written and ill. by Virginia Lee Burton, Houghton Mifflin. **Honor Books:** *Dash and Dart* written and ill. by Mary Buff and Conrad Buff, Viking; *Marshmallow* written and ill. by Clare Newberry, Harper.

1942   *Make Way for Ducklings* written and ill. by Robert McCloskey, Viking. **Honor Books:** *An American ABC* written and ill. by Maud and Miska Petersham, Macmillan; *In My Mother's House* by Ann Nolan Clark, ill. by Velino Herrera, Viking; *Paddle-to-the-Sea* written and ill. by Holling C. Holling, Houghton Mifflin; *Nothing at All* written and ill. by Wanda Gág, Coward.

1941   *They Were Strong and Good* written and ill. by Robert Lawson, Viking. **Honor Book:** *April's Kittens* written and ill. by Clare Newberry, Harper.

1940 *Abraham Lincoln* written and ill. by Ingri and Edgar Parin d'Aulaire, Doubleday. **Honor Books:** *Cock-A-Doodle Doo . . .* written and ill. by Berta and Elmer Hader, Macmillan; *Madeline* written and ill. by Ludwig Bemelmans, Viking; *The Ageless Story* ill. by Lauren Ford, Dodd, Mead.

1939 *Mei Li* written and ill. by Thomas Handforth, Doubleday. **Honor Books:** *The Forest Pool* written and ill. by Laura Adams Armer, Longmans; *Wee Gillis* by Munro Leaf, ill. by Robert Lawson, Viking; *Snow White and the Seven Dwarfs* written and ill. by Wanda Gág, Coward; *Barkis* written and ill. by Clare Newberry, Harper; *Andy and the Lion* written and ill. by James Daugherty, Viking.

1938 *Animals of the Bible* by Helen Dean Fish, ill. by Dorothy P. Lathrop, Lippincott. **Honor Books:** *Seven Simeons* written and ill. by Boris Artzybasheff, Viking; *Four and Twenty Blackbirds* by Helen Dean Fish, ill. by Robert Lawson, Stokes.

Newbery Award

Named in honor of John Newbery (1713–1767), the first English publisher of children's books, this medal has been given annually since 1922 by the American Library Association's Association for Library Service to Children. The recipient is recognized as author of the most distinguished book in children's literature published in the United States in the preceding year. The award is limited to citizens or residents of the United States.

1995 *Walk Two Moons* by Sharon Creech, HarperCollins. **Honor Book:** *Catherine, Called Birdy* by Karen Cushman, Clarion; *The Ear, the Eye, and the Arm* by Nancy Farmer, Orchard.

1994 *The Giver* by Lois Lowry, Houghton Mifflin. **Honor Books:** *Crazy Lady* by Jane Conly, HarperCollins; *Dragon's Gate* by Lawrence Yep, HarperCollins; *Eleanor Roosevelt: A Life of Discovery* by Russell Freedman, Clarion.

1993 *Missing May* by Cynthia Rylant, Orchard. **Honor Books:** *What Hearts* by Bruce Brooks, HarperCollins; *The Dark-Thirty: Southern Tales of the Supernatural* by Patricia McKissack, Knopf; *Somewhere in the Darkness* by Walter Dean Myers, Scholastic.

1992 *Shiloh* by Phyllis Reynolds Naylor, Atheneum. **Honor Books:** *Nothing but the Truth: A Documentary Novel* by Avi, Orchard; *The Wright Brothers: How They Invented the Airplane* by Russell Freedman, Holiday.

1991 *Maniac Magee* by Jerry Spinelli, Little, Brown. **Honor Book:** *The True Confessions of Charlotte Doyle* by Avi, Orchard.

1990 *Number the Stars* by Lois Lowry, Houghton Mifflin. **Honor Books:** *Afternoon of the Elves* by Janet Taylor Lisle, Orchard; *Shabanu: Daughter of the Wind* by Suzanne Fisher Staples, Knopf; *The Winter Room* by Gary Paulsen, Orchard.

1989 *Joyful Noise: Poems for Two Voices* by Paul Fleischman, HarperCollins. **Honor Books:** *In the Beginning: Creation Stories from Around the World* by Virginia Hamilton, Harcourt Brace; *Scorpions* by Walter Dean Myers, HarperCollins.

1988 *Lincoln: A Photobiography* by Russell Freedman, Clarion. **Honor Books:** *Hatchet* by Gary Paulsen, Bradbury; *After the Rain* by Norma Fox Mazer, Morrow.

1987 *The Whipping Boy* by Sid Fleischman, Greenwillow. **Honor Books:** *On My Honor* by Marion Dane Bauer, Clarion; *A Fine White Dust* by Cynthia Rylant, Bradbury; *Volcano* by Patricia Lauber, Bradbury.

1986 *Sarah, Plain and Tall* by Patricia MacLachlan, HarperCollins. **Honor Books:** *Commodore Perry in the Land of Shogun* by Rhoda Blumberg, Lothrop; *Dogsong* by Gary Paulsen, Bradbury.

1985 *The Hero and the Crown* by Robin McKinley, Greenwillow. **Honor Books:** *The Moves Make the Man* by Bruce Brooks, HarperCollins; *One-Eyed Cat* by Paula Fox, Bradbury; *Like Jake and Me* by Mavis Jukes, Knopf.

1984 *Dear Mr. Henshaw* by Beverly Cleary, Morrow. **Honor Books:** *The Wish Giver: Three Tales of Coven Tree* by Bill Brittain, HarperCollins; *A Solitary Blue* by Cynthia Voigt, Atheneum; *The Sign of the Beaver* by Elizabeth George Speare, Houghton Mifflin; *Sugaring Time* by Kathryn Lasky, Macmillan.

1983 *Dicey's Song* by Cynthia Voigt, Atheneum. **Honor Books:** *The Blue Sword* by Robin McKinley, Greenwillow; *Dr. De Soto* by William Steig, Farrar, Straus; *Graven Images* by Paul Fleischman, HarperCollins; *Homesick: My Own Story* by Jean Fritz, Putnam; *Sweet Whispers, Brother Rush* by Virginia Hamilton, Philomel.

1982 *A Visit to William Blake's Inn: Poems for Innocent and Experienced Travelers* by Nancy Willard, Harcourt Brace. **Honor Books:** *Ramona Quimby, Age 8* by Beverly Cleary, Morrow; *Upon the Head of the Goat: A Childhood in Hungary, 1939–1944* by Aranka Siegel, Farrar, Straus.

1981 *Jacob Have I Loved* by Katherine Paterson, Crowell. **Honor Books:** *The Fledgling* by Jane Langton, HarperCollins; *A Ring of Endless Light* by Madeleine L'Engle, Farrar, Straus.

1980 *A Gathering of Days: A New England Girl's Journal, 1830–32* by Joan Blos, Scribner. **Honor Book:** *The Road from Home: The Story of an Armenian Girl* by David Kherdian, Greenwillow.

1979 *The Westing Game* by Ellen Raskin, Dutton. **Honor Book:** *The Great Gilly Hopkins* by Katherine Paterson, Crowell.

1978 *Bridge to Terabithia* by Katherine Paterson, Crowell. **Honor Books:** *Anpao: An American Indian Odyssey* by Jamake Highwater, Lippincott; *Ramona and Her Father* by Beverly Cleary, Morrow.

1977 *Roll of Thunder, Hear My Cry* by Mildred D. Taylor, Dial. **Honor Books:** *Abel's Island* by William Steig, Farrar, Straus; *A String in the Harp* by Nancy Bond, Atheneum/McElderry.

1976 *The Grey King* by Susan Cooper, Atheneum/McElderry. **Honor Books:** *The Hundred Penny Box* by Sharon Bell Mathis, Viking; *Dragonwings* by Lawrence Yep, Harper & Row.

1975 *M. C. Higgins, The Great* by Virginia Hamilton, Macmillan. **Honor Books:** *Figgs and Phantoms* by Ellen Raskin, Dutton; *My Brother Sam Is Dead* by James Lincoln Collier and Christopher Collier, Four Winds; *The Perilous Guard* by Elizabeth Marie Pope, Houghton Mifflin; *Philip Hall Likes Me, I Reckon Maybe* by Bette Greene, Dial.

1974 *The Slave Dancer* by Paula Fox, Bradbury. **Honor Book:** *The Dark Is Rising* by Susan Cooper, Atheneum/McElderry.

1973 *Julie of the Wolves* by Jean George, Harper & Row. **Honor Books:** *Frog and Toad Together* by Arnold Lobel, Harper & Row; *The Upstairs Room* by Johanna Reiss, Crowell; *The Witches of Worm* by Zilpha Keatley Snyder, Atheneum.

1972 *Mrs. Frisby and the Rats of NIMH* by Robert C. O'Brien, Atheneum. **Honor Books:** *Incident at Hawk's Hill* by Allan W. Eckert, Little, Brown; *The Planet of Junior Brown* by Virginia Hamilton, Macmillan; *The Tombs of Atuan* by Ursula K. Le Guin, Atheneum; *Annie and the Old One* by Miska Miles, Atlantic/Little, Brown; *The Headless Cupid* by Zilpha Keatley Snyder, Atheneum.

1971 *Summer of the Swans* by Betsy Byars, Viking. **Honor Books:** *Kneeknock Rise* by Natalie Babbitt, Farrar, Straus; *Enchantress from the Stars* by Sylvia Louise Engdahl, Atheneum; *Sing Down the Moon* by Scott O'Dell, Houghton Mifflin.

1970 *Sounder* by William H. Armstrong, Harper & Row. **Honor Books:** *Our Eddie* by Sulamith Ish-Kishor, Pantheon; *The Many Ways of Seeing: An Introduction to the Pleasures of Art* by Janet Gaylord Moore, World; *Journey Outside* by Mary Q. Steele, Viking.

1969 *The High King* by Lloyd Alexander, Holt. **Honor Books:** *To Be a Slave* by Julius Lester, Dial; *When Shlemiel Went to Warsaw and Other Stories* by Isaac Bashevis Singer, Farrar, Straus.

1968 *From the Mixed-Up Files of Mrs. Basil E. Frankweiler* by E. L. Konigsburg, Atheneum. **Honor Books:** *Jennifer, Hecate, Macbeth, William McKinley, and Me, Elizabeth* by E. L. Konigsburg, Atheneum; *The Black Pearl* by Scott O'Dell, Houghton Mifflin; *The Fearsome Inn* by Isaac Bashevis Singer, Scribner; *The Egypt Game* by Zilpha Katley Snyder, Atheneum.

1967   *Up a Road Slowly* by Irene Hunt, Follett. **Honor Books:** *The King's Fifth* by Scott O'Dell, Houghton Mifflin; *Zlateh the Goat and Other Stories* by Isaac Bashevis Singer, Harper & Row, *The Jazz Man* by Mary H. Weik, Atheneum.

1966   *I, Juan de Pareja* by Elizabeth Borten de Trevino, Farrar, Straus. **Honor Books:** *The Black Cauldron* by Lloyd Alexander, Holt; *The Animal Family* by Randall Jarrell, Pantheon; *The Noonday Friends* by Mary Stolz, Harper & Row.

1965   *Shadow of a Bull* by Maia Wojciechowska, Atheneum. **Honor Book:** *Across Five Aprils* by Irene Hunt, Follett.

1964   *It's Like This, Cat* by Emily Cheney Neville, Harper & Row. **Honor Books:** *Rascal* by Sterling North, Dutton; *The Loner* by Esther Wier, McKay.

1963   *A Wrinkle in Time* by Madeleine L'Engle, Farrar. **Honor Books:** *Thistle and Thyme* by Sorche Nic Leodhas, Holt; *Men of Athens* by Olivia Coolidge, Houghton Mifflin.

1962   *The Bronze Bow* by Elizabeth George Speare, Houghton Mifflin. **Honor Books:** *Frontier Living* by Edwin Tunis, World; *The Golden Goblet* by Eloise McGraw, Coward; *Belling the Tiger* by Mary Stolz, Harper & Row.

1961   *Island of the Blue Dolphins* by Scott O'Dell, Houghton Mifflin. **Honor Books:** *America Moves Forward* by Gerald W. Johnson, Morrow; *Old Ramon* by Jack Schaefer, Houghton Mifflin; *The Cricket in Times Square* by George Selden, Farrar.

1960   *Onion John* by Joseph Krumgold, Crowell. **Honor Books:** *My Side of the Mountain* by Jean George, Dutton; *America Is Born* by Gerald W. Johnson, Morrow; *The Gammage Cup* by Carol Kendall, Harcourt Brace.

1959   *The Witch of Blackbird Pond* by Elizabeth George Speare, Houghton Mifflin. **Honor Books:** *The Family Under the Bridge* by Natalie S. Carlson, Harper; *Along Came a Dog* by Meindert DeJong, Harper; *Chucaro: Wild Pony of the Pampa* by Francis Kalnay, Harcourt Brace; *The Perilous Road* by William O. Steele, Harcourt Brace.

1958   *Rifles for Watie* by Harold Keith, Crowell. **Honor Books:** *The Horsecatcher* by Mari Sandoz, Westminster; *Gone-Away Lake* by Elizabeth Enright, Harcourt Brace; *The Great Wheel* by Robert Lawson, Viking; *Tom Paine, Freedom's Apostle* by Leo Gurko, Crowell.

1957   *Miracles on Maple Hill* by Virginia Sorensen, Harcourt Brace. **Honor Books:** *Old Yeller* by Fred Gipson, Harper; *The House of Sixty Fathers* by Meindert DeJong, Harper; *Mr. Justice Holmes* by Clara Ingram Judson, Follett; *The Corn Grows Ripe* by Dorothy Rhoads, Viking; *Black Fox of Lorne* by Marguerite de Angeli, Doubleday.

1956   *Carry On, Mr. Bowditch* by Jean Lee Latham, Houghton Mifflin. **Honor Books:** *The Secret River* by Marjorie Kinnan Rawlings, Scribner; *The Golden Name Day* by Jennie Lindquist, Harper; *Men, Microscopes, and Living Things* by Katherine Shippen, Viking.

1955   *The Wheel on the School* by Meindert Dejong, Harper. **Honor Books:** *The Courage of Sarah Noble* by Alice Dalgliesh, Scribner; *Banner in the Sky* by James Ullman, Lippincott.

1954   *. . . and Now, Miguel* by Joseph Krumgold, Crowell. **Honor Books:** *All Alone* by Claire Huchet Bishop, Viking; *Shadrach* by Meindert DeJong, Harper; *Hurry Home, Candy* by Meindert DeJong, Harper; *Theodore Roosevelt, Fighting Patriot* by Clara Ingram Judson, Follett; *Magic Maize* by Mary Buff and Conrad Buff, Houghton Mifflin.

1953   *Secret of the Andes* by Ann Nolan Clark, Viking. **Honor Books:** *Charlotte's Web* by E. B. White, Harper; *Moccasin Trail* by Eloise McGraw, Coward; *Red Sails to Capri* by Ann Weil, Viking; *The Bears of Hemlock Mountain* by Alice Dalgliesh, Scribner; *Birthdays of Freedom* (Vol. 1) by Genevieve Foster, Scribner.

1952   *Ginger Pye* by Eleanor Estes, Harcourt Brace. **Honor Books:** *Americans before Columbus* by Elizabeth Baity, Viking; *Minn of the Mississippi* by Holling C. Holling, Houghton Mifflin;

The Defender by Nicholas Kalashnikoff, Scribner; *The Light at Tern Rock* by Julia Sauer, Viking; *The Apple and the Arrow* by Mary Buff and Conrad Buff, Houghton Mifflin.

1951   *Amos Fortune, Free Man* by Elizabeth Yates, Aladdin. **Honor Books:** *Better Known As Johnny Appleseed* by Mabel Leigh Hunt, Lippincott; *Gandhi, Fighter without a Sword* by Jeanette Eaton, Morrow; *Abraham Lincoln, Friend of the People* by Clara Ingram Judson, Follett; *The Story of Appleby Capple* by Anne Parrish, Harper.

1950   *The Door in the Wall* by Marguerite de Angeli, Doubleday. **Honor Books:** *Tree of Freedom* by Rebecca Caudill, Viking; *The Blue Cat of Castle Town* by Catherine Coblentz, Longmans; *Kildee House* by Rutherford Montgomery, Doubleday; *George Washington* by Genevieve Foster, Scribner; *Song of the Pines* by Walter Havighurst and Marion Havighurst, Winston.

1949   *King of the Wind* by Marguerite Henry, Rand McNally. **Honor Books:** *Seabird* by Holling C. Holling, Houghton Mifflin; *Daughter of the Mountains* by Louise Rankin, Viking; *My Father's Dragon* by Ruth S. Gannett, Random House; *Story of the Negro* by Arna Bontemps, Knopf.

1948   *The Twenty-one Balloons* by William Pène du Bois, Lothrop. **Honor Books:** *Pancakes-Paris* by Claire Huchet Bishop, Viking; *Li Lun, Lad of Courage* by Carolyn Treffinger, Abingdon; *The Quaint and Curious Quest of Johnny Longfoot* by Catherine Besterman, Bobbs-Merrill; *The Cow-Tail Switch and Other West African Stories* by Harold Courlander, Holt; *Misty of Chincoteague* by Marguerite Henry, Rand McNally.

1947   *Miss Hickory* by Carolyn Sherwin Bailey, Viking. **Honor Books:** *Wonderful Year* by Nancy Barnes, Messner; *Big Tree* by Mary Buff and Conrad Buff, Viking; *The Heavenly Tenants* by William Maxwell, Harper; *The Avion My Uncle Flew* by Cyrus Fisher, Appleton; *The Hidden Treasure of Glaston* by Eleanore Jewett, Viking.

1946   *Strawberry Girl* by Lois Lenski, Lippincott. **Honor Books:** *Justin Morgan Had a Horse* by Marguerite Henry, Rand McNally; *The Moved-Outers* by Florence Crannell Means, Houghton Mifflin; *Bhimsa, The Dancing Bear* by Christine Weston, Scribner; *New Found World* by Katherine Shippen, Viking.

1945   *Rabbit Hill* by Robert Lawson, Viking. **Honor Books:** *The Hundred Dresses* by Eleanor Estes, Harcourt Brace; *The Silver Pencil* by Alice Dalgliesh, Scribner; *Abraham Lincoln's World* by Genevieve Foster, Scribner; *Lone Journey: The Life of Roger Williams* by Jeanette Eaton, Harcourt Brace.

1944   *Johnny Tremain* by Esther Forbes, Houghton Mifflin. **Honor Books:** *These Happy Golden Years* by Laura Ingalls Wilder, Harper; *Fog Magic* by Julia Sauer, Viking; *Rufus M.* by Eleanor Estes, Harcourt Brace; *Mountain Born* by Elizabeth Yates, Coward.

1943   *Adam of the Road* by Elizabeth Janet Gray, Viking. **Honor Books:** *The Middle Moffat* by Eleanor Estes, Harcourt Brace; *Have You Seen Tom Thumb?* by Mabel Leigh Hunt, Lippincott.

1942   *The Matchlock Gun* by Walter D. Edmonds, Dodd, Mead. **Honor Books:** *Little Town on the Prairie* by Laura Ingalls Wilder, Harper; *George Washington's World* by Genevieve Foster, Scribner; *Indian Captive: The Story of Mary Jemison* by Lois Lenski, Lippincott; *Down Ryton Water* by Eva Roe Gaggin, Viking.

1941   *Call It Courage* by Armstrong Sperry, Macmillan. **Honor Books:** *Blue Willow* by Doris Gates, Viking; *Young Mac of Fort Vancouver* by Mary Jane Carr, Crowell; *The Long Winter* by Laura Ingalls Wilder, Harper; *Nansen* by Anna Gertrude Hall, Viking.

1940   *Daniel Boone* by James Daugherty, Viking. **Honor Books:** *The Singing Tree* by Kate Seredy, Viking; *Runner of the Mountain Tops* by Mabel Robinson, Random House; *By the Shores of Silver Lake* by Laura Ingalls Wilder, Harper; *Boy with a Pack* by Stephen W. Meader, Harcourt Brace.

1939   *Thimble Summer* by Elizabeth Enright, Farrar & Rhinehart. **Honor Books:** *Nino* by Valenti Angelo, Viking; *Mr. Popper's Penguins* by Richard Atwater and Florence Atwater, Little,

Brown; *"Hello, the Boat!"* by Phyllis Crawford, Holt; *Leader by Destiny: George Washington, Man and Patriot* by Jeanette Eaton, Harcourt Brace; *Penn* by Elizabeth Janet Gray, Viking.

1938   *The White Stag* by Kate Seredy, Viking. **Honor Books:** *Pecos Bill* by James Cloyd Bowman, Little, Brown; *Bright Island* by Mabel Robinson, Random House; *On the Banks of Plum Creek* by Laura Ingalls Wilder, Harper.

1937   *Roller Skates* by Ruth Sawyer, Viking. **Honor Books:** *Phoebe Fairchild Her Book* by Lois Lenski, Stokes; *Whistler's Van* by Idwal Jones, Viking; *Golden Basket* by Ludwig Bemelmans, Viking; *Winterbound* by Margery Bianco, Viking; *Audubon* by Constance Rourke, Harcourt Brace; *The Codfish Musket* by Agnes Hewes, Doubleday.

1936   *Caddie Woodlawn* by Carol Brink, Macmillan. **Honor Books:** *Honk, The Moose* by Phil Strong, Dodd, Mead; *The Good Master* by Kate Seredy, Viking; *Young Walter Scott* by Elizabeth Janet Gray, Viking; *All Sail Set* by Armstrong Sperry, Winston.

1935   *Dobry* by Monica Shannon, Viking. **Honor Books:** *Pageant of Chinese History* by Elizabeth Seeger, Longman; *Davy Crockett* by Constance Rourke, Harcourt Brace; *Day on Skates* by Hilda Van Stockum, Harper.

1934   *Invincible Louisa* by Cornelia Meigs, Little, Brown. **Honor Books:** *The Forgotten Daughter* by Caroline Snedeker, Doubleday; *Swords of Steel* by Elsie Singmaster, Houghton Mifflin; *ABC Bunny* by Wanda Gág, Coward; *Winged Girl of Knossos* by Erik Berry, Appleton; *New Land* by Sarah Schmidt, McBride; *Big Tree of Bunlaby* by Padraic Colum, Macmillan; *Glory of the Seas* by Agnes Hewes, Knopf; *Apprentice of Florence* by Anne Kyle, Houghton Mifflin.

1933   *Young Fu of the Upper Yangtze* by Elizabeth Foreman Lewis, Winston. **Honor Books:** *Swift Rivers* by Cornelia Meigs, Little, Brown; *The Railroad to Freedom* by Hildegarde Swift, Harcourt Brace; *Children of the Soil* by Nora Burglon, Doubleday.

1932   *Waterless Mountain* by Laura Adams Armer, Longmans. **Honor Books:** *The Fairy Circus* by Dorothy P. Lathrop, Macmillan; *Calico Bush* by Rachel Field, Macmillan; *Boy of the South Seas* by Eunice Tietjens, Coward: *Out of the Flame* by Eloise Lownsbery, Longmans; *Jane's Island* by Marjorie Allee, Houghton Mifflin; *Truce of the Wolf and Other Tales of Old Italy* by Mary Gould Davis, Harcourt Brace.

1931   *The Cat Who Went to Heaven* by Elizabeth Coatsworth, Macmillan. **Honor Books:** *Floating Island* by Anne Parrish, Harper; *The Dark Star of Itza* by Alida Malkus, Harcourt Brace; *Queer Person* by Ralph Hubbard, Doubleday; *Mountains Are Free* by Julia Davis Adams, Dutton; *Spice and the Devil's Cave* by Agnes Hewes, Knopf; *Meggy Macintosh* by Elizabeth Janet Gray, Doubleday; *Garram the Hunter* by Herbert Best, Doubleday; *Ood-Le-Uk the Wanderer* by Alice Lide and Margaret Johansen, Little, Brown.

1930   *Hitty, Her First Hundred Years* by Rachel Field, Macmillan. **Honor Books:** *Daughter of the Seine* by Jeanette Eaton, Harper; *Pran of Albania* by Elizabeth Miller, Doubleday; *Jumping-Off Place* by Marian Hurd McNeely, Longmans; *Tangle-Coated Horse and Other Tales* by Ella Young, Longmans; *Vaino* by Julia Davis Adams, Dutton; *Little Blacknose* by Hildegarde Swift, Harcourt Brace.

Coretta Scott King Award

Established in 1969, this award commemorates the life and work of Martin Luther King, Jr., and honors Mrs. King for continuing the work for peace and world brotherhood. It is presented annually by the American Library Association to a black author (A) and illustrator (I) whose works encourage and promote world unity and peace and serve as an inspiration to young people in the achievement of their goals.

1993 *The Dark-Thirty: Southern Tales of the Supernatural* by Patricia McKissack, Knopf (A); *The Origin of Life on Earth: An African Myth* by David Anderson, ill. by Katherine Atkins Wilson, Sight Productions (I).

1992 *Now Is Your Time: The African American Struggle for Freedom* by Walter D. Myers, HarperCollins (A); *Tar Beach* by Faith Ringgold, ill. by Faith Ringgold, Crown (I).

1991 *Aida* by Leontyne Price, ill. by Leo Dillon and Diane Dillon, Harcourt Brace (I); *Road to Memphis* by Mildred D. Taylor, ed. by Phyllis Fogelman, 1990, Dial (A).

1990 *Long Hard Journey* by Patricia McKissack and Frederick McKissack, Walker (A); *Nathaniel Talking* by Eloise Greenfield, ill. by Jan S. Gilchrist, Black Butterfly (I).

1989 *Fallen Angels* by Walter D. Myers, Scholastic (A); *Mirandy and Brother Wind* by Patricia C. McKissack, ill. by Jerry Pinkney, Knopf (I).

1988 *The Friendship* by Mildred D. Taylor, ill. by Max Ginsburg, Dial (A); *Mufaro's Beautiful Daughter: An African Tale* ed. and ill. by John Steptoe, Lothrop (I).

1987 *Justin and the Best Biscuits in the World* by Mildred P. Walter, ill. by Catherine Stock, Lothrop (A); *Half a Moon and One Whole Star* by Crescent Dragonwagon, ill. by Jerry Pinkney, Macmillan (I).

1986 *The People Could Fly* by Virginia Hamilton, ill. by Leo Dillon and Diane Dillon, Knopf (A); *Patchwork Quilt* by Valerie Flournoy, ill. by Jerry Pinkey, Dial (I).

1985 *Motown and Didi: A Love Story* by Walter D. Myers, Viking (A).

1984 *Everett Anderson's Goodbye* by Lucille Clifton et al., ill. by Ann Grifalconi, Holt (A); *My Mamma Needs Me* by Mildred P. Walter, ill. by Pat Cummings, Lothrop (I).

1983 *Sweet Whispers, Brother Rush* by Virginia Hamilton, Philomel (A); *Black Child* written and ill. by Peter Magubane, Knopf (I).

1982 *Let the Circle Be Unbroken* by Mildred D. Taylor, Dial (A); *Mother Crocodile: An Uncle Amadou Tale from Senegal* adapted by Rosa Guy, ill. by John Steptoe, Delacorte (I).

1981 *This Life* by Sidney Poitier, Knopf (A); *Beat the Story-Drum, Pum-Pum* written and ill. by Ashley Bryan, Atheneum (I).

1980 *The Young Landlords* by Walter Dean Myers, Viking (A); *Cornrows* by Camille Yarbrough, ill. by Carole Byard, Coward (I).

1979 *Escape to Freedom* by Ossie Davis, Viking (A); *Something on My Mind* by Nikki Grimes, ill. by Tom Feelings, Dial (I).

1978 *Africa Dream* by Eloise Greenfield, ill. by Carole Byard Day/HarperCollins (A, I).

1977 *The Story of Stevie Wonder* by James Haskins, Lothrop (A).

1976 *Duey's Tale* by Pearl Bailey, Harcourt Brace (A)

1975 *The Legend of Africana* by Dorothy Robinson, ill. by Herbert Temple, Johnson (A, I).

1974 *Ray Charles* by Sharon Bell Mathis, ill. by George Ford, HarperCollins (A, I).

Boston Globe–Horn Book Award

These awards have been given annually in the fall since 1967 by *The Boston Globe* and *The Horn Book Magazine*. Through 1975, two awards were given: for outstanding text and outstanding illustration. In 1976 the award categories were changed to outstanding fiction or poetry, outstanding nonfiction, and outstanding illustration.

1992 **Fiction:** *Missing May* by Cynthia Rylant, Orchard; **Nonfiction:** *Talking with Artists* by Patricia Cummings, Bradbury; **Illustration:** *Seven Blind Mice* written and ill. by Ed Young, Philomel.

1991 **Fiction:** *The True Confessions of Charlotte Doyle* by Avi, ill. by Ruth E. Murray, Orchard; **Nonfiction:** *Appalachia: The Voices of Sleeping Birds* by Cynthia Rylant, ill. by Barry Moser,

Harcourt Brace; **Illustration:** *Tale of the Mandarin Ducks* by Katherine Paterson, ill. by Leo Dillon and Diane Dillon, Lodestar.

1990 **Fiction:** *Maniac Magee* by Jerry Spinelli, Little, Brown; **Nonfiction:** *Great Little Madison* by Jean Fritz, Putnam; **Illustration:** *Lon Po Po: A Red Riding Hood Story from China* by Ed Young, Philomel.

1989 **Fiction:** *Village by the Sea* by Paula Fox, Orchard; **Nonfiction:** *The Way Things Work* written and ill. by David Macaulay, Houghton Mifflin; **Illustration:** *Shy Charles* written and ill. by Rosemary Wells, Dial.

1988 **Fiction:** *The Friendship* by Mildred Taylor, Dial; **Nonfiction:** *Anthony Burns: The Defeat and Triumph of a Fugitive Slave* by Virginia Hamilton, Knopf; **Illustration:** *The Boy of the Three-Year Nap* by Diane Snyder, Houghton Mifflin.

1987 **Fiction:** *Rabble Starkey* by Lois Lowry, Houghton Mifflin; **Nonfiction:** *Pilgrims of Plimouth* by Marcia Sewall, Atheneum; **Illustration:** *Mufaro's Beautiful Daughters* by John Steptoe, Lothrop.

1986 **Fiction:** *In Summer Light* by Zibby O'Neal, Viking/Kestrel; **Nonfiction:** *Auks, Rocks and the Odd Dinosaur* by Peggy Thomson, Crowell; **Illustration:** *The Paper Crane* by Molly Bang, Greenwillow.

1985 **Fiction:** *The Moves Make the Man* by Bruce Brooks, Harper & Row; **Nonfiction:** *Commodore Perry in the Land of the Shogun* by Rhoda Blumberg, Lothrop; **Illustration:** *Mama Don't Allow* by Thatcher Hurd, Harper & Row.

1984 **Fiction:** *A Little Fear* by Patricia Wrightson, Atheneum/McElderry; **Nonfiction:** *The Double Life of Pocahontas* by Jean Fritz, Putnam; **Illustration:** *Jonah and the Great Fish* retold and ill. by Warwick Hutton, Atheneum/McElderry.

1983 **Fiction:** *Sweet Whispers, Brother Rush* by Virginia Hamilton, Philomel; **Nonfiction:** *Behind Barbed Wire: The Imprisonment of Japanese Americans During World War II* by Daniel S. Davis, Dutton; **Illustration:** *A Chair for My Mother* by Vera B. Williams, Greenwillow.

1982 **Fiction:** *Playing Beatie Bow* by Ruth Park, Atheneum; **Nonfiction:** *Upon the Head of the Goat: A Childhood in Hungary, 1939–1944* by Aranka Siegal, Farrar, Straus; **Illustration:** *A Visit to William Blake's Inn: Poems for Innocent and Experienced Travelers* by Nancy Willard, ill. by Alice Provensen and Martin Provensen, Harcourt Brace.

1981 **Fiction:** *The Leaving* by Lynn Hall, Scribner; **Nonfiction:** *The Weaver's Gift* by Kathryn Lasky, Warne; **Illustration:** *Outside over There* by Maurice Sendak, Harper & Row.

1980 **Fiction:** *Conrad's War* by Andrew Davies, Crown; **Nonfiction:** *Building: The Fight against Gravity* by Mario Salvadori, Atheneum/McElderry; **Illustration:** *The Garden of Abdul Gasazi* by Chris Van Allsburg, Houghton Mifflin.

1979 **Fiction:** *Humbug Mountain* by Sid Fleischman, Atlantic/Little, Brown; **Nonfiction:** *The Road from Home: The Story of an Armenian Girl* by David Kherdian, Greenwillow; **Illustration:** *The Snowman* by Raymond Briggs, Random House.

1978 **Fiction:** *The Westing Game* by Ellen Raskin, Dutton; **Nonfiction:** *Mischling, Second Degree: My Childhood in Nazi Germany* by Ilse Koehn, Greenwillow; **Illustration:** *Anno's Journey* by Mitsumasa Anno, Philomel.

1977 **Fiction:** *Child of the Owl* by Laurence Yep, Harper & Row; **Nonfiction:** *Chance Luck and Destiny* by Peter Dickinson, Atlantic/Little, Brown; **Illustration:** *Ganfa' Grig Had a Pig and Other Rhymes* by Wallace Tripp, Little, Brown.

1976 **Fiction:** *Unleaving* by Jill Paton Walsh, Farrar, Straus; **Nonfiction:** *Voyaging to Cathay: Americans in the China Trade* by Alfred Tamarin and Shirley Glubok, Viking; **Illustration:** *Thirteen* by Remy Charlip and Jerry Joyner, Parents.

1975 **Text:** *Transport 7–41–R* by T. Degens, Viking; **Illustration:** *Anno's Alphabet* by Mitsumasa Anno, Crowell.

1974   **Text:** *M. C. Higgins, The Great* by Virginia Hamilton, Macmillan; **Illustration:** *Jambo Means Hello* by Muriel Feelings, ill. by Tom Feelings, Dial.

1973   **Text:** *The Dark Is Rising* by Susan Cooper, Atheneum/McElderry; **Illustration:** *King Stork* by Trina Schart Hyman, Little, Brown.

1972   **Text:** *Tristan and Iseult* by Rosemary Sutcliff, Dutton; **Illustration:** *Mr. Gumpy's Outing* by John Burningham, Holt.

1971   **Text:** *A Room Made of Windows* by Eleanor Cameron, Atlantic/Little, Brown; **Illustration:** *If I Built a Village* by Kazue Mizumura, Crowell.

1970   **Text:** *The Intruder* by John Rowe Townsend, Lippincott; **Illustration:** *Hi, Cat!* by Ezra Jack Keats, Macmillan.

1969   **Text:** *A Wizard of Earthsea* by Ursula K. Le Guin, Houghton Mifflin; **Illustration:** *The Adventures of Paddy Pork* by John S. Goodall, Harcourt Brace.

1968   **Text:** *The Spring Rider* by John Lawson, Crowell; **Illustration:** *Tikki Tikki Tembo* by Arlene Mosel, ill. by Blair Lent, Holt.

1967   **Text:** *The Little Fishes* by Erik Christian Haugaard, Houghton Mifflin; **Illustration:** *London Bridge Is Falling Down* by Peter Spier, Doubleday.

Appendix B

Poetry and Rhymes for Reading

Bagert, B. (1992). *Let me be the boss.* Honesdale, PA: Boyds Mills.

Carle, E. (1989). *Eric Carle's animals animals.* New York: Philomel.

de Paola, T. (1985). *Tomie de Paola's Mother Goose.* New York: Putnam.

de Paola, T. (1988). *Tomie de Paola's book of poems.* New York: Putnam.

de Regniers, B. S., Moore, E., & White, M. M. (1969). *Poems children will sit still for.* New York: Citation.

de Regniers, B. S., Moore, E., White, M. M., & Carr, J. (1988). *Sing a song of popcorn: Every child's book of poems.* New York: Scholastic.

Fleischman, P. (1988). *Joyful noise: Poems for two voices.* New York: Harper & Row.

Hopkins, L. B. (Ed.). (1992). *Pterodactyls and pizza.* New York: Trumpet.

Livingston, M. C. (1987). *Cat poems.* New York: Holiday.

Livingston, M. C. (1988). *Space songs.* New York: Holiday.

Lobel, A. (1983). *The book of pigericks.* New York: Harper & Row.

Lobel, A. (1986). *The Random House book of Mother Goose.* New York: Random House.

Moss, J. (1989). *The butterfly jar.* New York: Bantam.

Moss, J. (1991). *The other side of the door.* New York: Bantam.

O'Neill, M. (1961). *Hailstones and halibut bones: Adventures in color.* Garden City, NY: Doubleday.

Opie, I., & Opie, P. (Eds.). (1992). *I saw Esau: The schoolchild's pocket book.* Cambridge, MA: Candlewick.

Prelutsky, J. (Ed.). (1983). *The Random House book of poetry for children.* New York: Random House.

Prelutsky, J. (1984). *New kid on the block.* New York: Greenwillow.

Prelutsky, J. (Ed.). (1986). *Read-aloud rhymes for the very young.* New York: Knopf.

Prelutsky, J. (1986). *Ride a purple pelican.* New York: Greenwillow.

Prelutsky, J. (1990). *Something big has been here.* New York: Greenwillow.

Silverstein, S. (1974). *Where the sidewalk ends.* New York: HarperCollins.

Silverstein, S. (1981). *A light in the attic.* New York: HarperCollins.

Slier, D. (Ed.). (1991). *Make a joyful sound: Poems for children by African-American poets.* New York: Checkerboard.

Viorst, J. (1981). *If I were in charge of the world and other worries.* New York: Atheneum.

Wildsmith, B. (1964). *Brian Wildsmith's Mother Goose.* New York: Franklin Watts.

Appendix C

Predictable Pattern Books

Pattern or predictable books contain distinct language patterns that make them easy for children to learn to read. Moreover, the repetitive and predictable language patterns are an enjoyable way for children to play with sounds, words, phrases, and sentences.

In general, pattern books should be read several times to allow children to learn the stories thoroughly. This can be done over several days or even weeks. Once the children have learned the text, the teacher can begin to direct their attention to individual sentences, phrases, words, and even letters and letter combinations. This is a natural progression from whole to part that allows students to discover how smaller units of language work without distorting or disrupting the process of reading and enjoying the story.

Sentence strips, word banks, and word sort activities are some of the tools that teachers can use to direct students' attention to words, phrases, and sentences in the stories. Teachers can have students predict individual words and phrases as well as portions of the plot after having read enough of the story to detect the patterns.

Because of the predictable and patterned nature of the stories, they are well suited for students who are writing their own version of the stories using the language patterns in the original text as a guide or scaffold. Students will find it fun and satisfying to compose similar stories to those they've heard and read and to share their compositions with their classmates.

The following books are easy to read, with strongly repetitive patterns and a minimum number of short sentences on each page:

Adams, Pam. (1974). *This old man*. New York: Grosset & Dunlap.
Aliki. (1989). *My five senses*. New York: Crowell.
Allenberg, J., & Allenberg, A. (1978). *Each peach, pear, plum*. New York: Viking Press.
Astley, Judy. (1990). *When one cat woke up*. New York: Dial.
Baer, Gene. (1989). *Thump, thump, rat-a-tat-tat*. New York: Harper & Row.
Barton, Byron. (1989). *Dinosaurs, dinosaurs*. New York: Crowell.
Becker, John. (1973). *Seven little rabbits*. New York: Scholastic.
Brandenberg, Franz. (1989). *Aunt Nina, good night*. New York: Greenwillow.
Brown, Margaret Wise. (1947). *Goodnight moon*. New York: Harper & Row.
Brown, Margaret Wise. (1964). *The important book*. New York: Parents' Magazine.
Brown, Ruth. (1981). *A dark, dark tale*. New York: Dial.

Carle, Eric. (1969). *The very hungry caterpillar*. New York: Philomel.

Carle, Eric. (1977). *The grouchy ladybug*. New York: Crowell.

Cowley, Joy. (1987a). *The jigaree*. Bothell, WA: Wright Group.

Cowley, Joy. (1987b). *Mrs. Wishy-Washy*. Bothell, WA: Wright Group.

Emberley, Ed. (1974). *Klippity klop*. Boston: Little, Brown.

Ets, Marie Hall. (1972). *Elephant in a well*. New York: Viking.

Galdone, Paul. (1973). *The little red hen*. New York: Scholastic.

Hennessy, B. G. (1990). *Jake baked the cake*. New York: Viking.

Hutchins, Pat. (1968). *Rosie's walk*. New York: Macmillan.

Hutchins, Pat. (1971). *Titch*. New York: Collier.

Hutchins, Pat. (1972). *Good-night owl*. New York: Macmillan.

Hutchins, Pat. (1982). *1 hunter*. New York: Greenwillow.

Hutchins, Pat. (1986). *The doorbell rang*. New York: Greenwillow.

Jonas, Ann. (1989). *Color dance*. New York: Greenwillow.

Keats, Ezra Jack. (1971). *Over in the meadow*. New York: Scholastic.

Kent, J. (1971). *The fat cat*. New York: Scholastic.

Kovalski, Maryann. (1987). *The wheels on the bus*. Little, Brown.

Kraus, Robert. (1970). *Whose mouse are you?* New York: Macmillan.

Langstaff, John. (1974). *Oh, a-hunting we will go*. New York: Atheneum.

Martin, Bill. (1983). *Brown bear, brown bear*. New York: Holt.

Martin, Bill. (1991). *Polar bear, polar bear*. New York: Holt.

McKissack, Patricia. (1986). *Who is coming?* Chicago: Children's Press.

McKissack, Patricia, & McKissack, Fredrick. (1988). *Constance stumbles*. Chicago: Children's Press.

Numeroff, Laura Joffe. (1985). *If you give a mouse a cookie*. New York: Harper & Row.

Numeroff, Laura Joffe. (1991). *If you give a moose a muffin*. New York: HarperCollins.

Peek, Merle. (1985). *Mary wore her red dress*. New York: Clarion.

Roffey, Maureen. (1988). *I spy at the zoo*. New York: Macmillan.

Rounds, Blen. (1989). *Old MacDonald had a farm*. Holiday.

Sendak, M. (1962). *Chicken soup and rice*. New York: Williams.

Seuss, Dr. (1957). *The cat in the hat*. New York: Random House.

Seuss, Dr. (1965). *Green eggs and ham*. New York: Random House.

Shaw, Nancy. (1989a). *Sheep in a jeep*. Boston: Houghton Mifflin.

Shaw, Nancy. (1989b). *Sheep on a ship*. Boston: Houghton Mifflin.

Wager, J. (1971). *The bus ride*. New York: Scott, Foresman.

Wescott, Nadine Bernard. (1980). *I know an old lady who swallowed a fly*. Boston: Houghton Mifflin.
West, Colin. (1986). *"Pardon?" said the giraffe*. New York: Lippincott.
Williams, Sue. (1992). *I went walking*. Orlando, FL: Harcourt Brace Jovanovich.
Wondriska, William. (1970). *All the animals were angry*. New York: Holt, Rinehart, & Winston.
Zemach, Margot. (1965). *The teeny tiny woman*. New York: Scholastic.
Zemach, Margot. (1976). *Hush, little baby*. New York: Dutton.

The following books are more difficult to read, with less obvious repetitive patterns as well as more and longer sentences:

Allen, Pamela. (1983). *Bertie and the bear*. New York: Coward-McCann.
Baker, Alan. (1990). *Two tiny mice*. New York: Dial.
Baker, Keith. (1990). *Who is the beast?* Orlando, FL: Harcourt Brace Jovanovich.
Brown, Marcia. (1957). *The three billy goats gruff*. New York: Harcourt Brace Jovanovich.
Brown, Margaret Wise. (1983). *Home for a bunny*. New York: Golden.
Carle, Eric. (1972). *The secret birthday message*. New York: Crowell.
Carle, Eric. (1984). *The mixed-up chameleon*. New York: Harper & Row.
Emberley, Edward R., & Emberley, Barbara. (1967). *Drummer Hoff*. New York: Simon & Schuster.
Flack, Marjorie. (1932). *Ask Mr. Bear*. New York: Macmillan.
Gág, Wanda. (1928). *Millions of cats*. New York: Coward-McCann.
Galdone, Paul. (1968). *Henny penny*. New York: Clarion.
Galdone, Paul. (1970). *The three little pigs*. New York: Seabury.
Galdone, Paul. (1972). *The three bears*. New York: Scholastic.
Hoberman, Mary Ann. (1978). *A house is a home for me*. New York: Viking.
Hogrogian, Nonny. (1971). *One fine day*. New York: Macmillan.
Kellogg, Steven. (1979). *Pinkerton, behave!* New York: Dial.
Lobel, Arnold. (1977). *Mouse soup*. New York: Harper & Row.
Lobel, Arnold. (1979). *A treeful of pigs*. New York: Greenwillow.
Mayer, M. (1973). *What do you do with a kangaroo?* New York: Scholastic.
Peppe, Rodney. (1970). *The house that Jack built*. New York: Delacorte.
Pomerantz, Charlotte. (1989). *Flap your wings and try*. New York: Greenwillow.
Quackenbush, R. (1972). *Old McDonald had a farm*. Philadelphia: Lippincott.
Ross, Tony. (1988). *Super dooper Jezebel*. New York: Farrar, Straus, & Giroux.
Sendak, M. (1963). *Where the wild things are*. New York: Scholastic.
Silverstein, Shel. (1964). *A giraffe and a half*. New York: Harper & Row.
Viorst, Judith. (1972). *Alexander and the terrible, horrible, no good, very bad day*. New York: Atheneum.
Williams, Linda. (1986). *The little old lady who was not afraid of anything*. New York: Crowell.
Wood, Audrey. (1984). *The napping house*. New York: Harcourt Brace Jovanovich.
Young, Ed. (1992). *Seven blind mice*. New York: Philomel.

Series Books

Beginning Readers

Asch, Frank. BEAR BOOKS. New York: Scholastic.
Allard, Harry. MISS NELSON BOOKS. Boston: Houghton Mifflin.
Bridwell, Norman. CLIFFORD (the dog) BOOKS. New York: Scholastic.
Bright, Robert. GEORGIE BOOKS. New York: Doubleday.
Brown, Marc. ARTHUR (the moose) BOOKS. Boston: Little, Brown.
Clifton, Lucille. EVERETT ANDERSON BOOKS. New York: Holt, Rinehart, & Winston.
Hill, Eric. SPOT BOOKS. New York: Putnam.
Hoban, Russell. FRANCES (the badger) BOOKS. New York: Harper & Row.
Lobel, Arnold. FROG AND TOAD BOOKS. New York: Harper & Row.
Pilkey, Dav. DRAGON BOOKS. New York: Orchard.
Rey, H. A., & Rey, Margaret. CURIOUS GEORGE BOOKS. Boston: Houghton Mifflin.
Rylant, C. HENRY AND MUDGE BOOKS. Scarsdale, NY: Bradbury.
Zion, Gene. HARRY (the dirty dog) BOOKS. New York: Harper & Row.

Transitional and Maturing Readers

Cleary, Beverly. HENRY HUGGINS BOOKS. New York: Morrow.
Cleary, Beverly. RAMONA BOOKS. New York: Morrow.
Cleary, Beverly. DEAR MR. HENSHAW and STRIDER. New York: Morrow.
Haywood, Carolyn. BETSY BOOKS. San Diego: Harcourt Brace.
Haywood, Carolyn. EDDIE BOOKS. San Diego: Harcourt Brace.
Hurwitz, Johanna. ALDO BOOKS. New York: Morrow.
Hurwitz, Johanna. RUSSELL BOOKS. New York: Morrow.
Kline, Suzy. HERBIE JONES BOOKS. New York: Putnam.
Lowry, Lois. ANASTASIA KRUPNIK BOOKS. Boston: Houghton Mifflin.
Martin, Ann. BABY-SITTERS BOOKS. New York: Scholastic.
Simon, Seymour. EINSTEIN ANDERSON BOOKS. New York: Puffin.
Stine, R. L. GOOSEBUMPS BOOKS. New York: Scholastic.
Warner, Gertrude Chandler. BOXCAR CHILDREN BOOKS. New York: Scholastic.
Wilder, Laura Ingalls. LITTLE HOUSE BOOKS. New York: Harper & Row.

Alphabet, Number, and Other Concept Books

ABC Books

Anno, M. (1974). *Anno's alphabet*. New York: Crowell. (Ages 5–7).

Base, G. (1986). *Animalia*. New York: Abrams. (Ages 6+).

Bridwell, Norman. (1984). *Clifford's ABC*. New York: Scholastic. (Ages 5–7).

Feelings, M. (1974). *Jambo means hello*. New York: Dial. (Ages 5–7).

Folsom, Marcia, & Folson, Michael. (1985). *Easy as pie: A guessing game of sayings* (Ill. by Jack Kent). New York: Clarion. (Ages 7–10).

Gardner, Beau. (1986). *Have you ever seen . . . ? An ABC book*. New York: Dodd, Mead. (Ages 3–6).

Geisert, Arthur. (1986). *Pigs from A to Z*. Boston: Houghton Mifflin. (Ages 2–8).

Hawkins, Colin, & Hawkins, Jacqui. (1987). *Busy ABC*. New York: Viking. (Ages 4–6).

Hoban, Tana. (1987). *26 letters and 99 cents*. New York: Greenwillow. (Ages 5–7).

Hughes, Shirley. (1987). *Lucy and Tom's a.b.c.* New York: Puffin. (Ages 4–7).

Kitamura, Satoshi. (1985). *What's inside: The alphabet book*. New York: Farrar, Straus, & Giroux. (Ages 3–8).

Lobel, Anita, & Lobel, Arnold. (1981). *On Market Street*. New York: Greenwillow. (Ages 4–7).

Martin, Bill, Jr., & Archambault, John. (1989). *Chicka chicka boom boom* (Ill. by Lois Ehlert). New York: Simon & Schuster. (Ages 4–6).

Musgrove, M. (1976). *Ashanti to zulu*. New York: Dial. (Ages 5–8).

Neumeier, Marty, & Glaser, Byron. *Action alphabet*. New York: Greenwillow. (Ages 3–8).

Potter, Beatrix. (1987). *Peter Rabbit's ABC*. New York: Warne. (Ages 2–4).

Steig, W. (1968). *CDB!* New York: Simon & Schuster. (Ages 5–8).

Van Allsburg, Chris. (1987). *The Z was zapped: A play in twenty-six acts*. Boston: Houghton Mifflin. (Ages 5–8).

Colors

Ehlert, Lois. (1988). *Planting a rainbow*. New York: Harcourt Brace Jovanovich. (Ages 4–8).

Hill, Eric. (1986). *Spot looks at colors*. New York: Putnam. (Ages 3–6).

Hoban, Tana. (1978). *Is it red? Is it yellow? Is it blue?* New York: Greenwillow. (Ages 4–8).

Hoban, Tana. (1988). *Of colors and things*. New York: Greenwillow. (Ages 4–8).

Imershein, Betsy. (1989). *Finding red finding yellow*. New York: Harcourt Brace Jovanovich. (Ages 4–8).

Leonni, Leo. (1959). *Little blue, Little yellow*. New York: Astor. (Ages 4–8).

Lionni, Leo. (1976). *A color of his own*. New York: Pantheon. (Ages 4–8).

Martin, Bill. (1983). *Brown bear, brown bear* (Ill. by Eric Carle). Holt. (Ages 3–7).

McMillan, Bruce. (1988). *Growing colors.* New York: Lothrop. (Ages 2–5).

Peek, Merle. (1985). *Mary wore her red dress, Henry wore his green sneakers.* New York: Clarion. (Ages 4–8).

Samton, Shelia White. (1987). *Beside the bay.* New York: Philomel. (Ages 3–5).

Sawicki, Norma. (1989). *The little red house* (Ill. by Toni Goffe). New York: Lothrop. (Ages 3–7).

Serfozo, Mary. (1988). *Who said red?* (Ill. by Keiko Narahashi). New York: McElderry. (Ages 3–6).

Sis, Peter. (1989). *Going up.* New York: Greenwillow. (Ages 4–7).

Counting Books

Aylesworth, Jim. (1988). *One crow: A counting rhyme* (Ill. by Ruth Young). Philadelphia: Harper-Collins. (Ages 2–6).

Bank, Molly. (1983). *Ten, nine, eight.* New York: Greenwillow. (Ages 3–6).

Boon, Emilie. (1987). *1 2 3, how many animals can you see?* New York: Orchard. (Ages 3–6).

Burningham, John. (1980). *The shopping basket.* New York: Crowell. (Ages 3–7).

Crews, Donald. (1986). *Ten black dots.* New York: Greenwillow. (Ages 3–6).

de Regniers, Beatrice Schenk. (1985). *So many cats!* (Ill. by Ellen Weiss). New York: Clarion. (Ages 3–5).

Fowler, Richard. (1987). *Mr. Little's noisy 1 2 3.* New York: Grosset & Dunlap. (Ages 3–8).

Hoban, Tana. (1972). *Count & see.* New York: Macmillan. (Ages 3–6).

Hoban, Tana. (1985). *1, 2, 3.* New York: Greenwillow. (Ages 3–6).

Hutchins, Pat. (1982). *1 hunter.* New York: Greenwillow. (Ages 3–6).

Inkpen, Mick. (1987). *One bear at bedtime.* Boston: Little, Brown. (Ages 3–7).

Kitchen, Bert. (1987). *Animal numbers.* New York: Dial. (Ages 3–5).

Mack, Stan. (1974). *10 bears in my bed.* New York: Pantheon. (Ages 3–6).

Peek, Merle. (1981). *Roll over.* New York: Clarion. (Ages 3–6).

Potter, Beatrix. (1988). *Peter Rabbit's 1 2 3.* New York: Warne. (Ages 3–5).

Stobbs, William. (1984). *1, 2 buckle my shoe.* Oxford: Oxford University Press. (Ages 3–6).

Tafuri, Nancy. (1986). *Who's counting?* New York: Greenwillow. (Ages 3–6).

Wadsworth, Olive A. (1985). *Over in the meadow: A counting out rhyme* (Ill. by Mary Maki Rae). New York: Viking. (Ages 2–5).

Other Concepts

Alhberg, Janet, & Ahlberg, Allen. (1978). *Each peach pear plum: An I spy book.* New York: Viking. (Ages 5–7).

Barton, Byron. (1986a). *Airplanes.* New York: Crowell. (Ages 3–6).

Barton, Byron. (1986b). *Boats.* New York: Crowell. (Ages 3–6).

Barton, Byron. (1986c). *Trains.* New York: Crowell. (Ages 3–6).

Barton, Byron. (1986d). *Trucks.* New York: Crowell. (Ages 3–6).

Carle, Eric. (1969). *The very hungry caterpillar.* New York: Philomel. (Ages 4–8).

Clifton, Lucile. (1978). *Some of the days of Everett Anderson* (Ill. by Evangeline Ness). New York: Holt. (Ages 5–8).

Demi. (1987). *Demi's opposites: An animal game book.* New York: Grosset & Dunlap. (Ages 3–8).

Gundersheimer, Karen. (1986). *Shapes to show.* New York: Harper & Row. (Ages 2–6).

Hill, Eric. (1986). *Spot looks at shapes.* New York: Putnam. (Ages 3–5).

Hoban, Tana. (1985). *Is it larger? Is it smaller?* New York: Greenwillow. (Ages 3–6).

Hooper, Meredith. (1986). *Seven eggs* (Ill. by Terry McKenna). New York: Harper & Row. (Ages 3–5).

Isadora, Rachel. (1985). *I see, I hear, I touch.* New York: Greenwillow. (Ages 2–4).

Provenson, Alice, & Provenson, Martin. (1978). *The year at Maple Hill Farm.* New York: Atheneum. (Ages 4–7).

Rogers, Fred. (1987a). *Making friends* (Photos by Jim Judkis). New York: Putnam/First Experience. (Ages 3–6).

Rogers, Fred. (1987b). *Moving* (Photos by Jim Judkis). New York: Putnam/First Experience. (Ages 3–6).

Roy, Ron. (1987). *Whose hat is that?* (Photos by Rosemarie Hausherr). New York: Clarion. (Ages 4–8).

Ward, Cindy. (1988). *Cookie's week* (Ill. by Tomie de Paola). New York: Putnam. (Ages 4–6).

Wells, Tony. (1987). *Puzzle doubles.* New York: Macmillan/Aladdin. (Ages 2–5).

Yetkai, Niki. (1987). *Bears in pairs* (Ill. by Diane deGroat). New York: Bradbury. (Ages 2–6).

Ziefert, Harriet. (1986a). *All clean!* (Ill. by Henrik Drescher). New York: Harper & Row. (Ages 3–6).

Ziefert, Harriet. (1986b). *All gone!* (Ill. by Henrik Drescher). New York: Harper & Row. (Ages 3–6).

Ziefert, Harriet. (1986c). *Bear all year: A guessing-game story* (Ill. by Arnold Lobel). New York: Harper & Row. (Ages 3–5).

Ziefert, Harriet. (1986d). *Run! Run!* (Ill. by Henrik Drescher). New York: Harper & Row. (Ages 3–6).

Appendix F

Common Word Families

Teachers can use word families (letter patterns or phonograms) as an alternative strategy for recognizing or decoding unknown words. One instructional approach is to focus on one or two word families at a time. Brainstorm short and long words that belong to the particular word families. List the words on chart paper and display the charts around the room for easy reading and spelling. When students come to unknown words, the teacher can cue the student to look for word families they know. Because words in word families rhyme, an excellent complement to word family instruction is reading and writing poetry.

ab: tab, drab	all: ball, squall
ace: race, place	am: ham, swam
ack: lack, track	ant: pant, chant
ad: bad, glad	ame: name, blame
ade: made, shade	amp: camp, clamp
ag: bag, shag	an: man, span
age: page, stage	and: land, gland
ail: mail, snail	ane: plane, cane
ain: rain, train	ang: bang, sprang
ake: take, brake	ank: bank, plank
alk: talk, chalk	eep: keep, sheep

ap: nap, snap

ape: tape, drape

ar: car, star

are: care, glare

ark: dark, spark

art: part, start

ash: cash, flash

ast: past, blast

at: fat, scat

ate: gate, plate

ave: gave, shave

aw: saw, draw

ay: hay, clay

eak: leak, sneak

eal: real, squeal

eam: team, stream

ean: mean, lean

eet: feet, sleet

eg: leg

ell: fell, swell

elt: felt, belt

en: Ben, when

end: tend, send

ent: sent, spent

ess: less, bless

est: rest, chest

et: get, jet

ew: flew, chew

ib: bib, crib

ice: rice, splice

ick: kick, stick

id: hid, slid

ide: wide, pride

ig: pig, twig

ear: year, spear

eat: beat, cheat

eck: peck, check

ed: bed, shed

eed: need, speed

eel: feel, kneel

een: seen, screen

ing: sing, string

ink: sink, shrink

ip: hip, flip

ipe: ripe, swipe

ire: tire, sire

ish: dish, swish

it: hit, quit

ite: bite, write

ive: five, hive

oat: boat, float

ob: job, throb

ock: lock, stock

og: fog, clog

oil: boil, broil

oke: woke, spoke

old: gold, scold

ight: tight, bright

ike: Mike, spike

ill: fill, chill

im: him, trim

in: tin, spin

ind: kind, blind

ine: mine, spine

ope: hope, slope

ore: bore, snore

orn: horn, thorn

ose: rose, close

oss: boss, gloss

ot: got, trot

ought: bought, brought

out: pout, about

ow: how, chow

ow: bow, throw

ox: fox, pox

oy: boy, ploy

ub: cub, shrub

uck: duck, stuck

ud: mud, thud

uff: puff, stuff

ole: hole, stole

oll: droll, roll

one: cone, phone

ong: long, wrong

ool: cool, fool

oom: room, bloom

oop: hoop, snoop

oot: boot, shoot

op: top, chop

ust: dust, trust

ug: dug, plug

um: sum, thumb

ump: bump, plump

un: run, spun

unch: bunch, scrunch

ung: hung, flung

unk: sunk, chunk

unt: hunt, grunt

ush: mush, crush

ut: but, shut

Maze and Cloze Activities

Maze and cloze activities are powerful ways to help students strengthen their abilities to use meaningful context to guide their word recognition. Teachers can develop maze and cloze activities by finding an exemplary text that students may be familiar with and deleting selected words from the passage. Words chosen for deletion should be those that can be identified using the context preceding or following the deletion. After students work in groups or alone to determine missing words, teacher and students should discuss how they were able to determine selected words. Several variations of the maze and cloze are possible, as the following examples show.

Maze

In a maze activity, deleted words are provided at the end of the passage so that students' task is less challenging. In effect, it is a multiple-choice cloze.

> Abraham Lincoln wasn't the sort of man who could lose himself in a _____. After all, he stood _____ feet four inches tall, and to top it off, he _____ a high silk _____. His height was mostly in his _____ bony legs. When the _____ sat in a _____, he seemed no taller _____ anyone else.
> Choices: (than, six, president, wore, chair, long, crowd, hat)

From Friedman R. (1987). *Lincoln: A photobiography*. New York: Clarion.

Cloze

> Wintertime was _____ quiet in the little town in Calabria where Strega Nona (Grandma Witch) and her helper Big Anthony _____. People came _____ Strega Nona to help them _____ their troubles. Big Anthony did _____ chores and tried to behave _____. And every morning Bambolona, the baker's daughter, came to deliver the _____.

From de Paola, T. (1979). *Big Anthony and the magic ring*. New York: Harcourt Brace.

Modified Cloze

This approach marks deleted words with initial letters.

Caleb the carpenter and Kate the weaver l_____ each other, b_____ not every single minute. O_____ in a while, they'd differ about this or th_____ and wind up in such a fierce quarrel you'd never believe they were h_____ and w_____.

From Steig, W. (1977). *Caleb and Kate*. New York: Farrar, Straus, & Giroux.

Modified Cloze

Here deleted words are marked with length-of-word cues.

Though his father was fat and merely owned _ candy and nut _____, Harry Tillian liked his papa. Harry stopped liking _____ and nuts when he was around seven, but __ spite of this, __ and Mr. Tillian had remained friends the ___ Harry turned twelve.

From Rylant, C. (1985). *Every living thing*. New York: Bradbury.

Appendix $\mathbf{H}$

Meaningful Prefixes, Suffixes, and Word Parts

Prefixes	Meanings	Examples
ante	before	antebellum
anti (ant)	against	antitoxin
archi (arch)	chief	archenemy
auto	self	autobiography
bene	good	benefit
bi	two	bicycle
centi	one hundred	centigrade
circum	around	circumnavigate
co	together	coauthor
com	with	combine
contra	against	contradiction
deca (dec, deka, dek)	ten	decade
ex	out	exodus
extra	beyond	extraordinary
hetero	different	heterosexual
homo	same	homophone
hyper	above	hyperactive
hypo	under	hypodermic
im	not	immature
inter	between	interurban
intra	within	intrastate
kilo	one thousand	kilowatt
macro	large	macrobiotic
mal	bad	maladjust
mega	large	megaphone
micro	small	microscope
mid	middle	midway
mis	bad	misbehave
mono (mon)	one	monologue

multi	many	multitude
omni	all	omnivorous
penta (pent)	five	pentagon
peri	all around	perimeter
phono	voice, sound	phonograph
poly	many	polysyllabic
post	after	postdoctoral
pre	before	prefix
re	again	rewrite
semi	half, partly	semicircle
super	over	supervisor
tele	distant	television
trans	across	transatlantic
tri	three	tricycle
ultra	beyond	ultramodern
un	not	unbeaten

Suffixes	Meaning	Examples
arium	place for	planetarium
ary	place for	library
ation	state of	starvation
cule	small	minuscule
dom	state of	freedom
enne	female	comedienne
er	comparative	smarter
ess	female	actress
est	comparative	smartest
ette	female	majorette
ette	little	cigarette
ful	full of	careful
ism	doctrine of	capitalism
ite	mineral	granite

Word Parts	Meaning	Examples
less	without	worthless
ment	state of	amazement
ology	study of	biology
orium	place for	emporium
ory	place for	laboratory
phobia	fear of	claustrophobia

Word Parts	Meaning	Examples
aero	air	aeronautics
alt	high	altitude
ambul	move	ambulance
anthr	man	anthropology
ast	star	asterisk
aud	hear	audience
belli	war	antebellum
biblio	book	Bible
bio	life	biology
cardi	heart	cardiology
chron	time	chronic
cycl	circle	bicycle
dem	people	epidemic
derm	skin	hypodermic
gam	marriage	monogamy
gram	written	grammar
graph	write	autograph
homo	man	homicide
hydr	water	hydrant
lab	work	laboratory
mania	madness	cleptomania
max	greatest	maximum
mort	death	immortal
narr	tell	narrate
neo	new	neonatal
nov	new	novice
opt	eye	optician
ped	foot	pedestal
phil	love	Philadelphia
phon	sound	phonics
photo	light	telephoto
port	carry	portable
psych	mind	psychiatrist
scop	see	microscope
scribe	write	inscribe
solv	loosen	dissolve
struct	build	construction
term	end	terminator
terr	land	Mediterranean

therm	heat	thermos
urb	city	urban
vag	wander	vagrant
ver	truth	verify
volv	roll	revolver
vor	eat	herbivorous

Appendix I

Magazines for Children

These magazines also publish student writing.

Boy's Life
1325 Walnut Hill Lane
P.O. Box 152079
Irving, TX 75015–2079

Chart Your Course!
P.O. Box 6448
Mobile, AL 36660

Chickadee
255 Great Arrow Ave.
Buffalo, NY 14207

Child Life
Children's Better Health Institute
1100 Waterway Blvd.
P.O. Box 567
Indianapolis, IN 46206

Children's Album
1320 Galaxy Way
Concord, CA 94520

Children's Digest
Children's Better Health Institute
1100 Waterway Blvd.
P.O. Box 567
Indianapolis, IN 46206

Children's Playmate
Children's Better Health Institute
1100 Waterway Blvd.

P.O. Box 567
Indianapolis, IN 46206

Cobblestone: The History Magazine for Young People
30 Grove St.
Peterborough, NH 03458

Creative Kids
P.O. Box 637
100 Pine Ave.
Holmes, PA 19043
or
P.O. Box 6448
350 Weinacker Ave.
Mobile, AL 36660–0448

Cricket: The Magazine for Children
Box 51145
Boulder, CO 80323–1145
or
P.O. Box 300
Peru, IL 61354

Daybreak Star: The Herb of Understanding
United Indians of All Tribes Foundation
P.O. Box 99100
Seattle, WA 98199

Faces: The Magazine about People
30 Grove St.
Peterborough, NJ 03458

Free Spirit: News and Views on Growing Up
123 N. Third St.
Minneapolis, MN 55401

Highlights for Children
P.O. Box 269
Columbus, OH 43272–0002

Hopscotch: The Magazine for Young Girls
Box 164
Bluffton, OH 45817–0164

Humpty Dumpty's Magazine
Children's Better Health Institute
1100 Waterway Blvd.
P.O. Box 567
Indianapolis, IN 46206

Jack and Jill
Children's Better Health Institute
1100 Waterway Blvd.
P.O. Box 567
Indianapolis, IN 46206

Kid City
P.O. Box 51277
Boulder, CO 80322–1277
or
One Lincoln Plaza
New York, NY 10023

Kidlife and Times
P.O. Box D
Bellport, NY 11713

Merlyn's Pen: The National Magazine of Student Writing
98 Main St.
East Greenwich, RI 02818

National Geographic World
17th and M Streets, N.W.
Washington, D.C. 20036

Odyssey
7 School St.
Peterborough, NJ 03458

Owl: The Discovery Magazine for Children
255 Great Arrow Ave.
Buffalo, NY 14207

P3: The Earth-based Magazine for Kids
P.O. Box 52
Montgomery, VT 05470

Prism
Box 030464
Ft. Lauderdale, FL 33303

Ranger Rick
8925 Leesburg Pike
Vienna, VA 22184–0001

Sesame Street Magazine
P.O. Box 55518
Boulder, CO 80322–5518

Shoe Tree
National Association for Young Writers
P.O. Box 452
Belvidere, NJ 07823

Sports Illustrated for Kids
Time and Life Building
Rockefeller Center
New York, NY 10020

Stone Soup
P.O. Box 83
Santa Cruz, CA 90563

Surprises
P.O. Box 326
Chanhassen, MN 55327

3–2–1 Contact
P.O. Box 53051
Boulder, CO 80322–3051

Turtle Magazine for Preschool Kids
1100 Waterway Blvd.
P.O. Box 567
Indianapolis, IN 46206

Wee Wisdom
Unity School of Christianity
Unity Village, MO 64065

Zillions
P.O. Box 51777
Boulder, CO 80321–1777
or
256 Washington St.
Mt. Vernon, NY 10553

A more complete description of these and other magazines for children can be found in Bromley, K., & Maddix, D. (1993). Publishing student work in magazines. *Reading Teacher, 47,* 72–77.

Bookmaking Ideas

Basic Materials

Paper & Covers	Fasteners	Tools
heavy cardboard	metal rings	scissors
boxes	yarn, thread	glue
oak tag	ribbon, twine	1" and 2" tape
newspaper	staples	paper cutter
construction paper	brass fasteners	needles
newsprint	nuts, bolts, & washers	stapler
manila paper	elastic bands	
wallpaper sample books		
flat boxes		
paper towel tubes		
clear contact paper		
tie-dye, batik		

Large Class Books

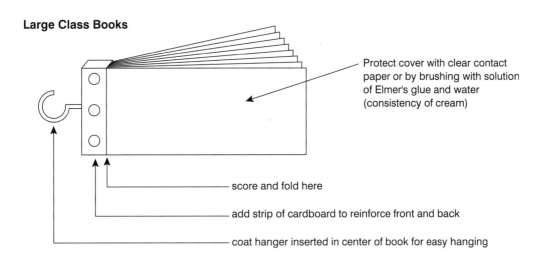

Protect cover with clear contact paper or by brushing with solution of Elmer's glue and water (consistency of cream)

score and fold here

add strip of cardboard to reinforce front and back

coat hanger inserted in center of book for easy hanging

— cut heavy cardboard covers to suit large sheets of paper.
— punch holes and fasten with nuts, washers, and bolts.
   (These can easily be removed to add pages.)

Small Books for Individual Use

Staples

Stitch with yarn or thread

Punch holes. Cut slots. Secure with rubber bands.

Apply Scotch tape to front and back covers. Punch holes through tape. Fasten with rings, brass fasteners, twists from plastic bags, shoe laces, etc.

Saddle Stitch Signature

1. Fold paper in half.
2. Bone (sharpen) fold using a folding bone or blunt stick.

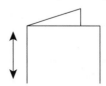

3. Jog the signature (set of folded pages) by tapping the top end on a table or flat surface.
4. Mark an odd number of holes on the fold. Mark the center hole first, then the two end holes the same distance from the top and bottom edges. Mark other holes if needed.

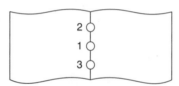

5. Punch holes using an awl, needle, or nail.
6. Cut thread 2 times longer than the signature. Wax thread. Thread needle. Knot the thread.

7. Sew signature pages together using a saddle stitch. Begin sewing in the center hole of the folio.

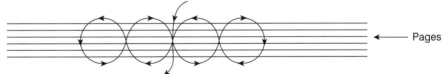

Pages

8. On the third time through the center hole, loop thread under the beginning stitch and then go back through the center hole.

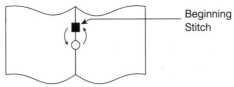

Beginning
Stitch

9. Tie a knot and clip extra thread. The knot will be on the inside of the book.

Creative Blank Books

Pages that have holes of varying sizes and numbers
Pages that are shaped
Pages that have different textures
Pages that fold out
Pages that have windows and doors
Pages that indicate direction (up-down-over-in)
Pages that progress in color (light-bright-dark-dull)
Pages that pop up

Experiment with Lettering

Sample Letter to Parents

This letter should be sent at the beginning of the school year.

Dear Parents:

One of the most important things we know about how children learn to read is that those children who read the most tend to be the best readers. The more you read, the better reader you become! For this reason I am asking you to take a few minutes (15–20 would be great) each day to read to or with your child.

The time you give to reading will allow your child to practice those reading strategies and skills he or she will be learning here at school. More important, however, is the message you will be sending to your child. Through your actions you will be saying that reading is important in your life and in your child's life and that you want him or her to become the best reader possible.

There are many ways you can read to or with your child. Here are a few suggestions:

Have your child sit next to you or on your lap as you read a good story to him or her. Be sure to read with an expressive voice and make sure your child can see the words and pictures.

Read together. Sitting side by side, read a story that your child has chosen aloud together. Let your voices blend together to create a real partnership in reading. If your child can read a section on his or her own without trouble, allow your voice to fade. On those sections that are challenging for your child, let your voice lead the way by reading slightly louder and ahead of your child. This has been proven to be a superb way to improve children's reading.

Echo reading. Allow your child to read back, phrase for phrase, a short text that you read to him or her.

Alternate reading. Switch who does the reading after every page or paragraph.

Repeat reading. Read a short story or poem to your child. (You can read the passage several times if you like, over several days.) Then allow your child to read the same passage to you.

Spend your time together quietly reading material of your own choosing. Although your child may be reading on his or her own, the fact that you are in the same room reading sends an important message to your child about the importance of reading.

Try to read with your child every day. Develop a routine for reading that will last a lifetime. Be sure to praise your child for good reading. And when he or she struggles over a word or phrase while reading, simply say the unknown word and continue. Don't make a lesson out of every mistake. (You can go back to the word after you've read.) Finally, don't just read—talk about the stories you read together and discuss your own reading habits and interests with your child. He or she needs to know that reading is an important part of everyday life.

Thank you for your help in making this year a successful one for your child in reading. Working together we can help your child become a successful and lifelong reader.

Sincerely,
Ms. Summers, Teacher

Appendix L

Professional Resources

Book Links (6 issues per year)
American Library Association
50 E. Huron St.
Chicago, IL 60611

Journal of Adolescent and Adult Reading (formerly **Journal of Reading**) (8 issues per year)
International Reading Association
800 Barksdale Road
P.O. Box 8139
Newark, DE 19714-8139

Language Arts (8 issues per year)
National Council of Teachers of English
1111 W. Kenyon Rd.
Urbana, IL 61801-1096

The New Advocate (4 issues per year)
Christopher-Gordon Publishers
480 Washington St.
Norwood, MA 02602

Primary Voices K–6 (4 issues per year)
National Council of Teachers of English
1111 W. Kenyon Rd.
Urbana, IL 61801-1096

The Reading Teacher (8 issues per year)
International Reading Association
800 Barksdale Rd.
P.O. Box 8139
Newark, DE 19714-8139

Reading and Writing Quarterly (4 issues per year)
Taylor and Francis, Ltd.
1900 Frost Rd., Suite 101
Bristol, PA 19007

Voices from the Middle (4 issues per year)
National Council of Teachers of English
1111 W. Kenyon Rd.
Urbana, IL 61801-1096

The WEB (Wonderfully Exciting Books)
    (3 issues per year; back issues available for purchase)
Ohio State University
200 Ramseyer Hall
29 Woodruff
Columbus, OH 43210

References

Allington, R. L. (1977). If they don't read much, how they ever gonna get good? *Journal of Reading, 21,* 57–61.

Allington, R. (1978, March). *Are good and poor readers taught differently? Is that why poor readers are poor readers?* Paper presented at the meeting of the American Educational Research Association, Toronto.

Allington, R. (1980). Teacher interruption behaviors during primary grade oral reading. *Journal of Educational Psychology, 72,* 371–377.

Allington, R. L. (1983). Fluency: The neglected reading goal. *The Reading Teacher, 36,* 556–561.

Allington, R. L. (1984). Content coverage and contextual reading in reading groups. *Journal of Reading Behavior, 26,* 85–96.

Allington, R. L. (1987, July/August). Shattered hopes: Why two federal reading programs have failed to correct reading failure. *Learning,* pp. 60–64

Allington, R. L., & McGill-Franzen, A. (1989). Different programs, indifferent instruction. In A. Gardner & D. Lipsky (Eds.), *Beyond separate education.* New York: Brookes.

Allington, R. L., Stuetzel, H., Shake, M. & Lamarche, S. (1986). What is remedial reading? A descriptive study. *Reading Research and Instruction, 24,* 15–30.

Anderson, B. (1981). The missing ingredient: Fluent oral reading. *Elementary School Journal, 81,* 173–177.

Anderson, R. C., & Freebody, P. (1981). Vocabulary knowledge. In J Guthrie (Ed.), *Comprehension and teaching: Research reviews* (pp. 77–117). Newark, DE: International Reading Association.

Anderson, R., Hiebert, E., Scott, J., & Wilkinson, I. (1985). *Becoming a nation of readers.* Washington, DC: U.S. Department of Education.

Anderson, R. C., Wilson, P. T., & Fielding, L. G. (1988). Growth in reading and how children spend their time outside of school. *Reading Research Quarterly, 23,* 285–303.

Aslett, R. (1990). *Effects of the oral recitation lesson on reading comprehension of fourth grade developmental readers.* Unpublished doctoral dissertation, Brigham Young University, Provo, UT.

Atwell, N. (1987). *In the middle: Writing, reading, and learning with adolescents.* Portsmouth, NH: Heinemann.

Barnes, D., Britton, J., & Rosen, H. (1971). *Language, the learner, and the school* (rev. ed.). Baltimore: Penguin.

Baumann, N. (1995). Reading millionaires—It works! *The Reading Teacher, 48,* 730.

Bird, L. B. (1989). The art of teaching: Evaluation and revision. In K. S. Goodman, Y. M. Goodman, & W. J. Hood (Eds.), *The whole language evaluation book* (pp. 15–24). Portsmouth, NH: Heinemann.

Bleich, D. (1978). *Subjective criticism.* Baltimore: Johns Hopkins University Press.

Bridge, C. (1979). Predictable materials for beginning readers. *Language Arts, 56,* 503–507.

Callaghan, M. (1935). All the years of her life. *New Yorker, 11*(17), 17–19.

Cambourne, B. (1995). Towards an educationally relevant theory of literacy learning: Twenty years of inquiry. *The Reading Teacher, 49,* 182-90

Carbo, M. (1978). Teaching reading with talking books. *The Reading Teacher, 32,* 267–273.

Cazden, C. (1981). Social context of learning to read. In J. Guthrie (Ed.), *Comprehension and teaching: Research reviews* (pp. 118–139). Newark, DE: International Reading Association.

Chittendon, E., & Courtney, R. (1989). Assessment of young children's reading: Documentation as an alternative to testing. In D. S. Strickland, & L. M. Morrow (Eds.), *Emerging literacy: Young children learn to read and write* (pp. 107–120). Newark, DE: International Reading Association.

Clay, M. (1986). Constructive processes: Talking, reading, writing, art, and craft. *The Reading Teacher, 39,* 764–770.

Cohen, D. (1968). The effect of literature on vocabulary and reading achievement. *Elementary English, 45,* 209–213, 217.

Commission on Chapter I. (1993). *Making schools work for children of poverty: A new framework.* Washington, DC: Author.

Cooper, H. (1977). Controlling personal rewards: Professional teachers' differential use of feedback and the effects of feedback on the students' motivation to perform. *Journal of Educational Psychology, 69,* 419–427.

Cunningham, P. M., & Cunningham, J. W. (1992). Making words: Enhancing the invented spelling-decoding connection. *The Reading Teacher, 46,* 106–115.

Cunningham, P. M., Hall, D. P., & Defee, M. (1991). Non-ability grouped, multilevel instruction: A year in a first-grade classroom. *Reading Teacher, 44,* 566–571.

Dalrymple, K. S. (1989). "Well, what about his skills?" Evaluation of whole language in the middle school. In K. S. Goodman, Y. M. Goodman, & W. J. Hood (Eds.), *The whole language evaluation book* (pp. 111–130). Portsmouth, NH: Heinemann.

Davidson, J. (1982). The group mapping activity for instruction in reading and thinking. *Journal of Reading, 26,* 52–56.

Davidson, J. (1986). The teacher-student generated lesson: A model for reading instruction. *Theory into Practice, 25,* 84–90.

Davidson, J. (1987, June). *Writing across the curriculum.* Paper presented at the meeting of the Language Experience Special Interest Council, DeKalb, IL.

257

Davis, F. B. (1944). Fundamental factors of comprehension in reading. *Psychometrika, 9,* 185–197.

Department of Education. (1985). *Reading in junior classes.* Wellington, New Zealand: Author.

Dowhower, S. L. (1987). Effects of repeated reading on second-grade transitional readers' fluency and comprehension. *Reading Research Quarterly, 22,* 389–407.

Dyson, A. (1984). "N spell my grandmama": Fostering early thinking about print. *The Reading Teacher, 38,* 262–271.

Elley, W. (1992). *How in the world do students read?* Hamburg, Germany: International Association for the Evaluation of Educational Achievement.

Estes, T. (1971). A scale to measure attitudes toward reading. *Journal of Reading, 15,* 135–138.

Evans, C. (1984). Writing to learn in math. *Language Arts, 61,* 828–835.

Fernald, G. M. (1943). *Remedial techniques in basic school subjects.* New York: McGraw-Hill.

Fisher, B. (1991). *Joyful learning.* Portsmouth, NH: Heinemann.

Fry, E. B., Fountoukidis, D. L., & Polk, J. K. (1985). *The new reading teacher's book of lists.* Englewood Cliffs, NJ: Prentice Hall.

Gambrell, L. (1994, November). *Motivation to read: Promising practices and future directions.* Paper presented at the meeting of the College Reading Association, New Orleans.

Gentry, R., & Henderson, E. (1980). Three steps to teaching beginning readers to spell. In E. Henderson & J. Beers (Eds.), *Developmental and cognitive aspects of learning to spell* (pp. 112–119). Newark, DE: International Reading Association.

Gillet, J., & Kita, M. (1979). Words, kids, and categories. *The Reading Teacher, 32,* 538–542.

Good, T. (1987). Two decades of research on teacher expectations: Findings and future directions. *Journal of Teacher Education, 38,* 32–47.

Goodman, K. S. (1992). I didn't found whole language. *The Reading Teacher, 46,* 188–199.

Goodman, Y. (1985a, Fall). Developing writing in a literate society. *Educational Horizons,* pp. 17–21.

Goodman, Y. (1985b). Kidwatching: Observing children in the classroom. In A. Jaggar & M. T. Smith-Burke (Eds.), *Observing the language learner* (pp. 9–18). Newark, DE: International Reading Association.

Goodman, Y. (1989). Evaluation of students: Evaluation of teachers. In K. S. Goodman, Y. M. Goodman, & W. J. Hood (Eds.), *The whole language evaluation book* (pp. 3–14). Portsmouth, NH: Heinemann.

Goodman, Y., & Watson, D. (1977). A reading program to live with: Focus on comprehension. *Language Arts, 54,* 868–879.

Graves, D. (1983). *Writing: Teachers and children at work.* Portsmouth, NH: Heinemann.

Graves, D., & Stuart, V. (1985). *Write from the start.* New York: Dutton.

Guthrie, J., Schafer, W., Wang, Y., & Afflerbach, P. (1995). Relationships of instruction to amount of reading: An exploration of social, cognitive, and instructional connections. *Reading Research Quarterly, 30,* 8–25.

Hansen, J. (1987). *When writers read.* Portsmouth, NH: Heinemann.

Hanser, C. (1986). The writer's inside story. *Language Arts, 63,* 153–159.

Harp, B. (Ed.). (1994). *Assessment and evaluation for student-centered learning.* Norwood, MA: Christopher-Gordon.

Harste, J. C. (1989). *New policy guidelines for reading: Connecting research and practice.* Urbana, IL: National Council of Teachers of English.

Harste, J. C., Woodward, V. A., & Burke, C. L. (1984). *Language stories and literacy lessons.* Portsmouth, NH: Heinemann.

Heathington, B., & Alexander, J. E. (1978). A child-based observation checklist to assess attitudes toward reading. *The Reading Teacher, 31,* 769–771.

Heckelman, R. G. (1969). A neurological impress method of reading instruction. *Academic Therapy, 4,* 277–282.

Herman, P. A. (1985). The effect of repeated readings on reading rate, speech pauses, and word recognition accuracy. *Reading Research Quarterly, 20,* 553–564.

Henderson, A. T. (1988). Parents are a school's best friend. *Phi Delta Kappan, 70,* 148–153.

Hoffman, J. V. (1987). Rethinking the role of oral reading in basal instruction. *Elementary School Journal, 87,* 367–373.

Hoffman, J. V., & Crone, S. (1985). The oral recitation lesson: A research-derived strategy for reading basal texts. In J. A. Niles & R. A. Lalik (Eds.), *Issues in literacy: A research perspective. Thirty-fourth yearbook of the National Reading Conference* (pp. 76–83). Rochester, NY: National Reading Conference.

Holdaway, D. (1979). *The foundations of literacy.* Sydney, Australia: Ashton Scholastic.

Jacobson, D. (1989). The evaluation process—in process. In K. S. Goodman, Y. M. Goodman, & W. J. Hood (Eds.), *The whole language evaluation book* (pp. 177–188). Portsmouth, NH: Heinemann.

Kitagawa, M. M. (1989). Guise, son of the shoemaker. In K. S. Goodman, Y. M. Goodman, & W. J. Hood (Eds.), *The whole language evaluation book* (pp. 101–109). Portsmouth, NH: Heinemann.

Koskinen, P. S., & Blum, I. H. (1984). Repeated oral reading and the acquisition of fluency. In J. A. Niles & L. A. Harris (Eds.), *Changing perspectives on research in reading/language processing and instruction. Thirty-third yearbook of the National Reading Conference* (pp. 183–187). Rochester, NY: National Reading Conference.

Koskinen, P. S., & Blum, I. H. (1986). Paired repeated reading: A classroom strategy for developing fluent reading. *The Reading Teacher, 40,* 70–75.

Manzo, A. (1975). The guided reading procedure. *Journal of Reading, 18,* 287–291.

Marek, A. M. (1989). Using evaluation as an instructional strategy for adult readers. In K. S. Goodman, Y. M. Goodman, & W. J. Hood (Eds.), *The whole language evaluation book* (pp. 157–164). Portsmouth, NH: Heinemann.

McCormick, S. (1994). A nonreader becomes a reader: A case study of literacy acquisition by a severely disabled reader. *Reading Research Quarterly, 29,* 156–176.

McCormick, S. (1995). *Instructing students who have literacy problems.* Englewood Cliffs, NJ: Prentice Hall.

McDermott, R. (1978). Pirandello in the classroom: On the possibility of equal educational opportunity in American culture. In M. Reynolds (Ed.), *Futures of exceptional children: Emerging structure* (pp. 41–64). Reston, VA: Council for Exceptional Children.

McKenna, M., & Kear, D. (1990). Measuring attitude toward reading: A new tool for teachers. *The Reading Teacher, 43,* 626–629.

Merriam, S. B. (1988). *Case study research in education.* San Francisco: Jossey-Bass.

Mervar, K., & Hiebert, E. H. (1989). Literature-selection strategies and amount of reading in two literacy approaches. In S. McCormick & J. Zutell (Eds.), *Cognitive and social perspectives for literacy research and instruction. Thirty-eighth yearbook of the National Reading Conference* (pp. 529–535). Chicago: National Reading Conference.

Moffett, J., & Wagner, B. (1992). *Student-centered language arts, K–12* (4th ed.). Portsmouth, NH: Boynton/Cook.

Morris, D., & Nelson, L. (1992). Supported oral reading with low-achieving second graders. *Reading Research and Instruction, 31,* 49–63.

Nagy, W. E. (1988). *Teaching vocabulary to improve reading comprehension.* Urbana, IL: National Council of Teachers of English.

Ogle, D. (1986). K-W-L: A teaching model that develops active reading of expository text. *The Reading Teacher, 38,* 564–570.

O'Masta, G. A., & Wolf, J. A. (1991). Encouraging independent reading through the reading millionaires project. *The Reading Teacher, 44,* 656–662.

Padak, N. (1987). *Reading placement and diagnosis: A guide for elementary teachers.* Springfield: Illinois State Board of Education.

Palmer, B., Codling, R., & Gambrell, L. (1994). In their own words: What elementary students have to say about motivation to read. *Reading Teacher, 48,* 176–178.

Patton, M. Q. (1990). *Qualitative evaluation methods* (2nd ed.). Newbury Park, CA: Sage.

Pikulski, J. J. (1994). Preventing reading failure: A review of five effective programs. *The Reading Teacher, 48,* 30–39.

Pinnell, G. S. (1989). Reading Recovery: Helping at-risk children learn to read. *Elementary School Journal, 90,* 161–183.

Pinnell, G. S., Fried, M. D., & Estice, R. M. (1990). Reading Recovery: Learning how to make a difference. *The Reading Teacher, 43,* 282–295.

Postlethwaite, T. N., & Ross, K. N. (1992). *Effective schools in reading: Implications for educational planners.* The Hague: International Association for the Evaluation of Educational Achievement.

Rasinski, T. V. (1990). *The effects of cued phrase boundaries in texts.* Bloomington, IN: ERIC Clearinghouse on Reading and Communication Skills (ED 313 689).

Rasinski, T. V. (1992). Promoting recreational reading. In K. Wood (Ed.), *Exploring literature in the classroom: Content and methods* (pp. 85–109). Norwood, MA: Christopher-Gordon.

Rasinski, T. V., & Fredericks, A. D. (1991). The Akron Paired Reading project. *The Reading Teacher, 44,* 514–515.

Rasinski, T. V., & Linek, W. (1993). *Do students in whole language classrooms really like reading?* Paper presented at the annual meeting of the College Reading Association, Richmond, VA.

Rasinski, T. V., Padak, N. D., Linek, W. L., & Sturtevant, E. (1994). Effects of fluency development on urban second-grade readers. *Journal of Educational Research, 87,* 158–165.

Read, C. (1971). Pre-school children's knowledge of English phonology. *Harvard Educational Review, 41,* 1–34.

Reutzel, D. R., & Fawson, P. C. (1990). Traveling Tales: Connecting parents and children through writing. *The Reading Teacher, 44,* 222–227.

Reutzel, D. R., & Hollingsworth, P. M. (1993). Effects of fluency training on second graders' reading comprehension. *Journal of Educational Research, 86,* 325–331.

Reutzel, D. R., Hollingsworth, P. M., & Eldredge, J. L. (1994). Oral reading instruction: The impact on student reading development. *Reading Research Quarterly, 29,* 40–62.

Rhodes, L. (1981). I can read! Predictable books as resources for reading and writing instruction. *The Reading Teacher, 34,* 511–518.

Rhodes, L. K., & Dudley-Marling, C. (1988). *Readers and writers with a difference.* Portsmouth, NH: Heinemann.

Rhodes, L., & Shanklin, N. (1993). *Windows into literacy.* Portsmouth, NH: Heinemann.

Ribowsky, H. (1985). *The effects of a code emphasis approach and a whole language approach upon emergent literacy of kindergarten children.* Urbana, IL: ERIC Clearinghouse on Reading and Communication Skills (ED 269 720).

Richek, M. A., & McTague, B. K. (1988). The "Curious George" strategy for students with reading problems. *The Reading Teacher, 42,* 220–226.

Rose, M. (1994, October). *A conversation with Mike Rose.* Graduate colloquium, Kent State University, Kent, OH.

Rupley, W., Wise, B., & Logan, J. (1986). Research in effective teaching: An overview of its development. In J. Hoffman (Ed.), *Effective teaching of reading: Research and practice* (pp. 3–36). Newark, DE: International Reading Association.

Samuels, S. J. (1979). The method of repeated readings. *The Reading Teacher, 32,* 403–408.

Schreiber, P. A. (1980). On the acquisition of reading fluency. *Journal of Reading Behavior, 12,* 177–186.

Schreiber, P. A. (1991). Understanding prosody's role in reading acquisition. *Theory into Practice, 30,* 158–164.

Schwartz, R., & Raphael, T. (1985). Concept of definition: A key to improving students' vocabulary. *The Reading Teacher, 39,* 198–205.

Shimron, J. (1994). The making of readers: The work of Professor Dina Feitelson. In D. Dickinson (Ed.), *Bridges to literacy* (pp. 80–99). Cambridge, MA: Blackwell.

Silvers, P. (1986). Process writing and the reading connection. *The Reading Teacher, 39,* 684–688.

Slavin, R. E., Madden, N. L., Karweit, N. L., Dolan, L., & Wasik, B. A. (1992). *Success for All: A relentless approach to prevention and early intervention in elementary schools.* Arlington, VA: Educational Research Service.

Smith, F. (1978). *Understanding reading* (2nd ed.). New York: Holt.

Smith, F. (1992). Learning to read: The never-ending debate. *Phi Delta Kappan, 73,* 432–441.

Sowers, S. (1985). Learning to write in a workshop: A study in grades one through four. In M. Farr (Ed.), *Advances in writing research. Vol. 1: Children's early writing development* (pp. 297–342). Norwood, NJ: Ablex.

Spurlin, J., Dansereau, D., Larson, C., & Brooks, L. (1984). Cooperative learning strategies in processing descriptive text: Effects of role and activity level of the learner. *Cognition and Instruction, 1,* 451–463.

Stahl, S. A. (1992). Saying the "p" word: Nine guidelines for exemplary phonics instruction. *The Reading Teacher, 45,* 618–625.

Stanovich, K. E. (1986). Matthew effects in reading: Some consequences of individual differences in the acquisition of literacy. *Reading Research Quarterly, 21,* 360–407.

Stauffer, R. (1980). *The language-experience approach to the teaching of reading* (2nd ed.). New York: Harper & Row.

Sweet, A., & Guthrie, J. (in press). How children's motivations relate to literacy development and instruction. *The Reading Teacher.*

Topping, K. (1987). Paired Reading: A powerful technique for parent use. *The Reading Teacher, 40,* 608–614.

Topping, K. (1989). Peer tutoring and Paired Reading: Combining two powerful techniques. *The Reading Teacher, 42,* 488–494.

Vacca, R. T., & Vacca, J. L. (1993). *Content area reading* (4th ed.). New York: HarperCollins.

Valencia, S., & Pearson, P. D. (1987). Reading assessment: Time for a change. *The Reading Teacher, 40,* 726–733.

Watson, B., & Konicek, R. (1990). Teaching for conceptual change: Confronting children's experience. *Phi Delta Kappan, 71,* 680–685.

Weiner, B. (1979). A theory of motivation for some classroom experiences. *Journal of Educational Psychology, 71,* 3–25.

Wigfield, A., & Asher, S. (1984). Social and motivational influences on reading. In R. Barr, M. Kamil, P. Mosenthal, & P. D. Pearson (Eds.), *Handbook of reading research* (Vol. 1) (pp. 423–452). New York: Longman.

Winograd, P., & Smith, L. (1987). Improving the climate for reading comprehension instruction. *The Reading Teacher, 41,* 304–310.

Author Index

Afflerbach, P., 43
Alexander, J. E., 34
Allington, R. L., 7, 21, 82
Anderson, B., 82
Anderson, R. C., 4, 21, 87, 103, 171
Asher, S., 33
Aslett, R., 82
Atwell, N., 6

Barnes, D., 110
Baumann, N., 43, 44
Berthoff, Ann, 132
Bird, L. B., 198
Bleich, David, 117
Blum, Irene, 73
Bridge, C., 27
Bridwell, Norman, 167
Britton, J., 110
Brooks, L., 20
Burke, Carolyn, 132, 193

Callaghan, M., 111
Cambourne, Brian, 38–39, 40, 42
Carbo, Marie, 75
Cazden, C., 20
Chittendon, E., 191, 193, 198, 205
Clay, Marie, 148
Cleary, B., 78
Codling, R., 32, 33, 39
Cohen, D., 90
Commission on Chapter I, 8
Cooper, H., 40
Courtney, R., 191, 193, 198, 205
Cowley, Joy, 80

Crone, S., 82
Cunningham, J. W., 57, 58
Cunningham, P. M., 57, 58, 165–166

Dalrymple, Karen, 197
Dansereau, D., 20
Davidson, Jane, 115, 116, 138, 149, 154
Davis, F. B., 87
Defee, M., 165–166
DePaola, Tomie, 60, 118, 119
Department of Education, 143
Dolan, L., 166
Dowhower, S. L., 72
Dudley-Marling, C., 189, 194
Dyson, Anne Haas, 149

Eldredge, J. L., 83
Elley, W., 163
Estes, T., 34
Estice, R. M., 164
Evans, Christine, 154

Fawson, Parker, 183, 186–187
Feitelson, Dina, 39
Fernald, Grace, 65
Fielding, L. G., 4, 171
Fisher, Bobbi, 24
Fleischman, Paul, 108
Fountoukidis, D. L., 98
Fredericks, A. D., 179
Freebody, P., 87
Fried, M. D., 164
Fry, E. B., 98

Gambrell, L., 32, 33, 39, 43
Gentry, R., 149
Gillet, J., 124
Good, T., 21, 40
Goodman, K. S., 4
Goodman, Yetta, 104, 143, 191, 192, 193, 194, 195, 196, 198
Graves, Donald, 143, 148
Guthrie, J., 32–33, 43
Gwynne, Fred, 100

Hall, D. P., 165–166
Hansen, J., 200
Hanser, C., 148
Harp, B., 190
Harste, Jerry, 27, 113, 193, 195
Heathington, B., 34
Heckelman, R. G., 74
Henderson, Ann, 171
Henderson, E., 149
Herber, 126
Herman, P. A., 72
Hiebert, E. H., 5, 21, 103
Hoffman, J. V., 82
Holdaway, D., 83
Hollingsworth, P. M., 82, 83
Hunt, Irene, 106

Jacobson, D., 198, 204

Karweit, N. L., 166
Kear, D., 34
Kita, M., 124
Kitagawa, M. M., 199

Konicek, R., 16, 17
Koskinen, Pat, 73

Lamarche, S., 7
Larson, C., 20
Lederer, Richard, 88
Linek, W. L., 5
Logan, J., 21

Madden, N. L., 166
Manzo, A., 135
Marek, Ann, 204
Martin, Bill, 6, 79, 155
McCormick, Sandy, 51
McDermott, R., 21
McGill-Franzen, A., 7
McKenna, M., 34
McTague, B. K., 107, 167
Mead, Margaret, 38
Merriam, S. B., 196, 198, 202
Mervar, K., 5
Moffett, J., 121
Morris, D., 83, 84
Morrow, L. M., 205

Nagy, William, 90
Nelson, L., 83, 84

Ogle, D., 128
O'Masta, G. A., 43, 177

Padak, N. P., 35, 80, 168
Palmer, B., 32, 33, 39
Parish, Peggy, 100

Patton, M. Q., 198, 202
Paulsen, Gary, 60
Pearson, P. D., 190
Pikulski, J. J., 169
Pinnell, G. S., 164
Polk, J. K., 98
Postlethwaite, T. N., 172

Raphael, T., 94
Rasinski, T. V., 5, 45, 78, 80, 168, 179
Read, Charles, 146
Reutzel, D. R., 82, 83, 183, 186–187
Rey, H. A., 167
Rey, Margaret, 167
Rhodes, L. K., 34, 156, 189, 190, 194
Ribowsky, H., 83
Richek, M. A., 107, 167
Robertson, J. I., 78
Rose, Mike, 37, 42
Rosen, H., 110
Rosenbloom, Joseph, 100
Ross, K. N., 172
Rupley, W., 21

Samuels, Jay, 72
Schafer, W., 43
Schreiber, Peter, 78
Schwartz, R., 94
Scott, J., 21, 103
Shake, M., 7
Shanklin, N., 34, 190
Shimron, J., 39
Silvers, P., 143
Silverstein, Shel, 80
Slavin, R. E., 166
Smith, F., 4, 19, 150
Smith, L., 20
Sowers, S., 148
Spurlin, J., 20

Stahl, Steven, 53–54, 58
Stanovich, Keith, 22
Stauffer, Russell, 54, 111, 130
Steig, William, 107, 118
Strickland, D. S., 205
Stuart, V., 143
Stuetzel, H., 7
Sweet, A., 32–33

Terban, Marvin, 100
Topping, Keith, 74–75, 178

Vacca, J. L., 126
Vacca, R. T., 126
Valencia, S., 190
Viorst, Judith, 107

Waber, Bernard, 109
Wagner, B., 121
Wang, Y., 43
Wasik, B. A., 166
Watson, B., 16, 17
Watson, D., 104, 132
Weiner, B., 33
White, E. B., 116
Wigfield, A., 33
Wilkinson, I., 21, 103
Williams, Sue, 80
Wilson, P. T., 4, 171
Winograd, P., 20
Wise, B., 21
Wolf, J. A., 43, 177
Woodward, V. A., 193

Yolen, Jane, 108

Zion, Gene, 167
Zolotow, Charlotte, 109

Subject Index

Ability, 33
Accommodation, 15–20
Affixes, 62
Agree or Disagree? program, 116–117
"All the Years of Her Life" (Callaghan), 111
Amelia Bedelia stories (Parish), 100
Analogies, vocabulary, 96–97
Analysis, portfolio assessment, 192–193
Anecdotal notes, observation, 198–199
Anguished English (Lederer), 88
Anticipation guides, 126–128
Approximations, 40–41
Attention focus during reading time, 21
Attitudes
    positive, 34–37
    about valuing reading, 42–43
Authentic materials, whole language instruction,
    9–10

Background knowledge, prereading activity, 128–129
Backpack programs, parents', 183, 186–187
Balderdash, 99
Behavior patterns in reading programs, 161
Bleich's Heuristic, 117
Block approach reading program, 165–166
Book It!, 45, 177
Bookmaking ideas, 248–251
Books
    access, 32
    choice, 32, 79–80
    about words, 100
Brainstorming, 125–126
Brown Bear, Brown Bear (Martin), 6, 79, 80, 155
Bull Run (Fleischman), 108

Categorization activities, vocabulary, 93–94
Challenge, 33
Character Sketches, 113
Charlotte's Web (White), 116
Checklists and charts, observation, 199–200
Children's Book Council, 45
Chocolate Moose for Dinner (Gwynne), 100
Choice time in instructional routines, 24–25
Choral reading, 76–77, 84
"Civil War, The," 108
Classroom Choices, 45–46
Classroom communities, 21
Classroom reading programs, 45–46
Classrooms
    arrangements, 26
    atmosphere in writing development, 147–148
    exemplary, 37–38
    primary grade, 5
    whole language, 5–7
Clifford the Big Red Dog (Bridwell), 167
Cloze activities, 60–61, 238–239
Cognitive strategies, 43
Commission on Chapter I, 8
Commission on Reading, 21, 103
Communication with parents, 175–177
Communities of learners, developing, 20–21
Community involvement, reading program, 45
Compare-and-Contrast Charts (CCC), 118, 119
Competition, 33
Compliance, 33
Compound words, 62
Comprehension with expository text, 123–138
    postreading, 133–137
        distinctive-features activity, 133–134

Guided Reading Procedure, 135–136
  herringbone activity, 135
  response activities, 136–137
prereading, 124–129
  anticipation guides, 126–128
  background knowledge, 128–129
  brainstorming, 125–126
  K-W-L charts, 128
  word sorts, 124–125
  principles of, 137–138
reading, 129–133
  dialectic or double-entry journals, 132
  Directed Reading-Thinking Activity, 130–132
  save last word for me activity, 132–133
Comprehension with narrative text, 103–121
  postreading, 115–121
    Agree or Disagree?, 116–117
    Bleich's Heuristic, 117
    Compare-and-Contrast Charts, 118, 119
    Group Mapping Activity, 115–116
    reader's theater, 118–120
    response journals, 120–121
    Sketch to Stretch, 117–118
    (Write and Share)^2, 116
  prereading, 105–109
    jackdaws, 105–107
    media and activities, 108
    readings, 107
    role playing, 108–109
    story mapping, 108
  reading, 109–115
    Character Sketches, 113
    Directed Reading-Thinking Activity, 110–112
    imagery, 114

Linguistic Roulette, 113–114
  Think-Pair-Share, 112–113
Concentration, 63, 99
Concept maps, 94–96
Conditions of learning, 38–41
Connected text, 10
Consistency
  parents' programs, 175
  reading programs, 163
Constructivist method of teaching, 16–17
Content area journals, 153–154
Contextual analysis, word recognition, 59–61
Contextual reading, 52
Conversations, observation, 200–203
Copy change, writing activity, 154–156
Corrections
  teachers' attitudes about, 28, 195–196
  teachers' cues for, 21
  writing development, 150
Corrective instruction and whole language, 9–11
Corrective reading and whole language, 7–9
Criticism, 40
Cultural logic, 18
Curiosity, 33
Curious George (Rey), 167
Curious George Strategy reading program, 167–168
Curriculum, reading program, 160

Daffy Definitions (Rosenbloom), 100
DEAR (Drop Everything and Read), 23
Demonstrations, 39
Devil's Arithmetic, The (Yolen), 108
Diablo Elementary School, 177
Diagnostic decisions, observation, 194–196

Diagnostic-prescriptive model, remedial reading, 7
Dialectic journals, 132
Dialogue journals, 152–153
Directed Reading-Thinking Activity (DR-TA)
    expository text, 130–132
    narrative text, 110–112
Distinctive-features activity, 133–134
Documenting home activities with parents, 175
Double-entry journals, 132

Effort, 33
Employment, 41
Engagement, 40
Environments
    instructional, 21–22
    learning, 38–41
Errors. *See* Corrections
Exemplary classrooms, 37–38
Expectations, 40
Experience/behavior questions, 202
Expository text. *See* Comprehension with expository
    text
Extrinsic motivation, 32–33

Fair Oaks School, Redwood City, California, 198
Fast Start program, 179–183, 184, 185
Feelings questions, 202
First graders, reading programs for, 169
Fluent reading, 69–85
    assessing, 70
    choral reading, 76–77, 84
    Fluency Development Lesson, 80–82, 84–85, 168
    marking phrase boundaries, 77–79
    model, 71–72
    Oral Recitation Lesson, 82, 85
    Paired Reading, 74–75, 84
    repeated reading, 72–74, 78, 84
    Shared Book Experience, 83, 85
    Support-reading Strategy, 83–84, 85
    tape-recorded passages, 75–76, 84
    text choice, 79–80
    and word recognition, 66
Functional principles, writing, 143

Games
    vocabulary instruction, 98–100
    word recognition, 62–64
Goals

reading development programs, 160
    whole language teachers, 4
Graphophonic knowledge, writing, 145
Group Mapping Activity, 115–116
Guided Reading Procedure (GRP), 135–136
Guppies in Tuxedos (Terban), 100

Hangman, 63
Harry the Dirty Dog (Zion), 167
Hatchet (Paulsen), 60
Herringbone, 135
Hinky Pinkies, 99–100
Hypothetical/future-oriented questions, 202

Ideal-position questions, 202
If I Were in Charge of the World and Other Worries
    (Viorst), 107
If You Give a Mouse a Cookie (Numeroff), 155
Imagery, 114
Immersion, 39
Incentive programs for parents, 177–178
Independent reading, 34–35
Instruction, vocabulary. *See* Vocabulary instruction
Instructional activities and materials for parents, 173,
    174–175
Instructional framework, 15–28
    accommodation, 15–20
        of conceptual needs and beliefs, 16–17
        of instructional needs and beliefs, 18–20
    developing communities of learners, 20–21
    reading materials, 26–27
    room arrangements, 26
    teacher's role in, 28
    time on tasks, 21–22
Instructional interaction, portfolio assessment,
    192–193
Instructional routines
    choice time, 24–25
    mini-lessons, 25
    reading aloud, 22–23
    reading program development, 160
    sustained silent reading, 23–24
Instructional support, 109–110
Integrative vocabulary instruction, 90
Intermediate-grades classroom, 6
International Reading Association, 45
Interpretive questions, 202
Interviews, 200–203

Intrinsic motivation, 32–33
Invented spelling, 54, 146
Involvement, 33
Ira Sleeps Over (Waber), 109
I Went Walking (Williams), 80

Jackdaws, 105–107
Journals
    content area, 153–154
    dialectic or double-entry, 132
    dialogue, 152–153
    personal, 152
    response, 120–121

Kent State University, 179
Key words, 55–56
Kidwatching, 193–194
Kinesthetic, 65
King Who Rained, The (Gwynne), 100
K-W-L charts, 128

Language experience activities, 6
Language Experience Approach (LEA), 54–55
Learned helplessness, 34
Learners, communities of, 20–21
Learning about written language, 142–143
Learning logs, 153–154
Learning to read by reading, 4
Letter patterns, 62
Light in the Attic, A (Silverstein), 80
Linguistic principles, writing, 144
Linguistic Roulette, 113–114
List Group Label (LGL), 91–93, 94
Little Pigeon Toad, A (Gwynne), 100
Luck, 33

Making Words program, 58–59
Marking phrase boundaries, 77–79
Massed and spaced practice, reading program,
    162–163
Match, 63, 99
Matthew Effect, 22
Maze activities, 238
Media and activities, comprehension, 108
Mini-lessons instructional routines, 25
Mistakes. *See* Corrections
Modeling, writing development, 150
Motivation, reading, 32–34

students, 10
variables affecting, 33–34
Mrs. Wishy Washy (Cowley), 80
Multimodality, word recognition, 65
Multiple Contexts/Multiple Exposures, 51

Name poems, 154
Narrative, 104. *See also* Comprehension with narra-
    tive text
National Assessment of Educational Progress (NAEP),
    43, 171
National Reading Research Center, 32
Negative attitudes. *See* Positive attitudes about
    reading
Neurological Impress Method (NIM), 74
New Reading Teacher's Book of Lists, The (Fry, Foun-
    toukidis, Polk), 98
No Promises in the Wind (Hunt), 106

Observations, 189–206
    anecdotal notes, 198–199
    attitudes and interests, 34–35
    checklists and charts, 199–200
    conversations and interviews, 200–203
    kidwatching, 193–194
    performance samples, 203–206
    portfolio assessment, 192–193
    professional judgment in diagnostic decisions,
        194–196
    reading conferences, 203–205
    reading programs, 162
    during school day, 196–197
Opinion/value questions, 202
Oral Recitation Lesson (ORL), 82, 85
Ownership, reading program, 169

Paired Reading
    fluent reading, 74–75, 84
    parents, 178–179
Parents, 171–187
    backpack programs, 183, 186–187
    communication, 175–177
    documenting home activities, 175
    Fast Start program, 179–183, 184, 185
    incentive programs, 177–178
    instructional activities and materials, 173,
        174–175
    Paired Reading, 178–179

Parents, *continued*
  program consistency, 175
  reading fun, 173–174
  reading involvement, 11
  and teachers, 172
  training for, 172–173
Pattern books, 224–226
Performance samples, observation, 203–206
Personal journals, 152
Philosophy
  reading program development, 160
  whole language, 4
Phonics, 53–54
Phrase boundaries, marking, 77–79
Pizza Hut's Book It! program, 45, 177
Planning instructional routines, 25
Polar Bear, Polar Bear, What Do You Hear? (Martin),
    79
Portfolio assessment, 191–193
Positive attitudes about reading, 31–47
  attitudes and interests, 34–37
  motivation, 32–34
  successful expectations, 37–42
  valuing reading, 42–46
Primary grade classrooms, 5
Print conventions, learning about, 142
Prior experience with books, 32
Professional development, teachers', 163
Professional judgment in diagnostic decisions, obser-
    vation, 194–196
Psychological safety, 38
Puzzles, vocabulary instruction, 98–100

Questions, interview, 202–203

Reader's theater, 118–120
Reading. *See also* Valuing reading
  aloud, 22–23
  learning to read, 4
  word recognition games, 62–64
Reading buddies, 73
Reading conferences, 203–205
Reading materials, instructional framework, 26–27
Reading Millionaires, 43–44, 177
Reading programs, 159–169
  behavior patterns, 161
  block approach, 165–166
  consistency over time, 163

Curious George Strategy, 167–168
Fluency Development Lesson, 168
focusing, 160–162
guidelines, 160
massed and spaced practice, 162–163
observations, 162
ownership, 169
professional development for teachers, 163
Reading Recovery, 164–165
schoolwide, 43–45
Success for All, 166–167
whole reader focus, 162
Reading Recovery reading program, 164–165
Reading Teacher, The, 45
Reading workshop, 6
Read-ins, 44–45
Recognition, 33
Relational principles, writing, 143
Remedial reading, 7–9
Repeated readings, fluency, 72–74, 78, 84
Repetition, vocabulary, 90–91
Response, 41
Response activities, 136–137
Response journals, 120–121
Responsibility, 40
Role playing, 108–109
Routines. *See* Instructional routines

Safety, classroom, 38
Say It (Zolotow), 109
Scattergories, 99
Scrabble, 63
Semantic maps, 92
Sentence concept, 144
Shared Book Experience (SBE), 83, 85
Sharing writing, 154–156
Sketch to Stretch, 117–118
Social interactions, 32, 33, 43
Spaced practice reading programs, 162–163
Spelling, 146, 149
SQUIRT (Super, Quiet, Uninterrupted, Independent
    Reading Time), 23
Standardized tests, 190
Stega Nona's Magic Lesson (DePaola), 60
Story mapping, 108
Story time, 22–23
Students
  conceptual needs and beliefs, 16–17

developing passion for, 4
instructional needs and beliefs, 18–20
reading motivation, 10
support for, 10–11
and teacher relationship, 6
Success
classroom, 41–42
conditions of learning, 38–41
exemplary classrooms, 37–38
focus, 11
positive attitude, 37–42
Success for All reading program, 166–167
Support-reading Strategy (SRS), 83–84, 85
Surveys, 34, 36–37
Sustained silent reading (SSR), 23–24

Tactile, 65
Talking about writing, 148
Talking books, 75–76
Tape-recorded reading, 75–76, 84
Teachers
correction attitudes, 28, 195–196
correction cues, 21
instructional framework, 28
models, 39–40
parental involvement, 172
professional development, 163
student relationship, 6
whole language, 4, 5
and word recognition, 51
and writing development, 149
Teacher-Student Generated Lessons, 138
Teaching, constructivist method of, 16–17
Tests, standardized, 190
Text. *See* Comprehension with expository text; Comprehension with narrative text
Think-Pair-Share, 112–113
Time
instructional environment, 21–22
reading program, 163
Too Hot to Hoot (Terban), 100
Traditional vocabulary instruction, 87–89
Training, parents, 172–173
Traveling Tales program, 183, 186–187

Valuing reading
attitudes, 42–43
classroom programs, 45–46

positive attitudes, 42–46
schoolwide programs, 43–45
Verbal encouragement, 40
Visual-auditory-kinesthetic-tactile approach (VAKT), 65
Vocabulary instruction, 87–101
analogies, 96–97
books about words, 100
categorization activities, 93–94
concept map, 94–96
effective, 90–91
games and puzzles, 98–100
learning new words, 89–90
List Group Label, 91–93, 94
repetition, 90–91
traditional, 87–89
word histories, 97–98

Wheel of Fortune, 63
Where the Sidewalk Ends (Silverstein), 80
Whole language
classrooms, 5–7
corrective instruction, 9–11
corrective reading, 7–9
definition, 3–4
philosophy, 4
Whole language teachers, 4, 5
Whole reader focus, reading program, 162
Wide reading word recognition, 66
Word banks, 55–56
Word families, 58, 234–237
Word histories, 97–98
Wordo, 63, 64, 98–99
Word recognition, 49–67
contextual analysis, 59–61
fluency and wide reading, 66
instruction, 51–52
key words and word banks, 55–56
Language Experience Approach, 54–55
longer words, 61–62
Making Words, 58–59
multimodality, 65
phonics, 53–54
principles, 50–51
reading and games, 62–64
strategies, 18–19
teacher's role, 51
word families, 58

Word recognition, *continued*
    word sorts, 56–57
    word walls, 57–58
Words, concept of, 144
Word sorts, 56–57, 124–125
Word walls, 57–58
Word War, 63
Work avoidance, 33
(Write and Share)², 116
Writing activities, 151–156
    copy change, 154–156
    dialogue journals, 152–153

learning logs or content area journals, 153–154
    personal journals, 152
Writing development, 141–151
    activities. *See* Writing activities
    classroom atmosphere, 147–148
    discovering what children know, 144–147
    learning about written language, 142–143
    modeling and corrections, 150
    talking about writing, 148
    teacher support of, 149
    why readers write, 143–144

About the Authors

Timothy Rasinski and Nancy Padak are Professors of Curriculum and Instruction at Kent State University where they teach courses in literacy education. They also serve as editors of *The Reading Teacher,* the most widely read professional journal in reading education.

Previously a classroom and Title I teacher in Nebraska, Tim Rasinski received his Ph.D. from The Ohio State University and has taught at the University of Georgia. He has written and edited several books on literacy education including *Case Studies in Whole Language* (coauthored with Rich Vacca), *Sensitive Issues: An Annotated Guide to Children's Literature, K-6* (coauthored with Cindy Gillespie), and *Parents and Teachers: Helping Children Learn to Read and Write.* Tim has also conducted research and written many articles on reading and writing education published in *Reading Research Quarterly, Reading Psychology, Reading Research and Instruction, Journal of Experimental Education, Education Forum,* and *The Reading Teacher,* among others.

Nancy Padak received her Ed.D. from Northern Illinois University, and has worked as a classroom teacher, Title I administrator, and a school district reading and language arts curriculum director in Illinois. She is Director of the University Reading and Writing Center at the Ohio Literacy Resource Center at Kent State University. Nancy's extensive research in literacy education has been published in *Journal of Reading, Journal of Educational Research, Language Arts,* and the Yearbooks of the National Reading Conference and the College Reading Association.

Tim and Nancy have worked intensively with children in public schools and in university reading clinics who have experienced difficulty in learning to read. They wrote this book in the hope that teachers who work with children struggling with reading can make reading a successful, exciting, and lifelong experience for those children.